33d CONGRESS, 2d *Session.* | SENATE. | Ex. Doc. No. 78.

REPORTS

OF

EXPLORATIONS AND SURVEYS,

TO

ASCERTAIN THE MOST PRACTICABLE AND ECONOMICAL ROUTE FOR A RAILROAD

FROM THE

MISSISSIPPI RIVER TO THE PACIFIC OCEAN.

MADE UNDER THE DIRECTION OF THE SECRETARY OF WAR, IN

1853-4,

ACCORDING TO ACTS OF CONGRESS OF MARCH 3, 1853, MAY 31, 1854, AND AUGUST 5, 1854.

VOLUME I.

WASHINGTON:
BEVERLEY TUCKER, PRINTER.
1855.

CONTENTS OF VOLUME I.

IN SENATE—February 24, 1855.

Resolved, That there be printed, for the use of the Senate, ten thousand copies of the several reports of surveys for a railroad to the Pacific, made under the direction of the Secretary of War; and also of the report of F. W. Lander, civil engineer, of a survey of a railroad route from Puget's Sound, by Fort Hall and the Great Salt lake, to the Mississippi river; and the report of John C. Frémont, of a route for a railroad from the head-waters of the Arkansas river into the State of California; together with the maps and plates accompanying said reports, necessary to illustrate the same; and that five hundred copies be printed for the use of the Secretary of War, and fifty copies for each of the commanding officers engaged in said service.

Attest: ASBURY DICKINS, *Secretary.*

THIRTY-SECOND CONGRESS, SECOND SESSION—Chapter 98.

Sect. 10. *And be it further enacted,* That the Secretary of War be, and he is hereby authorized, under the direction of the President of the United States, to employ such portion of the Corps of Topographical Engineers, and such other persons as he may deem necessary, to make such explorations and surveys as he may deem advisable, to ascertain the most practicable and economical route for a railroad from the Mississippi river to the Pacific ocean, and that the sum of one hundred and fifty thousand dollars, or so much thereof as may be necessary, be, and the same is hereby, appropriated out of any money in the treasury not otherwise appropriated, to defray the expense of such explorations and surveys.

Approved March 3, 1853.

THIRTY-THIRD CONGRESS, FIRST SESSION—Chapter 60.

Appropriation: For deficiencies for the railroad surveys between the Mississippi river and the Pacific ocean, forty thousand dollars.

Approved May 31, 1854.

THIRTY-THIRD CONGRESS, FIRST SESSION—Chapter 267.

Appropriation: For continuing the explorations and surveys to ascertain the best route for a railway to the Pacific, and for completing the reports of surveys already made, the sum of one hundred and fifty thousand dollars.

Approved August 5, 1854.

Erratum.—On page 3, report of Secretary of War, for "March 31" read *March* 3.

Note.—In the note to Table A, page 31, report of the Secretary of War, marked thus *, which reads, "These are the estimates of the office, those of Governor Stevens having been brought to the same standard of increased cost as the other routes, and his equipment reduced to that of the other routes. His estimates were $117,121,000 and $7,030,000;" the sum of $117,121,000 is the estimate for the whole route from St. Paul to Seattle. From St. Paul to Vancouver the estimate of Governor Stevens is $110,091,000.

INDEX

TO

REPORT OF THE SECRETARY OF WAR AND OFFICE REPORTS.

CHAPTER II.

Route near the forty-first and forty-second parallels of north latitude.

CHAPTER III.

Route near the thirty-eighth and thirty-ninth parallels of north latitude.

CHAPTER IV.

Route near the thirty-fifth parallel of north latitude.

CHAPTER V.

Route near the thirty-fifth parallel of north latitude.

CHAPTER VI.

MEMORANDA ON RAILWAYS BY BREVET CAPTAIN GEORGE B. MC'CLELLAN.

REPORT OF GENERAL JESUP.

REPORT

OF

THE SECRETARY OF WAR

ON THE

SEVERAL RAILROAD EXPLORATIONS.

REPORT OF THE SECRETARY OF WAR.

War Department,
Washington, February 27, 1855.

Sir: I have the honor, in obedience to the provisions of the 11th section of the army appropriation act, approved March 31, 1853, to lay before Congress printed reports of the engineers employed under the provisions of that act to make such explorations and surveys as this department might deem advisable, in order to ascertain the most practicable and economical route for a railroad from the Mississippi river to the Pacific ocean.

The great amount of labor required in the preparation of the general map, originally designed to accompany this report, and the unfinished condition of the original maps and other data, have delayed its completion beyond the period anticipated, but it is confidently believed that its engraving will be finished in time to accompany the extra copies of the report ordered by the two houses of Congress. It embraces the territory of the United States between the great lakes and the Mississippi river, on the east, and the Pacific ocean on the west. It is based upon the most reliable astronomical data within those limits; and the details having been compiled with care, from all the government explorations and surveys and other reliable authorities, it will present more minute information upon the region embraced by it than has heretofore been exhibited on any general map. It will show the relation to each other of the different railroad routes recently explored, their connexions with prominent points on Lakes Superior and Michigan, the Mississippi river and the Gulf of Mexico, and with the ports of the Pacific; and, exhibiting only such features as have been determined by reliable observers, it will be of great value in showing what further explorations are necessary, and in determining their direction and extent.

I have heretofore reported the nature of the explorations and surveys ordered in compliance with this act; and by a reference to the statements there made, it will be seen that in order to accomplish as much as possible within the limited period indicated, not only were there as many distinct corps employed as there were routes to be surveyed, but several parties were, in some cases, employed upon different sections of the same route. It appears, therefore, necessary, in submitting these several reports, many of which are quite voluminous and in detached parts, to present a general recapitulation of their results, indicating those distinguishing characteristics, the comparison of which will determine which of the routes surveyed best fulfils the condition of practicability and economy proposed by the act.

I will here repeat the general sketch of the country given in my first annual report, but corrected in accordance with the results of the recent explorations. This will serve, in the absence of a more elaborate description, to give some general idea of the nature of the country over which they extended.

The western portion of the continent of North America, irrespective of the mountains, is traversed from north to south by a broad, elevated swell or plateau of land, which occupies the greater portion of the whole space between the Mississippi river and the Pacific ocean. The crest of this plateau, or the water-shed of the country, is nearly midway between the Pacific coast and the Mississippi. It may be represented on the map by an undulating line traced between the headwaters of the streams which flow eastward and those which flow westward. It divides the whole area between the Mississippi and the Pacific into two nearly equal portions—that on the east being somewhat the larger. This crest of the water-shed has its greatest elevation in Mexico; and thence declines to its lowest point about the latitude of 32°, where it has a height of about 5,200 feet, between the waters of the Rio Grande and those of the San Pedro, a tributary of the Gila. From this parallel it increases in altitude northward, and reaches its maximum near the 38th parallel, where it is about 10,000 feet high. Thence it declines as we pass northward; and, in latitude 42° 24′, it has an elevation of, say, 7,490 feet; and in the latitude of about 47° it is reported to be at least 1,450 feet lower. The heights here given are those of the lowest passes over the crest or water-shed of the great plateau of the country, and not those of the mountain peaks and ridges which have their base upon it, and rise, in some cases, to the height of 17,000 feet into the region of perpetual snow.

The slope of the plateau on the east and south, towards the Mississippi and the Gulf of Mexico, is comparatively gentle, and in the northern part of Texas, that known by the name of the Llano Estacado, or Staked Plain, is by steps. It is traversed by the Missouri, the Platte, the Arkansas, and other large rivers, which rise among the mountains near the crest, and flow eastward and southward in channels sunk beneath the general surface-level of the plains.

Its crest, and nearly the entire distance thence to the Pacific, is occupied by high plains or basins, differing from each other in elevation from 1,000 to 3,000 feet, and by mountain peaks and ridges, varying in direction to almost every point of the compass, though they have a general course north and south. Many of these mountains, including those that bound this system, have obtained the name of chains, and a short classification of them will now be attempted, although it is to be premised that our knowledge of them is most imperfect, and the classification now made, future explorations will probably show to be erroneous. The only proper classification must be made by the geologist, after a thorough exploration for this purpose, which it will require a long period to accomplish.

These mountains may be considered as constituting three great systems, extending generally throughout our possessions in a north and south direction; and though this arrangement may not be the best or most accurate, yet it will enable us to take a comprehensive view of the whole as regards the construction of a railroad, since any direct line that can be traced from the Mississippi to the Pacific, except near the 48th and 32d parallels, will encounter each of these three systems in some point.

Calling the most eastern system No. 1, we find a portion of it, crossing the Rio Grande, and entering Texas at the Great Cañon. Its extension south into Mexico forms the east front of the Sierra Madre. Running northward, this system includes all the mountains on either side of the Rio Grande, enclosing its valley and the Salinas Basin. Those on the east form the divide between the Pecos and Salinas Basin, and between the Rio Grande and Canadian; on the west they divide the waters of the Rio Grande from those that flow to the Gulf of California. Those on the east are sometimes called the Rocky mountains, sometimes the Sierra Madre; and this last name is sometimes applied to those on the west. There seems to be a necessity for considering the mountains on both sides of the Rio Grande as one system. These may be said to unite near the headwaters of the Rio Grande and Arkansas, and here the mountains have their greatest development. The Sierra de la Plata extends to the southwest, the Elk mountains to the west, and the various chains forming the Park mountains to the north. The Park mountains, in latitude 41° 30′, sink into the plateau, forming the region of the South Pass; and the only continuation we have of this system is in the Black Hills, which continue to the north, with diminished elevation, till, in latitude 46° 15′, they are merged into the coteau through which the Upper Missouri makes its passage.

Among the mountains included in this system are the Sierra Madre, a portion of what is called the Rocky mountains, the Diabolo mountains, the Guadalupe mountains, Hueco mountains, Organ mountains, Sandia mountains, Santa Fe mountains, Sierra Blanca, Sierra Mojada, Sierra San Juan, Sierra de la Plata, Elk mountains, Park mountains, Medicine Bow mountains, and Black Hills.

System No. 1 is thus but partially gorged by the Rio Grande, whose passage of the Great Cañon is wholly impracticable for any method of communication; that of El Paso is practicable. It is completely cut through by the North Platte and Sweet Water, forming a practicable route; and is turned by the Upper Missouri.

Low mountains or hills are known to exist between the Black Hills and the Wind River chain, about the headwaters of the Yellowstone and Missouri; but this region is too little known to be treated of with confidence, and may have a decided effect in modifying this classification.

System No. 2. If, from the Great Northern Bend of the Missouri, we travel west for 450 miles, we come again upon what are called the Rocky mountains; and still further west lies the Cœur d'Alene, or Bitter Root range, the two enclosing the Bitter Root or St. Mary's valley; and both are considered as forming a part of this system. Following it to the south, it includes the Wind River chain, the Bear mountains, the Uinta mountains, and the Wahsatch, which last continue as far south as it has been explored, probably forming the divide between the Great Basin and the Colorado, till the junction of the latter with the Gila.

System No. 3. From the junction of the Gila and Colorado, we find continuous mountains running to the northwest, and terminating at Point Conception, on the Pacific. On the south they are joined by the mountains forming the peninsula of California, the junction being at the San Gorgonio Pass, in latitude 33° 45′.

On the north, two chains leave this range in latitude 35°. One, called the Coast range and Coast mountains, lies to the west of the San Joaquin and Sacramento valleys, the waters of which break through them at the Bay of San Francisco. The other, called the Sierra Nevada, lies to the east of these valleys. A great depression, forming a plateau, is known to exist in the Sierra Nevada in latitude 40° 30′, and another in latitude 42° 45′, near Lake Abert. This chain may, perhaps, be considered as terminating at or in these plateaus, or to find its continuation in the Cascade or Coast range, which extend into the British possessions, being broken through by the Columbia and partly by the Klamath rivers.

The Blue mountains, to the south of the Columbia, represented as having a general northeast direction, may be considered, along with the mountains mentioned since leaving the Colorado, as forming system No. 3.

The Humboldt River chain, running north and south, (where crossed,) and separating the waters of the Humboldt or Mary's river from those of the Great Salt Lake Basin, is a marked feature; but as to its connexion, north and south, with other ranges, nothing is certain.

There seem good reasons for believing that the east and west ranges, represented as separating the Columbia River basin from the Great Basin, as well as the range represented as extending west from the Vegas of Santa Clara, are only apparently such, the deception arising from the overlapping of the side spurs to chains, the general direction of which is north and south.

The "triangular space" lying between the Rio Grande, Gila, and Colorado, is everywhere, so far as known, exceedingly mountainous; the ranges, such as the Mogollon and San Francisco mountains, having a general northwest direction. Too broad an interval exists between the explorations of Lieutenant Whipple and those of Captain Gunnison, to enable us to speak with certainty of their relation to the systems already alluded to.

In portions of the mountain region, the waters find no outlet to the sea, but drain into lakes and ponds, or sinks, carrying with them all the impurities of the basins to which they belong, and are there uniformly brackish or very salt. Prominent examples of this are the Salinas Basin, of New Mexico, and the Great Salt Lake Basin in Utah.

From most portions of this interior mountain belt, the waters have been able to force their barriers and escape to the ocean. The valleys thus drained are, those of the southern tributaries of the Upper Missouri, that of the North Fork of the Platte, and its tributary the Sweet Water, between the first and second systems; that of the Upper Rio Grande del Norte, in the first system; that of the Great Colorado of the West and its tributaries, between the first and second systems; those of the waters of the Bay of San Francisco and of the Klamath river, in the third system; and that of the Columbia river and its tributaries, between the second and third systems. Some of these streams, as well as others in the enclosed basins, have in places worn for themselves, through the solid rock, the most stupendous chasms or cañons, often 2,000 feet in vertical height, many of which it is impossible to follow or to cross.

The position of this belt of mountain region, stretching from north to south, gives rise to a peculiarity of climate and soil. Fertility depends principally upon the degree of temperature and amount of moisture, both of which are much affected by increase of elevation; and the latter also depends on the direction of the wind. The upper or return current of the trade-wind, flowing backward towards the northeast, gives a prevalence of westerly winds in the north temperate zone, which tends to spread the moisture from the Pacific over the western portion of our continent. These winds, however, ascending the western slope of the mountain ridges, are deprived of their moisture by the diminished temperature of the increased elevation; and hence it is that the plains and valleys on the eastern side of the ridges are generally parched and barren, and that the mountain system, as a whole, presenting, as it were, a screen against the moisture with which the winds from the west come laden, has for its eastern margin a sterile belt, which probably extends along the whole range, with a width varying from 250 to 300 and 400 miles.

From the foregoing sketch it will be perceived that the lines of exploration must traverse three different divisions or regions of country lying parallel to each other, and extending north and south through the whole of the western possessions of the United States. The first is that of the country between the Mississippi and the eastern edge of the sterile belt, having a varying width of from 500 to 600 miles. The second is the sterile region, varying in width from 200 to 400 miles; and the third, the mountain region, having a breadth of from 500 to 900 miles.

Explorations show that the surface of the first division, with few exceptions, rises in gentle slopes from the Mississippi to its western boundary, at the rate of about six feet to the mile, and that it offers no material obstacle to the construction of a railroad. It is, therefore, west of this that the difficulties are to be overcome.

The concurring testimony of reliable observers had indicated that the second division, or that called the sterile region, was so inferior in vegetation and character of soil, and so deficient in moisture, that it had received, and probably deserved, the name of the desert. This opinion is confirmed by the results of the recent explorations, which prove that the soil of the greater part of this region is, from its constituent parts, necessarily sterile; and that of the remaining part, although well constituted for fertility, is, from the absence of rains at certain seasons, except where capable of irrigation, as uncultivable and unproductive as the other.

This general character of extreme sterility likewise belongs to the country embraced in the mountain region. From the western slopes of the Rocky mountains to the 112th meridian, or the western limit of the basin of the Colorado, the soil generally is of the same formation as that lying east of that mountain crest, mixed, in the latitudes of 35° and 32°, with igneous rocks; and the region being one of great aridity, especially in the summer, the areas of cultivable land are limited. The western slopes of the highest mountain chains and spurs within this region being of a constitution favorable to fertility, and receiving much larger depositions of rain than the plains, have frequently in their small valleys a luxuriant growth of grasses, which sometimes clothes the mountain-sides; and where the wash is deposited on mountain stream or river-bottom the soil is fertile, and can be cultivated, if the elevations are not too great, and the means of irrigation available. Such mountain-valleys and river-bottoms exist upon all the routes, and the difference in the areas found in the different latitudes is not sufficiently great to be of any considerable weight in determining the question of choice of route. It is probable that all the routes are nearly on an equality in this respect.

The cultivable valleys of the Rocky mountain district near the route of the 47th parallel do not probably exceed an area of 1,000 square miles, though there are extensive tracts of fine grazing lands. In this latitude the great sterile basaltic plain of the Columbia, and the barren table-lands, spurs, and mountain masses of the Cascade range, principally occupy the space between the Cœur d'Alene mountains and the main chain of the Cascade system. In this area, where the rocks are principally of igneous origin, there are likewise occasional valleys of cultivable soil. The western slopes of the Cascade mountains descend to the borders of Puget sound.

On the routes of the 41st and 38th parallels, in the region under consideration, the only large body of soil capable of productive cultivation, by the construction of suitable works for irrigation, is that of the basin of the Great Salt lake, estimated to be 1,108 square miles in extent, about one-tenth part of which, being susceptible of cultivation without the construction of irrigating canals, is now cultivated by the Mormons. Here also are extensive grazing lands.

The great elevated plain of the Rocky mountains in latitudes 41° and 42°, and that of latitude 38°, called the San Luis valley, are covered with wild sage, the narrow border of grass found upon the streams being the chief, almost only, production capable of supporting animal life. The slopes of the mountains bounding them are covered with grass.

The plains of the Great Basin, whose greatest width (500 miles) is in latitude 41°, are, with the exception heretofore stated, entirely sterile, and either bare or imperfectly covered with a scattered growth of wild sage. Where a stream or lake is found in this desolate region, its immediate borders generally support a narrow belt of grass and willows; the former being also found on the mountain slopes, where occasionally a scattered growth of stunted cedars is likewise seen. Water is found on the mountain-side. The predominating rocks, from the Wahsatch mountains to the Sierra Nevada, are of igneous origin. In the southern portion of the Basin the granitic rocks are more abundant than the volcanic.

On the routes of the parallels of 35° and 32° the valleys of the Pecos, Rio Grande, Gila, and Colorado of the West, contain the largest areas of fertile soil capable of irrigation and cultivation. That in New Mexico is estimated at 700 square miles, exclusive of the regions occupied by Indians, of which 200 square miles are now under cultivation. Here the grazing land is of very great extent, the table-lands, as well as the mountain-sides, being covered with grass. The valley of the Colorado of the West, between its mouth and the 35th parallel, contains 1,600 square miles of fertile soil, which can be irrigated from the river.

The plains south of the Gila in its lower course, and that west of the Colorado, extending to the Coast range, called the Colorado desert, as well as the contiguous portion of the Great Basin, are bare and exceedingly sterile in their aspect, and closely resemble each other. The soil of the Colorado desert, and much of this as well as other parts of the Great Basin, is, however, favorably constituted for fertility, but the absence of the essential, quickening element, water, leaves them utterly unproductive.

West of the Coast, Sierra Nevada, and Cascade mountains the country is better watered than that just considered; and the soil being mostly well constituted for fertility, is productive in proportion to the yearly amount of precipitation and the means of irrigation.

The general position and direction of the four routes to be explored were explained in my report of December 1, 1853, and copies of the instructions given to the parties were appended to it.

They were directed to observe and note all the objects and phenomena which have an immediate or remote bearing upon the railway, or which might seem to develop the resources, peculiarities, and climate of the country; to determine geographical positions, obtain the topography, observe the meteorology, including the data for barometric profiles, and two of the parties were to determine the direction and intensity of the magnetic force. They were to make a geological survey of the lines; to collect information upon, and specimens of, the botany and zoology of the country; and to obtain statistics of the Indian tribes which are found in the regions traversed. Thus would be obtained all the information for the general consideration of the question, as well as the data upon which the cost of construction and working a railroad depend.

If the results of the explorations made under these instructions do not furnish the data requisite to solve every question satisfactorily, they at least give a large amount of valuable information, and place the question in a tolerably clear light. We see now, with some precision, the nature and extent of the difficulties to be encountered, and, at the same time, the means of surmounting them.

As the readiest mode of communicating the nature and extent of the information contained in the reports herewith submitted, a brief description of each route, its characteristic features, facilities, difficulties, and probable cost of construction, will be given.

For a long distance west of the Mississippi, the enterprise of private companies, acting under State charters, has explored the country, and has projected or is constructing railroads, stretching towards the Pacific. As the examinations made under these auspices, and our general knowledge of that part of the country, afford the information necessary to determine all questions bearing upon the practicability of a railroad, it has been deemed unnecessary to incur the expense and delay of continuing the explorations directed by the act, eastward of the points reached, to which railroads are already projected, and consequently but one of the routes, the most northern, has its starting-point on the Mississippi. The connexion of the others with that river, as well as with the seaports of Atlantic and Gulf States, is shown by a table (B) hereto annexed, compiled from the best railroad maps.

ROUTE NEAR THE FORTY-SEVENTH AND FORTY-NINTH PARALLELS OF NORTH LATITUDE.

Taking the routes in their geographical order, that near the 47th parallel, the general direction of the exploration of which was intrusted to Governor Stevens, of Washington Territory, will be the first discussed.

The route was to cross the Rocky mountains at the sources of the tributaries of the Missouri and Columbia rivers, and, in approaching and leaving the mountains, to follow as far as practicable the valleys of these rivers and their tributaries.

The general direction of the Missouri from the Rocky mountains to the Great Bend, in latitude 48° 30′, is from west to east, and thence to latitude 43° 30′ southeast. The point where the direction changes is reached from St. Paul, on the Mississippi, by a line passing up on the east side of that river to Little Falls, 109 miles, and there crossing it; thence gaining the divide between the waters of Hudson's bay and those of the Missouri, keeping on this divide, and approaching, in longitude 103°, within a few miles of the 49th parallel; then passing southerly, between the 104th and 105th meridians, and entering the valley of the Missouri river. The route then follows this valley to the mouth of Milk river. The ground near the Missouri here becoming rough and broken, the route is obliged to leave it and follow the valley of Milk river 187 miles; then entering the prairies, which near the mountains are more favorable for location than near the Missouri river, it continues in a line nearly parallel to the river, across its tributaries, the Marias, Teton, and Sun rivers, and enters either Clark's or Cadotte's Pass.

As far as the crossing of Sun river, 1,093 miles from St. Paul, the route is over river bottom or prairie, the usual expense of construction over such ground being increased by the necessity of guarding against freshets by embankment on the river bottoms, of ballasting in the soft, sticky soil of Milk river, of providing supplies of water during the dry season, over certain portions of the route, by reservoirs and aqueducts, estimated to cost, with planting trees for supply of fuel, $3,000,000, and of transporting ties and lumber for distances of from 100 to

470 miles—forest-growth suitable for ties and lumber not being found at closer intervals on the route. These, in connexion with the uninhabited and uncultivable condition of the country for 740 miles, form the difficulties of this portion of the route, and will materially increase the cost of its construction.

The most difficult portion of the whole route is, however, that which is now entered upon, viz: from Sun river to the Spokane, a distance of 365 miles, embracing the Rocky mountains proper, and a secondary chain lying west of them, called Cœur d'Alene and the Bitter Root mountains.

Through the Rocky mountains seven passes were explored; but the only ones among them, upon which the information obtained was sufficiently thorough and complete to enable projects to be made, are two (Clark's and Cadotte's) lying near each other in latitude 47°, and connecting the headwaters of Dearborn river, a tributary of the Missouri, with the Blackfoot, a head branch of the Columbia.

The summit ridge of Clark's Pass has an elevation of 6,323 feet, and requires a tunnel 2½ miles long, at an elevation of 5,300 feet. Its connexion with the main line of survey along the valley of the Blackfoot river was not made, though "believed" practicable, with grades of 50 feet per mile. The interval unexamined is 4½ miles long. This pass has been adopted by Governor Stevens in the railroad estimate, and is probably practicable.

The approach to the other pass (Cadotte's) is difficult, owing to the numerous deep ravines of the tributaries of a branch of Dearborn river, which the road must cross. The summit of the pass has an elevation of 6,044 feet; requires a tunnel 4¼ miles long, at an elevation of 5,000 feet, with grades of approach of 60 feet, and of departure of 40 feet, per mile.

A tunnel 4¼ or even 2½ miles in length, in rock or part rock, at a depth below the summit of 1,000 feet, in a severely-cold climate, 800 or 1,000 miles distant from a thickly-inhabited district, is a work of vast difficulty; and the necessity of the construction of one of these two tunnels, in connexion with the character of the approach, and the difficult nature of the work required, continuing westward as far as the crossing of the Spokane river, in all a distance of 365 miles, is one of the most serious objections to the route.

From either pass the route seeks the Blackfoot river, with the view of reaching Clark's fork, which opens the only pass through the Bitter Root mountains, the practicability of which was determined. In order to reach Clark's fork, two routes were examined. The first follows the Blackfoot river to its junction with Hell-Gate, a distance of 93 miles. The valley is narrow and wooded, the stream winding, and for twenty miles there is a narrow gorge. Numerous bridges will be required. The Hell-Gate, a few miles after being joined by the Blackfoot, empties into the St. Mary's, called below this junction the Bitter Root. The construction of the road along this stream to its junction with Clark's fork will be a work of great difficulty and expense, requiring short curves, steep gradients, numerous bridges, heavy side-cutting, and high embankments, in consequence of the spring freshets, (from twenty to thirty feet of vertical rise.) From the nature of the examination, its practicability cannot be considered as established.

The other route, (shorter, and probably less difficult,) having followed the Blackfoot but a short distance, crosses to the Jocko, descends this to the Flathead, and descends the latter to its junction with the Bitter Root, forming Clark's fork, bounded closely by high, rocky mountains. Having reached Clark's fork, the route continues along this river as far as Lake Pend d'Oreille, between rugged, rocky mountains, which at several points crowd upon the river. The valley of this river is heavily timbered, principally with pine, and, with the lake, it is subject to freshets fifteen feet in height. Leaving Lake Pend d'Oreille at its lower extremity, the route crosses to the Spokane without difficulty. At the Spokane river the continuous mountain region and the forest terminate, and "all great difficulties of location upon the route cease." The earth-excavation and embankment throughout this section (from the east base of the Rocky mountains to the Spokane river, 365 miles) will be large in amount, and expensive; there will be frequent rock-excavation, and the bulk of the rock-excavation in the entire route will be in this section. It is evident that the difficulties of construction will be great, and the cost excessive.

Upon the passes of the Rocky mountains, Governor Stevens says: "It is not doubted there are other passes in this portion of the Rocky mountain range, even better than those explored; they are indicated by the general depression of the mountain range, with the greater frequency of the streams stretching out to meet each other from the opposite slopes of the mountains; and I consider it important that, in future operations, a whole season should be devoted to their thorough examination, and that instrumental surveys should be made of the pass found to be the most practicable."

Leaving the Spokane, the route enters the Great Plain of the Columbia, a table-land stretching from the Cœur d'Alene to the Cascade mountains, a distance of 200 miles. Its central and western portions are of trap formation, and are described on the map as sandy, rocky, and sterile. Its summit, 800 feet above the Spokane river, is readily attained, the treeless plain is crossed in a distance of 110 miles, and a suitable point for crossing the Columbia river, 400 or 450 yards wide, reached, 140 miles distant from the Spokane. This point is about equally distant from the navigable waters of the Pacific in Puget sound and in the Columbia river. The whole intermediate space is occupied by the Cascade mountains, with their secondary chains, spurs, and high, broken table-lands, through which there are but two passes reported practicable for a railroad—that of the Columbia river and that of the Yakima, sometimes erroneously called the Snoqualme.

The Yakima Pass gives the most direct route to Puget sound, the distance by it being 150 or 160 miles shorter than by the Columbia River Pass. It requires a tunnel through rock, (siliceous conglomerate,) either 4,000 yards long, 3,000 feet above the sea, or a tunnel 11,840 yards long, 2,400 feet above the sea. The reconnaissance did not extend westward from the summit more than three miles. The evidence respecting the amount of snow found on the summit of the pass at the close of winter, makes it probable that it is then 20 feet deep there. This question should be satisfactorily settled, and the reconnaissance completed, before the practicability of the pass can be considered established. In the opinion of the officer making the reconnaissance—Captain McClellan, Corps of Engineers—the pass is barely practicable, and only at a great cost of time, labor, and money. Under every favorable condition of position the construction of either of the proposed tunnels would be seriously objectionable; but where the position itself is so unfavorable, the final advantages should be very great to determine the selection of this route. The information now possessed is sufficient to decide against this route.

The route by the pass of the Columbia follows that river from the Great Plain, being generally located, as far as the Dalles, in bottom-lands which present no difficulties. From the Dalles to near Vancouver, 90 miles, the rocky bluffs close upon the river, and the work required will be similar to that of the Hudson River railroad along the mountain region. In the opinion of Mr. Lander, "the high floods to which the Columbia river is subject, are serious obstacles to obtaining the best location for cheap construction offered by its valley." In 1854, the rise of the river during the flood was 10 feet above spring level, and 17 feet above summer level.

The Columbia river is navigable for sea-going vessels to Vancouver, the point now reached; but the unfavorable character of the entrance to that river, and the great superiority of the ports on Puget sound, seemed to render it expedient to adopt some one of the latter as the Pacific terminus of this route. Continuing down the Columbia, therefore, through bottom-lands, to the mouth of the Cowlitz, the route enters the wide and comparatively flat and wooded valley of that river, ascends it, and, crossing over the wooded and prairie plains, which, "though not fully explored, are sufficiently well known to insure the unusually favorable character of the country for the construction of a railway," reaches Seattle, the best port on the east side of Puget sound.

From the Rocky mountains to Seattle, wood, stone, and other building materials, are found along the line of the route, or at points so accessible to it, that it may be considered well supplied with them throughout.

The information upon the character of the soil upon the route does not admit of satisfactory conclusions to be deduced. It is sufficient, however, to show that in this latitude, as in that of the Arkansas, the uncultivable region begins about the 99th meridian. Immediately under the Rocky mountains the soil improves, probably from the mountain wash. The tertiary and cretaceous formations extend, in these latitudes, from about the 97th meridian to the eastern base of the Rocky mountains, and, under the meteorological conditions found in this space, are unsuitable for agricultural purposes. There are some very limited exceptions to this general character in portions of river bottoms. These tertiary formations in the arid regions of Asia and Africa form the great deserts of those countries.

The country west of the Rocky mountains to the Pacific slopes may likewise be described as one of general sterility. The eastern portion of the Great Plain of the Columbia is represented to be grassed; its middle and western parts almost entirely sandy, rocky, and sterile. The mountain masses, spurs, and table-lands of the Cascade chain, east of the main crest, are sterile. There are exceptions to this general sterility in the mountain valleys, where the soil is better constituted for fertility, and the rains more abundant; but, although portions of these are suitable for agricultural purposes, they are better adapted to grazing. The sum of the areas of cultivable soil in the Rocky mountain region does not exceed, if it equals, 1,000 square miles. West of the Cascade mountains there are rich river bottoms, clay formations that are arable, and prairies offering good grazing.

The principal favorable characteristics of this route are its low profile, low grades, and the low elevation of the mountain passes, and its connexion with the Missouri and Columbia rivers. The reported sum of the ascents and descents is the least of all the routes; this proportion may, however, be changed when the minor undulations are measured. The principal unfavorable features are, in construction, the tunnel required on the Rocky mountains, and the difficulty and expense of construction from the eastern approach of the Rocky mountains to the Spokane river, and the expense of the construction along the Columbia river, from the Dalles to near Vancouver. These, when considered carefully, are serious objections to the route, not only in the money, but the time, they will consume. In thickly-populated countries their construction would be difficult and costly; situated as they are—the Rocky mountain region especially—the difficulties, cost, and time required, are greatly increased.

The severely-cold character of the climate throughout the whole route, except the portion west of the Cascade mountains, is one of its unfavorable features; and, for national considerations, its proximity to the dominions of a powerful foreign sovereignty must be a serious objection to it as a military road.

Its cost has been estimated by Governor Stevens, by the Columbia River valley and the Cowlitz, at $117,121,000; the cost of work at eastern prices having had 25 per cent. added to it from the Bois des Sioux to the Rocky mountains, and 40 per cent. thence to the Pacific. It has been thought safer to add 100 per cent. to the cost at eastern prices from the eastern slope of the Rocky mountains to the Pacific. This would swell the estimate to $150,871,000.

Should Governor Stevens have included a full equipment in his estimate, $10,000,000 should be subtracted from this sum to bring the estimate in accordance with those of the other routes, and the cost then becomes $140,871,000.

The length of the route from St. Paul to Vancouver is 1,864 miles. The sum of ascents and descents, as far as reported, is 18,100 feet, which will be equivalent, in the cost of working the road, to an increased horizontal distance of 343 miles: this added to the length of the line of location, gives for equated length 2,207 miles.

From St. Paul to Seattle, by the Columbia route, is 2,025 miles, which the sum of ascents and descents increases to an equated distance of 2,387 miles.

The work upon this route, under Governor Stevens, embraced a wider field of exploration than that upon any other explored, and a great amount of topographical and general information was collected in relation to the country traversed. The necessary astronomical observations were not made to determine accurately the longitudes of the several stations, and the loss of his barometrical observations, after the completion of the field-work, left no means of revising and verifying the profile of the route.

The examination of the approaches and passes of the Cascade mountains, made by Captain McClellan, of the Corps of Engineers, presents a reconnaissance of great value, and though performed under adverse circumstances, exhibits all the information necessary to determine the practicability of this portion of the route, and reflects the highest credit on the capacity and resources of that officer.

ROUTE NEAR THE FORTY-FIRST AND FORTY-SECOND PARALLELS OF NORTH LATITUDE.

About one-half of the route in this latitude, extending from the Missouri river to Fort Bridger, on a tributary of Green river, has not been explored with a special reference to the practicability of constructing a railroad, and the reports do not contain all the details necessary to the elucidation of the subject. The information respecting it is to be found in the reports of Col. Fremont and Capt. Stansbury.

From Fort Bridger to Fort Reading, on the Sacramento river, the exploration has been made by Lieut. E. G. Beckwith, under the appropriation for that purpose.

The route may commence on the Missouri, either at Fort Leavenworth, about 245 miles from the Mississippi at St. Louis, or at Council Bluffs, about 267 miles from the Mississippi at Rock Island, ascend the Platte and enter the eastern chain of the Rocky mountains (the Black Hills) by the North fork and its tributary, the Sweet Water. Another route, by the South fork and a tributary called Lodge Pole creek, has been suggested by Capt. Stansbury as shorter and less expensive; but the information respecting it is not sufficiently full to make further mention of it necessary.

From the Missouri river to the entrance of the Black Hills, 30 miles above Fort Laramie, 520 miles from Council Bluffs, and 755 miles from Fort Leavenworth, the route resembles others from the Mississippi to the Rocky mountains, and needs no special mention. Its cost per mile will be about the same.

The route west of this point crosses many lateral streams that have cut deep ravines into the soil, and leaves the Platte just below the Hot Spring Gap, above which it is walled in by cañons. To avoid these, the route crosses a range of hills 800 feet above the river, and descending to the Sweet Water, a branch of the Platte, follows that stream to its source, where the summit of the plateau of the South Pass (elevation 7,490 feet) is attained. The valley of the Sweet Water is generally rather open, but occasionally it cuts through mountain spurs, forming cañons.

From the first gorge in the Black Hills to the summit of the pass, 291 miles, the work will be difficult and expensive, and is assimilated in amount to that of the Baltimore and Ohio railroad.

From the South Pass the route follows down Sandy creek, a tributary of Green river, to the crossing of the latter, and thence to Fort Bridger, (elevation 7,254 feet,) on Black's fork, likewise a tributary of Green river. The amount of work on this section would be considerably less than on the preceding.

From Council Bluffs to Fort Bridger the distance is 942 miles; from Fort Leavenworth 1,072 miles.

The route now ascends the divide between the waters of Green river and those of the Great Salt lake, by the valley of Black's fork, or of one of its tributaries, with grades of 69.5 and 40.3 feet per mile. The summit is a broad terrace at the foot of the Uinta mountains, and has an elevation of 8,373 feet. From this point the line descends over the undulating country separating the Uinta and Bear River mountains, crossing the head of Bear river, and, entering the valley of White Clay creek at its head, follows down that stream to its junction with Weber river.

The Wahsatch mountains now intervene between this plateau country and the Great Salt lake, and the passage through them may be effected by following Weber river, or by ascending to near the sources of the Timpanogos; and descending that stream—both being affluents, directly or indirectly, of the Great Salt lake—the distances are about the same to their common point on that lake.

There are cañons upon both these streams. That of the Timpanogos is 10 miles in length, and narrow, being from 100 to 300 yards in width. It is direct in its general course, but must be bridged at several points, to avoid short curves. The sides are of blue limestone, and will require rock-blasting at some points. The river, 30 yards wide, descends with a powerful current, and, when most swollen, is six feet above its ordinary level.

On Weber river there are two cañons. The upper is rather a gorge or defile, 8½ miles long. The mountains rise to a great height above it, and are rocky and precipitous, and much broken by ravines. The river is winding, and it will be necessary to cross it frequently. The lower cañon, near the borders of the valley of Great Salt lake, is four miles long, direct, with an average width of 175 yards, the stream being 30 yards wide, and impinging frequently with great force against the base of the mountains, which, however, are sufficiently retreating to admit of the practicable passage of a railway.

Entering the valley of Great Salt lake from either this or the Timpanogos cañon, there is no obstacle to the construction of a railway passing by the south end of the lake, and crossing the Jordan, Tuilla valley, and Spring or Lone Rock valley, to its west side.

By the valley of the Timpanogos, the distance from near Fort Bridger to the south end of the Great Salt lake, on the western side of the valley of the Jordan, is 182.55 miles; the greatest grade required, 84 feet to the mile. The amount of work required on this section, excepting that along the cañon, will not, in the opinion of Lieutenant Beckwith, be great.

From the western shore of Great Salt lake to the valley of Humboldt river, the country consists alternately of mountains, in more or less isolated ridges, and of open level plains, rising gradually from the level of the lake on the east, to the base of the Humboldt mountains on the west; that is, from 4,200 feet to 6,000 feet above the sea. West of the Humboldt mountains the country is of the same character, the plains declining until, at the west shore of Mud lake, usually called the foot of the Sierra Nevada, the elevation is 4,100 feet.

The mountains in this space of 500 miles, (by the route travelled 600 miles,) between the Great Salt lake and the foot of the Sierra Nevada, have a general north and south course. Occasionally cross-spurs close in the valleys to the north and south, but more frequently this isolation is only apparent. The mountains are sharp, rocky, and inaccessible in many parts, but are low and easily passed in others. Their general elevation varies from 1,500 to 3,000 feet above the valleys, and but few of them retain snow upon their highest peaks during the summer. They are liberally supplied with springs and small streams, but the latter seldom extend far into the plains. At the time of melting snows there are many small ponds and lakes, but at other seasons the waters are absorbed by the soil near the base of the mountains. Grass is found in abundance upon nearly every range, but timber is very scarce—a small scattered growth of cedar only being seen upon a few ranges. East of the Humboldt mountains the growth of cedars is more abundant, and the grass better, than to the west. The valleys rarely have a width east and west of more than five or ten miles, but often have a large extent north and south. They are irregular in form, frequently extending around the ends of mountains, or uniting to succeeding valleys by level passages. The greater part of the surface of these valleys is merely sprinkled by several varieties of sombre artemisia, (wild sage,) presenting the aspect of a dreary waste. Though there are spots more thickly covered with this vegetation, yet the soil is seldom half covered with it, even for a few acres, and is nowhere suitable for settlement and cultivation. Immediately west of Great Salt lake there is a plain of mud, clay, and sand, impregnated with salt, seventy miles in width from east to west by its longest line, and forty at a narrower part further south, thirty miles of which must be piled for the passage of a railroad across it. A railroad may be carried over this series of valleys and around the mountain masses, at nearly the general level of the valleys.

The route in this manner reaches the foot of the Humboldt mountains, a narrow but elevated ridge, containing much snow during most of the year, and crosses them by a pass nine miles long, about three of which are occupied by a narrow, rocky ravine, above which the road should be carried on the sloping spurs of the mountains on the western descent; elevation of summit 6,579 feet above the sea. At the time when passed, 21st May, snow covered the high peaks above it, and a few drifts extended into the ravines down to the level of its summit.

The descent is now made to the open valley of Humboldt river, which is followed for about 190 miles. The steepest grade proposed in the pass of Humboldt mountain is 89 feet per mile for eight miles, but this can be reduced by gaining distance to any desirable extent.

The Humboldt river, as described by Colonel Fremont, is formed by two streams rising in mountains west of the Great Salt lake. Its general direction is from east to west, coursing among broken ranges of mountains; its length about three hundred miles. It is without affluents, and terminates near the foot of the Sierra Nevada in a marshy lake. It has a moderate current—is from two to six feet deep in the dry season, and probably not fordable anywhere below the junction of the two streams during the melting of the snows. The valley varies in width from a few miles to twenty, and, excepting the immediate river-banks, is a dry, sandy plain, without grass, wood, or arable soil. Its own immediate valley (bottom) is a rich alluvion, covered with blue grass, herds-grass, clover, and other nutritious grasses, and its course is marked through the plain by a line of willow.

Of the three lines from the Humboldt river to the foot of the Sierra Nevada, the best is that by the Noble's Pass road, as it avoids the principal range of mountains crossed on the line followed a few miles south. The line followed crosses two ranges of the general character of the Basin mountains, and reaches the foot of the Madelin Pass of the Sierra Nevada, on the west shore of Mud lake, in a distance of 119 miles, and at an elevation of 4,079 feet above the sea.

In this latitude the Sierra Nevada was found to be a plateau about 5,200 feet above the sea, 40 miles in width from east to west, enclosed at these limits by low mountains, the summits of the passes through which are 400 and 500 feet above the base. The plain is covered with irregular spurs, ridges, and isolated peaks, rising a few hundred feet, limiting it in a north and south direction sometimes to a space of a few hundred yards, and at others to that of ten miles. These spurs, &c., on the eastern portion of the plateau, are sparsely covered with cedar; on the western, heavily covered with pine.

There is no drainage from this plain, the waters of a few small streams and springs forming grassy ponds upon its surface. In its general features it is similar to the Great Basin, excepting that as more rain falls upon it, the vegetation is comparatively luxuriant.

There are two routes by which this plain may be reached from the Great Basin, and the descent made to the Sacramento river. That by the Madelin Pass, the more northern, is most probably the better of the two, and is the only one necessary to be considered. Leaving Mud lake, it ascends by the valley of Smoky creek for three miles, through a narrow gorge (from 100 to 150 yards wide) in an outlying spur of the Sierra Nevada.

After this the route is over more open ground, varying, in degree, to the summit of the passage through the eastern ridge bounding the Sierra Nevada plateau. The pass is thus far of a very favorable character—the length of the ascent is 22.89 miles; the difference of elevation, 1,172 feet; the altitude of the summit, 5,667 feet; and the steepest slope is 75 feet per mile.

The plateau being gained, is crossed by a nearly level line to the low ridge bounding it on the west, the summit elevation of which, 5,736 feet, is attained by following a ravine valley.

The descent to the Sacramento along one of its tributaries is now commenced, and is at first rapid. A cut is proposed at the summit, 120 feet deep, running out to the surface at either end, making a length of four miles, and a grade of 124 feet to the mile for 2.4 miles. It may be preferable to tunnel or to cut only one-half the depth proposed. The open plain of Round valley, on the Sacramento, is reached 15 miles from the summit, (difference of elevation 1,300 feet,) located for one-half that distance on the mountain side, which is broken by ravines.

The route now lies over the smooth plain of Round valley for 15 miles, to the head of the first cañon on the Sacramento. This cañon is a formidable obstacle to be overcome. Its entire length is nearly 14 miles, succeeded by an open valley of similar extent, which is followed by a second cañon, nine miles in length, of the same character as the first. From the mouth of Canoe creek, four miles below the foot of the second cañon, for the space of 96 miles the course of the Sacramento lies entirely through heavily-timbered mountains, which rise precipitously from the river-banks to the height of from 1,500 to 2,000 feet above the stream. Its course is very sinuous, with all varieties of curves greater than a right-angle, and is seldom entirely straight for two miles consecutively. The construction of this portion of the route, 136 miles in length, would be one of no ordinary difficulty or expense under the most favorable circumstances of dense population, and the facilities of railroad construction which it would afford. It is impossible, with the data presented, to form a reliable opinion of its probable cost.

Seventeen miles above Fort Reading the open valley of the Sacramento is attained, over which a railroad may be carried to the bay of San Francisco, 250 or 300 miles distant.

The distance from Fort Bridger to Fort Reading by the line of Lieutenant Beckwith's profile is 1,012 miles; from Fort Leavenworth to Fort Bridger, 1,072 miles—making the whole distance from Fort Leavenworth to Fort Reading, on the Sacramento, 2,084 miles, and to Benicia 2,264 miles.

The distance from Council Bluffs to Benicia by the above route is 2,134 miles.

Using the line along which the route can be located in the Great Basin, about 103 miles shorter than that travelled, the distances become, from Fort Bridger to Fort Reading, 909 miles; from Fort Leavenworth to Fort Reading, 1,980 miles; and to Benicia, 2,161 miles.

The distance from Council Bluffs to Benicia becomes 2,031 miles.

The points of supply for ties, lumber, &c., are at distances apart of 500, 300, 200, and 700 miles, as timber is only found at the eastern extremity of the route, on the Black Hills, Wind River mountains, the Uinta and Wahsatch mountains, and on the western slopes of the Sierra Nevada. The scattered growth of cedar upon the Basin mountains may, perhaps, be found available for ties.

Should the coal-beds of Green river prove to be of such quality and extent as to admit of being profitably mined, the points of supply of fuel—the same as those just designated for lumber—will be importantly increased. Coal may then be had for nearly the cost of mining it at the eastern terminus of the road, for cost of mining near its middle, and at its western terminus for the cost of mining, and freight to that point from Puget sound.

Fuel for working-parties will generally be found contiguous to the route.

The winter climate is known to be severe on the plains east of the Rocky mountains in this latitude. That it is more severe, and of long duration, upon the great table-land of the Rocky mountains, is to be inferred. Lieut. Beckwith found the sun had not yet begun to melt the snow upon the terrace divide on the western border of the plateau, and about 1,000 feet above it, when he crossed the former, on the 10th April. The snow was here from twelve to sixteen inches deep, and had accumulated in deep drifts on the northeast slopes of the hills and ravines. Captain Stansbury found the Uinta mountains covered with snow for a considerable distance from their summits on the 19th August. The quantity of snow that falls upon the great undulating plain between Fort Laramie and Fort Bridger is not exactly known. It is probable that no unusual difficulty may be apprehended from it on this plain, or on the terrace divide, where crossed by Lieut. Beckwith; but the fall of snow in the Wahsatch and other mountains is very much greater, and accumulates in their gorges, ravines, and cañons, to great depths. Apparently, Lieut. Beckwith does not apprehend unusual difficulties from this cause along the proposed railroad route in this region, or in that of the Madelin Pass.

The supply of water upon the Rocky mountain plateau must be very limited at certain seasons of the year: the distances apart of these supplies are not given.

Abundant supplies of water were found by Lieut. Beckwith on the mountains of the Great Basin. The season of the year when he crossed it—the spring—was the most favorable in this respect.

On this route, as on others, from the 98th or 99th meridian to the western slopes of the Sierra Nevada, a distance of 1,400 miles, the soil is uncultivable, excepting the comparatively limited area of the Mormon settlement, and an occasional river-bottom and mountain valley of small extent.

West of the Black Hills the plains are covered with artemisia, rarely furnishing any grazing except along the water-courses—the mountains being generally clothed, to a greater or less extent, with grass. The barren aspect of the Great Basin has been already described. In that desolate region there are but few and very limited areas where the conditions of soil, water, and temperature requisite for cultivation, are found.

The features of this route, favorable to the economical construction of a railroad, are apparent from the description of it which has just been given. Its unfavorable features may be briefly described: as the costly construction, for nearly three hundred miles along the Platte and Sweet Water, in ascending to the summit of the South Pass; in the cañon of the Timpanogos; in the two cañons of the Sacramento, fourteen and nine miles in length; and in the very sinuous course of the river, for the space of ninety-six miles, through heavily-timbered mountains rising precipitously from the stream—the cost of constructing a railroad along which cannot be properly estimated until minute surveys are made.

Although the route passes over elevated regions, the sum of ascents and descents is the next least after that of the 47th parallel, which is to be attributed to the table-land character of the mountain districts.

It partakes of the character of the route near the 47th parallel, in the long and severe winters on the plains east of the Rocky mountains and westward to the Great Basin.

The cost, as estimated in the office, from Council Bluffs to Benicia, a distance of 2,031 miles, is $116,095,000.

The statistics of the route will be found in the table appended.

The survey of the western portion of this route by Lieutenant Beckwith, has resulted in the discovery of a more direct and practicable route than was believed to exist from the Great Salt lake to the valley of the Sacramento. Since his report was made, a brief communication from Brevet Lieutenant Colonel Steptoe, commanding the troops in Utah, has announced the discovery of a still more direct route from Great Salt lake to San Francisco. The new portion of this route passes to the south of Humboldt or Mary's river, and, entirely avoiding the difficulties experienced by travellers along that stream, proceeds to the valley of Carson river, being well supplied with water and grass. From Carson river it crosses the Sierra Nevada by the passes at the head of that river, and descends to the valley of the Sacramento, being practicable throughout for wagons.

In the absence of instrumental surveys affording data for the construction of profiles, no opinion can be formed as to the practicability of this route for a railroad. Should it be found practicable, however, it will lessen the length of the route of the 41st parallel, and still further diminish its difficulties, already known to be less than on any other route except that of the 32d parallel.

ROUTE NEAR THE THIRTY-EIGHTH AND THIRTY-NINTH PARALLELS OF NORTH LATITUDE.

The general consideration that determined the position of the route to be examined near the 38th and 39th parallels of latitude, was its central position geographically, it being about midway between the northern and southern boundary lines of the United States, which is likewise the position, nearly, of the Bay of San Francisco; the two termini of the route, St. Louis and San Francisco, being respectively in latitudes 39° and 38°, nearly. Moreover, a route near these parallels would probably give the shortest road from the Bay of San Francisco to the navigable waters of the Mississippi.

The exploration of the route conducted by Captain J. W. Gunnison, corps of Topographical Engineers, commenced on the Missouri at the mouth of the Kansas, about 245 miles from the Mississippi at St. Louis. The Kansas, and its branch called the Smoky Hill fork, were followed to a convenient point for crossing to the Arkansas, the valley of this latter river having been entered west of the Great Bend and near the meridian of 99°. The route then ascended the valley of the Arkansas to the mouth of Apishpa creek, fifty miles above Bent's Fort; leaving it here, and crossing to the entrance of the Rocky mountains, here called the Sierra Blanca, at the Huerfano Butte, on the river of that name, a tributary of the Arkansas. The elevation at this point is 6,099 feet; its distance from Westport, mouth of the Kansas river, by the railroad route, 654 miles.

Of the several passes through the Rocky mountains connecting the tributaries of the Huerfano with those of the Rio del Norte, but one, the Sangre de Cristo, was found practicable for a railroad, the new and only practicable approach to this pass being explored by Capt. Gunnison. By side location the summit, 9,219 feet above the sea, 692 miles from Westport, was attained, and the descent made to the valley of the Rio Grande with practicable though heavy grades; and thence the grades were favorable to the vicinity of Fort Massachusetts.

The western chain of the Rocky mountains is now to be crossed in order to gain and traverse the basins of the two great tributaries of the Colorado of the West, Grand and Green rivers. For this purpose the valley of San Luis, an extensive, uncultivable plain, covered for the most part with wild sage, was ascended with easy grades to Sahwatch creek, one of whose affluents rises in a pass of the Rocky mountains, here called the Sahwatch mountains, known by the name of the Coo-che-to-pa Pass.

The approach to the summit of the pass, 10,032 feet above the sea, 816 miles from Westport, is not favorable, the pass in this part having a defile character, overhung occasionally by walls of igneous rock. To cross the summit, a grade of 124 feet per mile for several miles, and a tunnel nearly two miles long, are required. The descent, with grades varying from 41 to 108 feet per mile, is by the valley of Pass creek, along which much cutting and filling will be necessary, as the hills are cut by numerous ravines. For 16 miles before the junction of Pass creek with Coo-che-to-pa creek, the former passes through a broken cañon. After following Coo-che-to-pa creek seven miles, the valley of Grand river is attained.

The route follows the valley of this river 173 miles, then crosses the divide to Green river, 68 miles, and by the tributaries of the latter approaches the pass through the Wahsatch mountains. A tunnel three-quarters of a mile long is here required, the eastern approach to which is by means of a grade of 125 feet per mile for 6½ miles, and a descent to the west for 5 miles of 131 feet per mile. Thence westward along the valley of Salt creek for 18 miles the grade is 95 feet per mile, 16 miles of which is through a rocky cañon, intersected by lateral streams. The route then enters the valley of the Sevier, the exploration terminating on this river, 86 miles further on, and 1,348 miles from Westport.

From the western border of the State of Missouri to the Rocky mountains, 650 miles, no timber suitable for railroad purposes will be found, upon which reliance can be placed. From the Coo-che-to-pa Pass to the Great Basin, 500 miles, there is none available on the route, and the nearest supplies on the mountains bordering the Great Basin are in latitudes 40° and 41°.

With building-stone it is about as well supplied as the other routes. Of water there is a sufficient supply, except between Grand and Green rivers, a distance of 70 miles, where, at certain seasons of the year, little or none is found.

The soil west of the meridian of 99° is, under the present meteorological conditions, uncultivable, except in limited portions of river-bottoms and small mountain valleys; these latter, from their great elevation, being better adapted to grazing than agricultural pnrposes. This description is completely in accordance with the geological formation and meteorological condition; the former, from the meridian of 99° west, being apparently tertiary, excepting in the high mountain passes.

This route may be considered to possess, in common with that of the 41st parallel, the large body of fertile soil in Utah Territory occupied by the Mormons, the area of which is about 1,108 square miles.

The coal field of Missouri lies at the eastern extremity of this route; the indications of coal in the Grand and Green River basins make it highly probable that seams sufficiently thick for profitable mining exist there.

In regard to grade and construction, it is unnecessary to enter into any discussion of that portion of the route from Westport to the Sangre de Cristo Pass. It presents no peculiar difficulties or advantages, but is similar to the routes of the 47th and 41st parallels.

It would appear that the Sangre de Cristo and Coo-che-to-pa Passes are practicable in grade; but the construction of the road through the Coo-che-to-pa Pass, and the western approach to it, would be costly under favorable circumstances of population, &c., not only on account of the tunnel, but of the numerous ravines that are crossed west of the pass, and the cañon that follows.

The following brief enumeration of the character and extent of the difficulties to be encountered between the Coo-che-to-pa Pass and the Great Basin, make it evident that the route must be considered impracticable.

From the head of the cañon on Grand river, not far below the mouth of Coo-che-to-pa creek, to the Uncompahgra river, a distance of 70 miles, the ground is cut up with deep, wide, precipitous ravines, the largest several hundred feet deep. These ravines cannot be turned near the mountains without encountering similar difficulties, and at a cost greater than that of a route along the river. Thus the route is forced upon Grand river, and along its cañon, 60 miles in length, broken and interrupted by the deep ravines already mentioned and numerous smaller gullies. The roadway throughout the greater part of this distance must be blasted out of solid rock, and these wide ravines, from 100 to 200 feet deep, where they cut through the cañon, crossed by viaducts or filling.

Then follow 50 miles to the mouth of Blue river, the construction still of a difficult and costly character, from the cañons of the river and broken nature of the ground. From Blue to Green river is 100 miles, over which the road will require numerous bridges and culverts, and a costly road-bed foundation of broken stone or piling over a clayey soil, which in wet weather is almost impassable.

From Green river to the Wahsatch Pass, about 80 miles, the construction would still be of a costly character, the country being of the same ravine and chasm-like nature as that between the mouth of Coo-che-to-pa creek and Uncompahgra river, though on a smaller scale.

Next follows the Wahsatch Pass, the work in which is difficult and expensive. The greatest grade is 131 feet per mile; a tunnel not quite three-quarters of a mile long is requisite; and finally, a cañon 16 miles long on Salt creek, the walls of which are frequently broken by lateral streams, gives the only route along which the road can be brought, by cutting in solid rock at very great expense.

The difficulties of engineering and the cost of construction of this portion of the route from the Coo-che-to-pa Pass to Sevier river, in the Great Basin, a distance of about 500 miles, would be so great that it may be pronounced impracticable; and it is evident, from the report of Lieutenant Beckwith, that, to use his own language, "no other line exists in the immediate vicinity of this, worthy of any attention in connexion with the construction of a railroad from the Mississippi river to the Great Basin."

It is unnecessary, therefore, to consider the route further, or to enter into any discussion connected with the probable practicability and cost of constructing and working a railroad over other portions of the route where counterbalancing advantages are not found to compensate, in any degree, for the enormous cost of that under consideration.

Laying aside the utterly impracticable nature of this route, the following considerations will show its disadvantages as regards expenses of working, supposing it constructed:

From Westport to the west base of the Un-kuk-oo-ap mountains is 1,323 miles; sum of ascents, 23,190 feet; of descents, 19,052 feet; length of equivalent horizontal line for the route, 2,123 miles.

Of the direct route from the point at the western base of the Un-kuk-oo-ap mountains, near where the survey under Capt. Gunnison terminated, to the Tah-ee-chay-pah Pass, there is no survey or positive information. There is every reason to belive that it is, for the most part, a desert of the same general character as other portions of the Great Basin. Supposing the route to be a straight line, with uniform descent from the Un-kuk-oo-ap mountains to the entrance of the Tay-ee-chay-pah Pass, in latitude 35° 5′, (no pass being known to be practicable to the north of it in this portion of the Sierra Nevada,) the distance will be 430 miles, and the descent 1,830 feet; the equated horizontal distance, 464 miles.

From the entrance of the Tay-ee-chay-pah Pass to San Francisco is 326 miles; sum of ascents, 1,308 feet; sum of descents, 4,608 feet; equated length, 440 miles. Adding these together, with the equated distance from the mouth of the Kansas to the west base of the Un-kuk-oo-ap mountains, we have the total equated distance from Westport to San Francisco, 3,027 miles—the length of the straight horizontal line, which supposes no obstacle to be avoided, being only 1,500 miles.

The distance from Sevier river to Great Salt lake is 120 miles; sum of ascents and descents, 1,600 feet; equated distance, 150 miles; thence to Benicia, by the route near the 41st parallel, explored by Lieut. Beckwith, is 872 miles; sum of ascents and descents, 15,200 feet: making the equivalent horizontal line 1,160 miles; which added to the equated distance from Westport to Sevier river, 2,050 miles, we have a total of 3,360 miles, as the equated distance by this route from Westport to Benicia.

Neither in soil, climate, productions, population, nor in any other respect, does it possess advantages superior to other routes favoring the construction and working of a railroad.

The exploration of this route, conducted by Capt. Gunnison, of the Corps of Topographical Engineers, exhibits the high professional skill and sound judgment which characterized that officer. The extensive and reliable information which he collected, and the exact manner in which his operations were conducted, up to the period when he lost his life in the discharge of his duty, show how thoroughly he would have completed the task he had commenced, and how great a loss the service sustained in his untimely death. Several of his civil assistants fell with him, and the charge of the survey devolved upon Lieut. Beckwith, of the artillery, who has made, from the field-notes left by Capt. Gunnison, a thorough report of his explorations. Satisfied of the impracticability of the line he had traversed, Lieut. Beckwith commenced an exploration eastward from the Great Salt lake, to connect that position with the line of the 41st parallel, and then returning to Salt lake, continued the survey westward to the waters of the Pacific. This work, in all its parts, has been well done, and the topography well represented. More than ordinary credit is due to this officer, as the task performed by him was not in the line of his usual duties, and was executed without the aid of assistants, and with the means left to the party after a season of field operations.

ROUTE NEAR THE THIRTY-FIFTH PARALLEL OF NORTH LATITUDE.

The general features which have determined the position of this route, the exploration of which was conducted by Lieut. A. W. Whipple, Topographical Engineers, are the extension, west and east, of the interlocking tributaries of the Mississippi, the Rio Grande, and the Colorado of the West. It would appear to possess also a greater yearly amount of rain than the regions immediately north and south of it—and, as a consequence, a better supply of fuel and timber.

Commencing at Fort Smith, on the Arkansas river, about 270 miles from the Mississippi at Memphis, the route, as far as the Antelope Hills on the Canadian, a distance of 400 miles, may follow either the valleys of the Arkansas and Canadian, or a shorter line perhaps, but over more ground, south of the Canadian, this latter route branching again, and following either the valley of the Washita, or the dividing ridge between it and the Canadian.

From the Antelope Hills the route continues along the bottom of the Canadian, on the right bank, to the mouth of Tucumcari creek, about 250 miles, and ascends by the valley of Tucumcari, or by that of Pajarito creek, to the dividing-ridge between the Canadian and the Pecos rivers, elevation about 5,543 feet, and enters the valley of the latter. It follows this valley until, by means of a tributary, it rises to the high table-land, or basin, lying east of the Rocky mountains, elevation about 7,000 feet, crosses the elevated Salinas basin, 30 miles wide, the lowest point being 6,471 feet, and gains the divide in the Rocky mountains, elevation about 7,000 feet; from which point it descends to Albuquerque, or Isleta, on the Rio Grande, through the San Pedro Pass; or it may descend to the Rio Grande by the valley of the Galisteo river, north of Sandia mountain. A third route is indicated along the valley of the Pecos to its headwaters; thence to an affluent of the Galisteo; and thence, as before, to the Rio Grande.

Isleta, on the Rio Grande, is 854 miles from Fort Smith, and 4,945 feet above the sea.

Crossing the ridge separating the Rio Grande from the Puerco, the route follows the valley of its tributary, the San José, to one of its sources in a pass of the Sierra Madre, called the Camino del Obispo; at the summit, (elevation 8,250 feet,) a tunnel three-fourths of a mile long, at an elevation not less than 8,000 feet, is required, when the descent is made to the Zuñi river and near the Pueblo of Zuñi; the route then crosses, over undulating ground, to the Puerco of the West, at the Navajo spring.

Another route across the Sierra Madre, about twenty miles further north, was examined by Mr. Campbell, which is apparently far more favorable. The profile, however, is not from reliable instrumental examination. The height of the summit is about 7,750 feet above the sea. The Puerco of the West heads in this pass, and the route follows the valley of this stream, (intersecting the other line at Navajo spring,) to its junction with the Colorado Chiquito; then the valley of that stream to the foot of the southeastern slopes of the San Francisco mountains, elevation 4,775 feet; distance from Fort Smith 1,182 miles, and from the crossing of the Rio Grande 328 miles. Here it ascends to the dividing ridge between the waters of the Gila on the south, and of the Colorado of the West on the north, and continues (or nearly so) upon it for about 200 miles, to the Aztec Pass, elevation 6,281 feet; distance from Fort Smith 1,350 miles. The highest point reached upon this undulating ridge is 7,472 feet, at Leroux's spring, at the foot of the San Francisco mountain. From the Aztec Pass, the descent to the Colorado of the West is made by a circuitous route northward along valleys of its tributaries, the largest and last being Bill Williams's fork, the mouth of which, on the Colorado, is 1,522 miles from Fort Smith, and at an elevation above the sea of about 208 feet.

The Colorado is now ascended 34 miles, when the route, leaving it at the Needles, follows what was erroneously supposed to be the valley of the Mohave river, but which proved to be the valley of a stream, dry at the time, whose source was in an elevated ridge, which probably divides the Great Basin from the waters of the Colorado. The summit having been attained, at an elevation of 5,262 feet above the sea, the descent is made to Soda lake, the recipient at some seasons of the waters of the Mohave river, 1,117 feet above the sea, with an average grade of 100 feet to the mile for 41 miles—the steepest grade yet required on this route. From Soda lake the ascent to the summit of the Cajon Pass, elevation 4,179 feet, in the Sierra Nevada, is made by following the valley of the Mohave river. The summit of this pass, by the line of location, is 1,798 miles from Fort Smith, and 242 from the point of crossing the Colorado. Here a tunnel of $2\frac{1}{2}$ or $3\frac{4}{10}$ miles through white conglomerate sandstone is required, descending to the west with an inclination of 100 feet to the mile, which grade will be the average for 22 miles into the valley of Los Angeles, if the broken character of the hills should be found, upon careful examination, to admit of such side location as would reduce to that degree the natural grades varying between 90 and 171 feet per mile. Thence to the port of San Pedro the ground is favorable for location.

The principal characteristics of this route, in comparison with others, are, probably, its passing through or near more numerous cultivable areas, its more abundant natural supply of water as far west as the Colorado, and the greater frequency and extent of forest growth on the route between the Rio Grande and the Colorado. These two latter characteristics entail a third, however, of an unfavorable nature—the large sum of ascents and descents.

Near the meridian of 99° the change from fertile land to uncultivable is complete, excepting in the river bottoms, which are more or less fertile. Some portions of the upper valley of the Canadian, the upper valley of the Pecos, the valleys of the Rio Grande, Zuñi, Colorado Chiquito, San Francisco, Colorado of the West, and its tributaries, possess a fertile soil, requiring generally irrigation to make it productive. That portion of the southwest corner of the Great Basin traversed by this route, and over which the explorations of Lieut. Williamson also extended, is well constituted for fertility, its barrenness resulting from the absence of rain. Generally the uncultivable plains have an abundance of nutritious grass, though there are extensive tracts where little or none is found.

The route may be considered sufficiently well supplied with good building-stone, since sandstones suitable for the bridge-building required are reported to exist in the generally soft trias formation, extending from Delaware mountain, on the Canadian, to the Rocky mountains, a distance of 600 miles.

Forest growth, furnishing timber of size suitable for ties and lumber for railroad uses, is found in the following localities: continuously on the route east of longitude 97°; in or near the Pecos valley; in the Rocky mountains and Sierra Madre; in the Mogollon mountains, (south of the route,) in which the Colorado Chiquito and some of its tributaries rise; on the slopes of the San Francisco mountain; and continuously, with short intervals, for more than 120 miles; and on the Sierra Nevada. The distances apart of these points of supply are respectively 540 miles, 100 miles, 150 miles; from the Sierra Madre to San Francisco mountain, 250 miles; then for a space of about 120 miles the supply may be considered continuous; thence to the Sierra Nevada, 420 miles. If the road be built from the two termini, the greatest spaces over which ties, lumber, &c., must be brought by it are 400 and 500 miles. The route, therefore, in comparison with others, is favorably circumstanced in this respect.

The same localities will supply fuel; and, in addition, the coal-fields of Delaware mountain will furnish the eastern portion of the route where wood cannot be economically used. It is reported that coal exists in several localities in the Rocky mountains, both east and west of the Rio Grande, near this route, but there is no positive and reliable information that it has been found in sufficient quantities for profitable mining.

The route for 540 miles east of the Sierra Nevada must receive its fuel from the ports of the Pacific.

Over portions of this route, as upon all others, no fuel whatever, not even sufficient for working parties, will be found. The greatest distance over which this total absence of fuel exists, is between the Colorado and Mohave rivers, 115 miles.

The exact distances over which water is not found at certain seasons are not stated.

Between the 100th meridian and the Pacific there are spaces destitute of it, where, from the known character of the geological structure, there is no doubt that sufficient supplies can be obtained either by deep common wells, artesian wells, or reservoirs.

These more abundant supplies of timber and water, west of the Rio Grande, are attained at the expense of great elevation and somewhat rugged ground.

The Galisteo Pass in the Rocky mountains, and the passes in the Sierra Madre, being wide openings, or valleys, rather than mountain passes, no difficulty need be apprehended from snow, even if it fell to greater depths than those known; over the remainder of the route no difficulty from this cause is to be met with.

The sum of the ascents from San Pedro to Fort Smith is 24,641 feet; of descents, 21,171 feet; equivalent, in the cost of working the road, to an increased horizontal distance of 924.5, which added to the length of the line of location, 1,892 miles, gives for length of equated distance 2,816 miles.

The general features of the country indicated lines for examination at more than one point, which will probably greatly improve the route by reducing the ascents and shortening distances. The party was, however, unable to examine them.

The heaviest grades that will probably be required on the route from Fort Smith to San Pedro, do not equal those in use on the Baltimore and Ohio railroad.

The description of the topographical features of the route is not sufficiently minute to enable one to form a satisfactory opinion of the difficulties of ground to be encountered, and, consequently, of the probable cost of the formation of the road-bed. Lieut. Whipple assimilates the several portions of the route to roads already built, possessing, as nearly as possible, similar features and difficulties.

Four hundred and eighty (480) miles of the route are assimilated to the Hudson River railroad, 151 miles to the Worcester and Albany railroad, (Western railroad,) and 374 miles to the Baltimore and Ohio railroad—making 1,005 miles assimilated to railroads among the most costly that have been constructed in the United States.

The impression given by the description of the route in the report induces the opinion that the ground is more favorable than the comparison of Lieut. Whipple supposes.

Assuming this assimilation to be correct, and bringing the estimate to a uniform standard of increased cost over eastern prices and of equipment, the estimated cost of the route from Fort Smith to San Pedro becomes $169,210,265.

This estimate is believed to be, as above stated, in excess; but the data for reducing it have not yet been reported to the department.

Should it be desired to reach San Francisco by the Tulares and San Joaquin valleys, the route should leave the Mohave valley some 30 miles before reaching the entrance to the Cajon Pass, 1,768 miles from Fort Smith—elevation about 2,555 feet—and proceed across the southwest corner of the Great Basin towards the Tah-ee-chay-pah Pass, reaching its entrance at an elevation of 3,300 feet, in a distance of about 80 miles. The route from this point is coincident with that hereafter described for the 32d parallel.

The sum of ascents from San Francisco to Fort Smith, by the route from Mohave river to Tayee-chay-pah Pass, is 25,570 feet; of descents, 25,100 feet; the equivalent in miles of horizontal road is 963 miles, which added to the location-distance between those two points, 2,174 miles, gives for equated length of road 3,137 miles.

The exploration of the route by Lieut. Whipple, and his report thereon, are entitled to the highest commendation, for the completion of the work in all its parts, the full and exact observations which he made for the determination of longitudes and latitudes, and the wide range of scientific research which he instituted into all the collateral branches connected with the question which his exploration was designed to solve.

ROUTE NEAR THE THIRTY-SECOND PARALLEL OF NORTH LATITUDE.

Among the considerations which determine the general position of the route near the 32d parallel, are the low elevation of the mountain passes in this latitude, and their favorable topographical features, as well as those of the table-lands, extending over more than 1,000 miles of the route; the favorable character of the surface generally, on the route, by which the most costly item of construction in railroads, the formation of the road-bed, is, in a great measure, avoided; the shortness of the line, 1,600 miles, from the navigable waters of the Mississippi to the Pacific, and the temperate climate on the elevated portions in this southern latitude.

The explorations made upon this route are, from Preston, on Red river, to the Rio Grande, by Capt. John Pope, Topographical Engineers; from the Rio Grande, near Fort Fillmore, to the Pimas villages, on the Gila, by Lieut. John G. Parke, Topographical Engineers. From the Pimas villages to the mouth of the Gila, the reconnaissance in New Mexico and California of Major W. H. Emory, Topographical Engineers, in 1846, has been used; and from the mouth of the Gila to San Francisco, the exploration of Lieut. R. S. Williamson, Topographical Engineers, has furnished the data.

Fulton, on the Red river, about 150 miles from the Mississippi, may be considered the eastern terminus of the route, although the examination of Capt. Pope extends only to Preston, 133 miles further west. A direct line from Fulton to the point on the eastern border of the Llano Estacado selected by Capt. Pope for crossing it, would give more favorable ground than that traversed by him between Preston and this point; the latter in a distance of 352 miles gives generally easy grades and cheap construction through a country alternately wooded and open, abundantly supplied with water and fuel, and with forest growth suitable for ties and lumber for two-thirds of the length. From Fulton to the eastern border of the Llano Estacado is 485 miles, 370 of which are wooded.

The exploration of Capt. Pope comprised three distinct belts of country, the first of which has been just described above. The second is the Llano Estacado, whose mean elevation is 4,500 feet, the smooth surface of which along the route proposed, 125 miles from the eastern border to the Pecos river, presents in this respect great facilities for the construction of a railroad. It is, however, at certain seasons of the year destitute of water, is scantily supplied with grass, and not a single tree is to be seen upon it. Its geological formation is such as to render the success of obtaining water by artesian wells, at moderate depths, highly probable. During, and for some time subsequent to the rainy season, there are here, as on most other arid plains, numerous ponds, the contents of which might be collected in reservoirs; but the distance from the Colorado Springs to the Pecos, 125 miles, is not so great as to form a serious obstacle to the working of a railroad.

Between the Pecos and the Rio Grande, 163 miles, three mountain chains rise from the table-lands, the Guadalupe, Hueco, and Organ mountains. The Guadalupe mountain is crossed without a tunnel, elevation of summit 5,717 feet, and with a grade of 108 feet to the mile for 22 miles. A high viaduct and heavy cutting and filling for three miles near the summit, form the costly and difficult part of the pass. The Waco Pass is still more favorable, the greatest grade being about 80 feet to the mile; the elevation of the summit, 4,812 feet. The Organ mountain is turned just before reaching the Rio Grande at Molino and El Paso.

A peculiarity of the mountains in the western part of the continent, in this and other latitudes, is, that they have no intervening deep secondary valleys between the main chain and the plains. Over the usually uniform and smooth surface of these last, the general elevation of which, between the Pecos and the Rio Grande, is from 4,000 to 4,500 feet, the valley of the Rio Grande is attained near Molino, at an elevation of 3,830 feet, and at a distance of 787 miles from Fulton.

The region between the Rio Grande and the Pimas villages on the Gila, just above which point the latter leaves the mountain region, may be described as a great plain, interrupted irregularly and confusedly by bare, rugged, abrupt, isolated mountains or short ranges, around or through the passes in which a railroad may be constructed with quite practicable grades. The mean elevation of this plain, or series of basins into which the ridges divide it, is about 4,100 feet; the mean elevation of the summits of the passes through the ridges is 4,700 feet, the highest, through the Chiricahui range, being 5,180 feet. Except through the passes, the surface is so smooth as to require but little preparation to receive the superstructure of a railroad; and even in the two most difficult of the passes, the natural slope of the ground may be used for a railroad until the construction of the road reduces the cost of materials and supplies to the lowest rates. In one of these two passes (the Chiricahui) the steepest natural slope is 194 feet per mile for 2¼ miles. In the second pass the steepest natural slope is 240 feet per mile for three-fourths of a mile. Both these grades are within the power of a thirty-ton engine, carrying 200 passengers and baggage.

In one case deep cutting in rock, or a tunnel near the surface, at the summit, with heavy side cutting and high embankments for short distances; and, in the other, a short cut of 60 feet, probably through rock, are proposed by Lieut. Parke, to attain grades of 46 feet and 90 feet per mile, or less by increasing distance.

The great difficulty experienced in crossing this district is in the long distances over which no water is found at certain seasons. The survey by Lieut. Parke was made during the dryest season of the year, and, irrespective of the springs found at intermediate points, the whole distance between the two rivers, Rio Grande and Gila, may be divided into five spaces, varying from 80 to 53 miles in length, at the termination of which large permanent supplies of water are found at the most unfavorable season of the year.

These spaces and points are—

From the Rio Grande to the Rio Mimbres	71 miles.
From the Rio Mimbres to the stream of the Valle de Sauz	72 "
From the Valle de Sauz to the San Pedro	80 "
From the San Pedro to Tuczon	53 "
From Tuczon to the Gila	79 "

Not counting the stream of the Valle de Sauz, the distance from the Rio Mimbres to the San Pedro is 152 miles; which distance is not so great that railroad trains could not cross it without water, special arrangements having been made for the purpose. But this is the worst aspect of the case. At other seasons the supply of water is more abundant, and lakes and ponds are formed upon the plains, which may be drained into tanks; and the geological formation is such as to indicate the existence of sufficient supplies of water beneath the surface, which may be brought to it by artesian wells.

The line proposed by Lieut. Parke leaves the Rio Grande near Fort Fillmore, 35 miles from Molino, between which points the river, where confined to one channel, is about 300 yards wide, crosses the district just described, and enters the valley of the Gila near the Pimas villages, the elevation above the sea being 1,365 feet. The route then follows this river to its junction with the Colorado, a distance of 223 miles, with a general slope of 5.6 feet per mile. The Gila, in this distance, flows through a plain with occasional mountains, ridges, and peaks; its valley is highly favorable to cheap construction from its generally smooth surface, and from not being liable to freshets.

From the point now attained, the nearest port in our territory is San Diego, but the passes of the intervening Coast range are very difficult, if not impracticable, and the route is forced northward to the San Gorgonio Pass, which is much the most favorable of the passes in the Coast range explored by Lieut. Williamson for this route. It is an open valley, from two to five miles wide, the surface smooth and unbroken, affording, in its form and inclination, every facility to the building of a railroad. The entrance of this pass is 133 miles from the mouth of the Gila, in a straight line over the Colorado desert, a smooth and nearly horizontal plain, requiring but little preparation for the superstructure of a railroad. Thirty-five miles of this is a gravel plain; the remainder is alluvial soil, which only needs irrigation to be highly productive. On this latter soil, water is found at a depth of 30 feet.

The steepest natural slope, in ascending to the summit of this valley pass, (elevation 2,808 feet,) is 132 feet per mile for two miles.

San Diego and San Pedro can be reached by lines of about equal length from the San Gorgonio Pass. To the former, the first section of the route to San Luis Rey (about 75 miles long) would pass through a country generally favorable to the construction of a railroad, being a plain with numerous hills from 500 to 1,000 feet high, irregularly distributed on its surface, between and around which a road may be carried with favorable grades. Between San Luis Rey and San Diego, however, about 40 or 45 miles, the coast is cut into numerous deep intricate gullies by the drainage of the plain.

To San Pedro, about 125 miles, the route lies almost wholly over the same description of ground as that constituting the first section of the San Diego route, and avoids the obstacles presented by the second. It is, therefore, assumed that the terminus of this route should be at San Pedro, the point which it has now reached. It may, however, be proper to remark that San Pedro is an open roadstead, and would require the construction of a breakwater to constitute it a safe harbor.

From the report of Capt. Pope, it would appear that the belt of fertile land which lies on the west side of the Mississippi throughout its length, extends on this route nearly to the headwaters of the Colorado of Texas, in about longitude 102°—that is, about three degrees further west than on the more northern routes. The evidence adduced in support of this opinion is not, however, conclusive; and, until it is rendered more complete, the fertile soil must be considered in this, as in other latitudes, to terminate about the 99th meridian. Thenoe to the Pacific slopes the route is over uncultivable soil, though generally grassed, the exceptions being, as on the route of the 35th parallel, in portions of the valleys of the Pecos, Rio Grande, Gila, and Colorado of the West. The table-lands and mountain slopes are usually well covered with grama-grass, and in New Mexico have supported immense herds of cattle. There are exceptions to this, however, on the greater portion of the Llano Estacado, on portions of the plains between the Rio Grande and the Gila; and (comprised in that space) from Tuczon to the Gila, 80 miles, there is no grass on the route travelled, nor is it to be found on the Lower Gila valley; occasional patches of bunch-grass only being found on the plain, and a species of grama-grass sometimes upon the mountain sides. No grass is found on the Colorado desert, 135 miles along the line of location.

The length of the route through this generally uncultivable soil is 1,210 miles. Upon descending from the summit of the San Gorgonio Pass, on the route to San Pedro, the soil is fertile, and either well watered or can be irrigated.

The climate throughout the route is salubrious, the heat due its southern latitude being moderated by the elevation of the table-lands. On the Colorado desert it is torrid, but not unhealthy, and much of the country west of the Sierra Nevada and Coast range is celebrated for health and agreeableness.

The principal characteristic of this route is the great extent of high, arid, smooth, and nearly horizontal table-lands which it traverses, reaching an elevation of 4,000 feet upon the dividing ridge between the Brazos and Colorado rivers of Texas, near which elevation it continues until it descends from the pass of the Sierra de Santa Catarina to the Gila river, a space of nearly 600 miles. The elevation at the summit of the Llano Estacado is 4,700 feet, and in the passes of the Guadalupe and Hueco mountains, east of the Rio Grande, 5,700 and 4,800 feet, respectively. Between the Rio Grande and the Gila, the greatest elevation, which is twice attained, is 5,200 feet; the mean elevation, before the descent to the Gila is commenced, being 4,100 feet. From the eastern edge of the Llano Estacado to the pass of San

Gorgonio, 1,052 miles, the route crosses three rivers, the Pecos, the Rio Grande, and the Great Colorado of the West. The peculiar features of the arid region over which the route lies from the eastern edge of the Llano Estacado to the summit of the San Gorgonio Pass, prove, when closely examined, to be most favorable to the construction of a railroad, since they obviate to a great degree the necessity of the most costly item of railroad construction, the preparation of the road-bed for the superstructure; this preparation, with few and limited exceptions, throughout a distance of about 1,000 miles, having been already made by nature. This item amounts to from one-half to three-fourths of the whole cost of a railroad. Draining and ballasting are also dispensed with at the same time. Over the remaining portions of the route, the ground is generally favorable to the construction of the road-bed. The mountain passes are, of their kind, highly favorable, those west of the Rio Grande requiring no difficult engineering for location through them, and but little rock excavation or expensive embankment and side-cutting. The Guadalupe and Hueco Passes are more difficult.

The most unfavorable supposition for supplies of ties and lumber for the construction of that portion of the route between the eastern limit of the Llano Estacado and the summit of the San Gorgonio Pass, 1,052 miles, is that they are to come from either end of the road, from 300 miles east of the Llano Estacado, and from the port of San Pedro on the Pacific, 1,400 miles apart.

It is supposed that the road is to be built from both ends, in sections not greater than 50 miles each, and made to aid in building itself, transporting its own material, &c., so far as the proper adjustment of economy of time and means will admit; this would bring the mean cost of lumber over this distance of 1,052 miles to $52½ per 1,000 feet, and the mean cost of ties to $1,760 per mile.

The worst case having been examined, it remains to be said that ties and lumber can be obtained on and near this portion of the route from the Guadalupe and Hueco mountains, from the headwaters of the Rio Mimbres, from the Pinal Lleno, from the Salinas river (tributary of the Gila) and headwaters of the San Francisco, and from the San Bernardino mountains of the Coast range; which sources of supply, the length apart of the most distant being 500 miles, may be found to materially obviate the necessity of transporting lumber from the two ends of the road.

The coal of the Brazos and that from Puget sound may be used over the 1,200 miles from San Pedro, to within 200 miles of the Brazos, at a mean cost per ton of $16.

The portions of the route where unusual means must be resorted to for supplies of water, have already been pointed out. Under the most unfavorable suppositions, the cost per mile, over these portions, of obtaining water by artesian wells, will not probably exceed $1,000, an expenditure greatly overbalanced by the saving in road-bed formation, from the regularity and smoothness of surface of the arid regions.

The mode and probable cost of obtaining water at short distances in these dry regions, by artesian wells, reservoirs, and deep common wells, are discussed in the accompanying detailed reports. The practicability of the method by artesian wells is now being subjected to trials.

If these should fail, of which, however, in the Llano Estacado, there is little probability, the permanent streams and large springs are sufficiently near for the purposes of a railroad; and since its construction over these districts will require small working parties, the expense of supplying them with water and fuel, when necessary, will not largely increase the cost of construction. It is probable that the region between the Rio Grande and the Gila, 350 miles by the route explored, is more arid than corresponding regions on the more northern routes, but the construction of works of an unusual kind on railroads for supplies of water, are as essential on all these routes as upon that now under consideration.

The length of this route from Fulton to San Pedro is.................................. 1,618 miles.
The sum of the ascents and descents.. 32,784 feet;
To overcome which is equivalent, in the cost of working the road, to traversing a
horizontal distance of 621 miles; and the equated length of the road is......... 2,239 miles.
The estimated cost is.. $68,970,000

EXTENSION OF THE ROUTE OF THE THIRTY-SECOND PARALLEL TO SAN FRANCISCO.

For a connexion with the Bay of San Francisco, the most direct route from the San Gorgonio Pass would be through one of the passes leading from the plain of Los Angeles to the valley of Salinas river. The practicability of these passes is yet to be determined, and an exploration is now being made for this purpose. With the information now possessed, the Bay of San Francisco must be reached by crossing the Coast range to the Great Basin, passing over its southwestern extremity, then crossing the Sierra Nevada and descending to the Tulares valley.

The best pass by which to reach the Great Basin is the "New Pass," made known by Lieut. Williamson's explorations.

Descending from the summit of the San Gorgonio Pass to the town of San Bernardino, 24 or 25 miles distant, with natural slopes less than 80 feet per mile, excepting for 1.3 mile, where the slope is 127 feet per mile, the route to the Mission and Low Pass of San Fernando (about 100 miles from the summit of San Gorgonio) is over a country giving gently undulating grades, and in other respects favorable to construction, in fertile soil, building-stone, water, and fuel.

The San Fernando Pass is about eight miles through. Its summit has an elevation of 1,949 feet. A tunnel is required one-third of a mile long, through soft sandstone, 203 feet below the summit. An ascent of 620 feet is made on the south side, with grades of 155 feet per mile for four miles along the natural slopes, which cannot be reduced by side location without great expense, and a descent of four miles of 115 feet per mile, with heavy side-cutting in earth on the north side. The ascent to the New Pass in the valley of Santa Clara is now begun, and with a cut of 50 feet for a short distance at the summit in drift, the summit is attained in 29 miles over natural slopes without side location, and with grades varying from 55 to 105 feet per mile. For the space of one mile on the ascent, the mountains close in precipitously, and the streams wind abruptly; and it may be necessary here to cut two or perhaps three short tunnels, from 100 to 300 feet long, through slaty granite. The elevation of the summit is 3,164 feet. Descending to the Great Basin, cutting and filling will be required for two or three miles to adjust the natural slope to the grade west of the summit. After that, and until descending into the Tulares valley by the Tah-ee-chay-pah Pass, a distance of about 70 miles, the ground will require little preparation for the superstructure. The lowest level descended to in the Great Basin is about 2,900 feet.

The Tah-ee-chay-pah Pass, first explored throughout by Lieut. R. S. Williamson, is the most favorable in this part of the Sierra Nevada. Its summit is a nearly horizontal prairie for 7½ miles. The elevation of its entrance from the Great Basin is 3,300 feet, from which the natural slope ascends at the rate of 22 feet to the mile for 12 miles, then at 80 feet per mile for 9 miles, to the prairie summit.

The descent to the Tulares valley is 15½ miles by the natural slopes, which vary from 153 to 192 feet per mile, a side location in earth-cutting giving an average grade of 144 feet per mile for 17 miles, which may be reduced still further by an extension to 21 miles—the Tulares valley being entered at an elevation of 1,489 feet. There are two intervals of 13 and 17 miles in the Great Basin where there is no water. Artesian wells here, as in the similar formations between the Rio Grande and the Gila, will probably reach supplies at moderate depths. Deep common wells may be successfully resorted to.

The natural slopes of the three passes just considered are within the power of a 30-ton engine with a load of 200 passengers, each with 100 pounds of baggage.

Supposing 20-ton engines used, and that they carried the maximum loads adapted to the other portions of the road, where the greatest grades are 40 feet to the mile, it would be necessary to divide this load into three parts to pass a grade of 150 feet per mile; and the grades being brought to that, its disadvantage consists in the expense of two additional engines worked through the passes.

From the head of the Tulares valley, the navigable waters of the Bay of San Francisco may be reached in several ways.

The eastern side of the Tulares and San Joaquin valleys is intersected by numerous streams from the Sierra Nevada. The western is bounded by the Coast chain, and has few streams. That part of the Tulares valley between Kern and San Joaquin rivers, a space of 150 miles, having a soft alluvial soil, is, at certain seasons, miry; a road, therefore, extending through it, should keep near the foot-slopes of the mountains. From the Tah-ee-chay-pah Pass to the best point of crossing Kern river, 21½ miles, the route passes over a dry, dusty plain, destitute of water and fuel, the soil of which is not well constituted for fertility.

From the crossing of Kern river to the second crossing of the San Joaquin, near Grayson's, the numerous river-beds or bottoms should be crossed on piles, the spaces varying from 50 to 300 feet—the greatest width to be spanned not exceeding 100 feet. From Tah-ee-chay-pah Pass to the Straits of Martinez, the location distance would be 288 miles. The most direct route to San Francisco from the Tah-ee-chay-pah Pass will be found through one of the passes known to exist in the mountain range separating the Tulares and San Joaquin valleys from those of the Salinas and San José rivers. The distance through it is about 10 miles; the elevation of the passes about 600 feet. From Tah-ee-chay-pah Pass the route should cross to the western side of the Tulares valley, around the head of the lakes, and enter the Salinas valley as soon as practicable.

The soil of the Tulares valley, north of Kern river, and of the San Joaquin valley, is well constituted for fertility, and needs merely the proper amount of water to be highly productive. Sufficient water and fuel for working parties can be found at convenient distances on this section, (excepting where it crosses the Great Basin, and approaching Kern river; the amount of deficiency on these portions having been already given.) Lumber and good building-stone are found at various points in the mountains, accessible from their foot-slopes. For fuel for locomotives, the coal of Puget sound and Vancouver's island *must probably be depended upon.*

The topographical features of this extension of the route are, with the exception of the mountains, favorable to cheap construction. The mountain passes are likewise of a favorable character, their only objectionable feature being their high grades. The nature and extent of this objection has been already stated, and, it is seen, is not serious.

From Fulton to San Francisco the distance is 2,039 miles; the sum of the ascents and descents 42,008 feet, which is equivalent to 795 miles; and the equated length of the road is 2,834 miles; the estimated cost is $93,120,000.

To Lieut. Williamson, assisted by Lieut. Parke, was intrusted the survey of a route from the Bay of San Francisco to the junction of the Gila and Colorado rivers, connecting with the ports of San Pedro and San Diego on the one side, and on the other with the most practicable mountain passes. His work has been thoroughly and handsomely executed, presenting much new and valuable information of the mountain passes on the southern portion of the Sierra Nevada and Coast range. The geological examination, made under his orders, is highly creditable and instructive.

The examination of the middle section of the route of the 32d parallel, by Lieut. Parke, was very thorough, and highly creditable, though executed with small means; and his report very satisfactorily exhibits the character and essential features of the country over which he passed. The scientific labors of the boundary survey, which had been previously performed in this region, rendered it unnecessary to do more than make what may be strictly called a railroad exploration.

The examination of the eastern portion by Capt. Pope, assisted by Lieut. Garrard, of the dragoons, was made under the most disadvantageous circumstances, the party having been organized at a remote point, where neither instruments, nor assistants specially instructed in the scientific branches connected with the survey, could be procured. It was, however, creditably performed, and satisfactorily exhibits the topography and general character of the country along the line surveyed.

CONCLUSION.

To aid in a comparison of the several routes, reference is made to a table prepared by Capt. A. A. Humphreys, and hereto appended.

With regard to the estimates of cost, although believed to be as accurate as can be made under present circumstances, they are to be considered as intended not so much to show the absolute sums of money which would build the several roads, as to represent the relative quantities of materials and labor required for the purpose. If now tested in the actual construction of any one of the roads, they will doubtless be found to contain many errors; but as the same data have been assumed on all the routes, the same amount of error will probably be found in each, and the actual expense will thus preserve the same proportion.

With regard to the equated lengths of the several roads, or, in other words, the influence of ascents and descents upon the expense of working, it is proper to direct attention to the remarks of the engineer, appended to the tables, in which he states that, on all the routes, the amount reported will be subject to increase when the minor undulations of the ground shall be measured; and this increase will be greatest on those routes and in those portions where the features of the country are less regular—that is, where there are most of such minor undulations to be measured. The equated distances also affect the cost of working a road only under certain circumstances, which may or may not exist on the contemplated route.

A comparison of the results stated above, and of those exhibited in the tables referred to, conclusively shows that the route of the 32d parallel is, of those surveyed, "the most practicable and economical route for a railroad from the Mississippi river to the Pacific ocean."

This is the shortest route; and not only is its estimated cost less by a third than that of any other of the lines, but the character of the work required is such that it could be executed in a vastly shorter period. It is obvious that a road on any of these routes, with the exception perhaps of the 47th parallel, must be built continuously from the two extremities, and an obstacle that arrests its progress at any point defers the commencement of all the work in advance. The tunnels and much of the other work on the more northerly routes in the most desolate regions are such as could not be commenced until a road was constructed up to those points, and would then require a long period for their completion.

On the southernmost route, on the contrary, the progress of the work will be regulated chiefly by the speed with which cross-ties and rails can be delivered and laid, the nature of the country being such that throughout the whole line the road-bed can easily be prepared in advance of the superstructure. The few difficult points, such as the Pass of the Guadalupe and Hueco mountains, and the passes between the Rio Grande and Gila, would delay the work but an inconsiderable period.

This peculiarity of the ground presents another advantage in the fact that temporary tracks could be laid upon the natural surface of the earth to almost any extent, to serve for the transportation of materials and supplies.

The climate on this route is such as to cause less interruption to the work than on any other route.

Not only is this the shortest and least costly route to the Pacific, but it is the shortest and cheapest route to San Francisco, the greatest commercial city on our western coast; while the aggregate length of railroad lines connecting it at its eastern terminus with the Atlantic and Gulf seaports is less than the aggregate connexion with any other route, as will be seen by reference to the appended table B.

With regard to the circumstances which affect the cost of working and maintaining the road, they are more favorable than on any other route. In this dry climate the decay of cross-ties and other timber would be very slow, and the absence of severe frost would have a most important influence upon the permanence of the road-bed, and heavier grades could be adopted than in a climate where ice and snow prevail.

The snows on all the other routes, except that of the 35th parallel, could not fail at certain seasons to suspend the working of the road, for on all, such snows are known to have fallen as would interpose an effectual barrier to the passage of trains. Such an occurrence in this desolate region would be attended with more serious consequences than in inhabited districts.

In only one important respect is this route supposed to be less favorable than some of the others, and that is, in the supply of fuel. The difference, however, in favor of the others is not great, unless the existence of coal at certain points along those routes where it is indicated should be verified by further examination. The cost of fuel is about one-fifth of the whole expense of maintaining and working a railroad.

The grades of the several routes, and other similar information, will be found upon the sheets of profiles compiled in the office.

In the determination of the explorations proper to be made—in the examination of the reports of the suveying parties, the preparation of the profiles, and of a general map to exhibit, in their geographical relation to each, all the routes of which an instrumental examination had been made—I am greatly indebted to the assistance which has been rendered by the officers of the corps of topographical engineers employed in the office established here in connexion with the explorations directed by the act; and I will here especially acknowledge my obligations to Major W. H. Emory, whose extensive knowledge of the western regions of our country, no small part of which he had actually explored, and whose sound judgment in all things connected with topographical reconnaissances and field operations, gave me important aid in the organization of the work and the subsequent office examinations necessary to systematize its results.

When, in August, 1854, Major Emory's duties as commissioner to run the boundary-line between Mexico and the United States separated him from further connexion with these explorations, he was succeeded by Capt. A. A. Humphreys, whose high scientific attainments and power of exact analysis had been manifested in several important positions which he had held, and are further shown in the able and comprehensive examination, herewith submitted, of the reports of the several parties of exploration.

Lieut. G. K. Warren, first under Major Emory, and subsequently under Captain Humphreys, has been specially intrusted with the preparation of the material and the construction of the general map, together with the compilation of profiles of all the routes which had been instrumentally surveyed, and the collection of all general information which would aid in the determination of the question before the department. In these duties he has recently had the zealous and efficient aid of Lieut. H. L. Abbott.

These laborious and important duties have been performed by the officers above named with the most commendable diligence and intelligence, and much of whatever success belongs to the preparation and presentation of the matter collected is due to these officers.

Capt. McClellan, of the corps of enginers, after the completion of his field operations, was directed to visit various railroads, and to collect information of facts established in the construction and working of existing roads, to serve as data in determining the practicability of constructing and working roads over the several routes explored. The results of his inquiries will be found in a very valuable memoir herewith submitted.

Very respectfully, your obedient servant,

JEFF'N DAVIS, *Secretary of War.*

Hon. LINN BOYD,

Speaker of the House of Representatives.

A.

Table showing the lengths, sums of ascents and descents, equated lengths, cost, &c., of the several routes explored for a railroad from the Mississippi to the Pacific. (For the grades, see the profiles accompanying the report.)

	Distance in straight line.	Distance by proposed railroad route.	Sum of ascents and descents.	Length of level route of equal working expense.	Comparative cost of different routes.	Number of miles of route through arable land.	Sterile region. No. miles of route through lands generally uncultivable, arable soil being found in small areas.	Sterile region. No. of square miles of sums of areas of largest bodies of arable land in uncultivable region.	No. of miles at an elevation above 0, and less than 1,000 feet.	No. of miles at an elevation greater than 1,000 and less than 2,000 feet.	2,000 and 3,000.	3,000 and 4,000.	4,000 and 5,000.	5,000 and 6,000.	6,000 and 7,000.	† 7,000 and 8,000.	8,000 and 9,000.	9,000 and 10,000.	Summit of the highest pass on the route.	
	Miles.	*Miles.*	*Feet.*	*Miles.*															*Feet.*	
Route near 47th and 49th parallels, from St. Paul to Vancouver.	1,445	1,864	18,100	2,207	*$130,781,000	374	1,490	‖ 1,000	470	580	720	130	97	28	...	...	..	..	6,044	Tunnel at elevat'n of 5,219 feet.
Extension thence to Seattle	......	161	1,000	180	*10,090,000	161	....	....	161											
Route near the 41st and 42d parallels, via South Pass from Council Bluffs to Benicia.	1,410	2,032	29,120	2,583	116,095,000	632	1,400	‖ 1,100	180	170	210	160	580	2[illegible]5	270	107	20	..	8,373	
† Route near the 38th and 39th parallels, from Westport to San Francisco by the Coo-che-to-pa and Tah-ee-chay-pah Passes.	1,740	2,080	49,986	3,125	Cost so great that the road is impracticable.	620	1,460	‖ 1,100	340	276	165	348	466	170	60	155	80	20	10,032	Tunnel at elevat'n of 9,540 feet.
The same, from Westport to San Francisco by the Coo-che-to-pa and Madelin Passes.	1,740	2,290	56,514	3,360	.....do.....	670	1,620	1,100	275	308	190	143	725	284	110	155	80	20	10,032	Tunnel at elevat'n of 9,540 feet.
Route near the 35th parallel, from Fort Smith to San Pedro.	1,360	1,892	48,812	2,816	‡ 169,210,265	416	1,476	2,300	305	347	260	185	160	305	235	95	..	..	7,472	
Branch road to San Francisco, from the Mohave river.	......	406	7,500	506	19,935,000	322	84	....	290	10	72	35								
Route near the 32d parallel, from Fulton to San Pedro.	1,400	1,618	32,784	2,239	68,970,000	408	1,210	2,300	485	300	100	170	503	60	...	...	..	..	5,717	
Extension to San Francisco	......	440	10,150	632	25,100,000	376	70	....	290	50	65	35								

* These are the estimates of the office, those of Gov. Stevens having been brought to the same standard of increased cost as the other routes, and his equipment reduced to that of the other routes. His estimates were $117,121,000 and $7,030,000.

† Supposing the route to be a straight line, with uniform descent from the Un-kuk-oo-ap mountains (near Sevier river) to the entrance of the Tah-ee-chay-pah Pass, the most favorable supposition.

‡ This estimate for the route near the 35th parallel is thought to be largely in excess.

‖ These sums do not include the areas of cultivable soil as far west as the Cascade and Sierra Nevada mountains.

The sum of the minor undulations (not included in the sum of ascents and descents here given) will probably be greater for the route of the 47th parallel than for the other routes; that for the route near the 32d parallel will probably be the least of all.

With the amount of work estimated for the roads in this report, the equated lengths corresponding to the sum of ascents and descents has but little practical value. With a full equipment and heavy freight business, the sum of ascents and descents becomes important. A comparison of the degree of curvature of the routes cannot be made.

NOTE TO TABLE A.

The sum of the ascents and descents given for the various routes, does not take into consideration those minor undulations which sometimes largely increase the aggregate.

I think it probable that when detailed surveys are made, it will be found that this sum for the route near the 47th parallel will be more increased than those for the other routes, and that the sum for the route near the 32d parallel will be less increased than the others.

The equated lengths corresponding to these sums, may give erroneous impressions. If the loads to be habitually carried over the roads are within the power of the engines over the greatest grades proposed, then the sums of ascents and descents really have little meaning or value. The wear and tear of rail and machinery, and consumption of fuel, would be somewhat greater on the road having the largest sum; but the difference would not be worth taking into account, unless there was an equality in all other respects between the routes.

If there are some grades so steep as to require the division of the loads habitually carried over other portions, the cost of the extra locomotives, and of working them over those portions, will show the extent of the disadvantage and yearly cost.

So far as any estimate has been made by me of the amount of work to be done on the roads, these sums of ascents and descents have little practical value, since those portions of the routes have been indicated where it may be considered advisable to use steep natural slopes with extra engines, to expedite the completion of the road, and save expensive road-bed preparation. With a full equipment and heavy freight business, the sum of ascents and descents becomes important.

The nature of the surveys does not admit of a comparison of the degree of curvature on the several routes.

B.

Distances of the eastern termini of the several Pacific railroad routes to the Mississippi river, Boston, New York, Charleston, and New Orleans, by railroads built, building, and projected, as measured on the "Railroad Maps."

	Miles.
1. St. Paul to Boston	1,316
to New York	1,190
to Charleston	1,193
to New Orleans	1,198
Aggregate	4,897
2. Council Bluffs to Rock Island, (Miss. river)	267
to Boston	1,374
to New York	1,252
to Charleston	1,195
to New Orleans	1,075
Aggregate	5,163
3. Westport, mouth of Kansas, (near Fort Leavenworth,) to St. Louis, (Miss. river)	245
to Boston	1,415
to New York	1,220
to Charleston	1,045
to New Orleans	875
Aggregate	4,800
4. Fort Smith, on the Arkansas, to Memphis, (Miss. river)	270
to Boston	1,540
to New York	1,345
to Charleston	960
to New Orleans	655
Aggregate	4,770
5. Fulton to Gaines, (Miss. river)	150
to Boston	1,530
to New York	1,335
to Charleston	950
to New Orleans	402
Aggregate	4,367

LIST OF DOCUMENTS ACCOMPANYING THE REPORT OF THE SECRETARY OF WAR.

AN EXAMINATION

BY DIRECTION OF THE

HON. JEFFERSON DAVIS, SECRETARY OF WAR,

OF THE

REPORTS OF EXPLORATIONS FOR RAILROAD ROUTES

FROM

THE MISSISSIPPI TO THE PACIFIC, MADE UNDER THE ORDERS OF THE WAR DEPARTMENT IN 1853–'54, AND OF THE EXPLORATIONS MADE PREVIOUS TO THAT TIME, WHICH HAVE A BEARING UPON THE SUBJECT:

BY

CAPT. A. A. HUMPHREYS & LIEUT. G. K. WARREN,

CORPS TOPOGRAPHICAL ENGINEERS.

TABLE OF CONTENTS.

AN EXAMINATION

OF THE

REPORTS AND EXPLORATIONS FOR RAILROAD ROUTES FROM THE MISSISSIPPI TO THE PACIFIC.

WAR DEPARTMENT,
Office of Pacific Railroad Surveys, Washington, February 5, 1855.

SIR: In accordance with your instructions, I submit the following result of the examination of the reports of the explorations, made under the orders of the War Department, to determine the most practicable and economical route for a railroad from the Mississippi to the Pacific; as well as of the explorations and surveys previously made which have a bearing upon this subject.

It has been found impossible to complete the general map of the country embracing these and former explorations, owing to the great amount of labor required in its preparation, the unfinished condition of the original maps and other data upon which it is to be founded; and the heavy duties imposed upon the officer having it in charge.

This map should be accompanied by a report giving the authorities and data upon which it rests, with explanations of the adjustment of discrepant authorities; and also a brief memoir upon the physical geography of the regions embraced within its limits. Such a memoir necessarily formed a preliminary to a report upon the most practicable and economical route for a railroad from the Mississippi to the Pacific; but the unfinished condition of the maps and material collected in the departments of science necessary to elucidate the subject, and the insufficiency of the material, when prepared, for so comprehensive a subject, precluded the possibility of its being undertaken at the present time, more especially as the labors of all in the office were required in the preparation of the details necessary to discuss the greater or less degree of practicability and economy of each route separately.

The report herewith submitted partakes more of the character of memoranda upon the different routes, than of a report upon the whole subject; and, in fact, it was prepared as such, with the intention, principally, of aiding your examination of the reports of the officers charged with the explorations, rather than as a general report upon all the routes. These memoranda would have served as the basis of a general report, but time does not admit of their being placed in that shape, and they are consequently submitted in their present condition, with this explanation of the cause of their deficiency in comprehensiveness of matter, and in arrangement.

Upon relieving Major Emory, in August last, from the charge of the Pacific Railroad office, I found that the preparation of the material for the general map, a work of great labor, and the superintendence of its construction and drawing, had been intrusted to Lieut. G. K. Warren, topographical engineers, whose zeal and ability in the performance of this and the general office duty, Major Emory acknowledged in warm terms. Lieut. Warren has continued in charge of the office duties, which include the critical examination of the reports, maps, profiles, and all original data submitted by the exploring parties and others, and reports upon the result; the preparation of the general map and its engraving; the compilation of profiles of all the routes recently explored and previously examined barometrically; the preparation of all the maps, profiles, and other drawings made in the office, comprising the duplication of the originals received from the exploring parties; the preparation of reports upon those routes and portions of routes and lines formerly explored, but not with a special view to the railroad question. In addition to this, he has likewise largely aided me in making this report.

This laborious service has been executed by him with great intelligence, zeal, and energy.

Lieut. H. L. Abbot, topographical engineers, was assigned to duty in this office in October last, and has most zealously aided Lieut. Warren in the compilation of the office profiles, and assisted me in investigations connected with this report.

I would especially call your attention to the admirable arrangement of the profiles which have been compiled in the office, by Lieuts. Warren and Abbot, exhibiting so well all the information upon, and the data and statistics of the routes, (as far as it is possible to compress them into so small a space,) as to serve the purpose of a brief report.

In making this examination I have had the advantage of frequent personal conferences with the chiefs of the exploring parties, and with Dr. John Evans and W. P. Blake, esq., geologists.

I have also availed myself of the information contained in the memoranda upon various practical points connected with the construction and working of railroads; prepared in the office by Bvt. Capt. George B. McClellan, corps of engineers, as suggested by my letter to the department of the 7th October last.

Very respectfully, your obedient servant,

A. A. HUMPHREYS,

Captain Topographical Engineers.

Hon. Jefferson Davis,

Secretary of War.

CHAPTER I.

ROUTE NEAR THE FORTY-SEVENTH AND FORTY-NINTH PARALLELS OF NORTH LATITUDE.

Although the report of Governor I. I. Stevens of his exploration of the northern route is clearly and forcibly written, yet, as all the facts bearing upon a particular portion of the route are not always to be found in one place, I have thought that it would facilitate the review to recapitulate the leading characteristics of the railroad route proposed, with such additional investigations and opinions as appeared to be necessary. The great extent of ground examined, the number of subjects treated, and the voluminous character of the report, seemed to require this somewhat laborious process.

The general direction and position of the extreme northern route is mainly determined by the following considerations:

1. From the great northern bend of the Missouri, (lat. 48° 30′, about,) near the mouth of White-earth river, to Council Bluffs, (lat. 43° 30′,) the river flows in a general southeast direction. Throughout this portion of its course the country on either side is generally rough and broken; to the east lies the Coteau du Missouri, a high, rolling prairie, and to the west a rough and rugged country (including the "Mauvaises Terres," and excepting the smooth table-land divide between the Yellow Stone and Missouri) extends to the base of the mountains. To the east and north, the Coteau du Missouri sinks into the prairie, and near the parallel of 49° can be completely turned. The northern route should, therefore, seek the shortest practicable line between this point and the navigable waters of the Mississippi. St. Paul, at the head of navigation of the Mississippi, appears the most suitable eastern terminus of the road. The manner in which these two points are connected will be discussed hereafter.

2. After passing the Coteau du Missouri, the valley of the Missouri and its tributaries, in direction and acclivity, furnish the best approach to the Rocky mountains, the passes of which, near the sources of the Missouri, in latitude 47°, have an elevation of about 6,000 feet, being nearly 1,500 feet lower than the Great South Pass.

3. The Rocky mountains once crossed, the route to the Pacific is then determined by the course of the tributaries of the Columbia.

Finally, the navigable character of the Missouri, of the Columbia, and of the great lakes, as well as the Mississippi—all of which can be made to aid in the construction of this road—gives to it, at first glance, a character of great importance. Its objectionable features are also apparent in its high northern latitude, and consequent severity of climate, which greatly detracts from the importance of the aid from navigation by obstructing the rivers with ice, and in the long intervals through which labor in the open air must be suspended, and, finally, in its contiguity to the soil of a powerful foreign sovereignty.

The northern railroad route may be said to commence at St. Paul, in about latitude 45°, at the head of steamboat navigation of the Mississippi. The road ascends the left bank of the Mississippi, passing over fertile prairies or oak uplands to Little Falls, the best point for crossing the river, a distance of 109 miles, without rock-cutting, and with light grades, seldom exceeding ten feet per mile. For structures, both of wood and stone, the material is good, and near at hand.

Crossing the Mississippi river with 325 feet of bridge, the line is directed to the prairie of the Bois des Sioux, an extensive flat plain. Between this and the Mississippi is a high, rolling prairie, forming part of the divide between the waters of Hudson's bay and those of the Mississippi. The road passes successively through a wooded and fertile prairie country, and crosses the tributaries of the Minnesota river at their sources. From the Mississippi to the Bois des Sioux the distance is 110 miles; the rise is about 750 feet; the grades generally ten feet per mile, though occasionally thirty feet. Lumber and stone are to be supplied from the Mississippi and west of it; the excavation and embankments are light.

The line passes for 40 miles over the almost absolute plain of the Bois des Sioux, leaving its western edge near and north of Dead Colt Hillock, here entering the rolling prairie, keeping south of the Shayenne river, whose valley is 150 to 200 feet below the general level of the prairie, and along the dividing ridge between it and the Rivière à Jacques; then crossing the latter river at a width of 120 feet, it is directed towards the valley of Mouse river, bounded on the south by the high plateau of the Coteau du Missouri. Keeping along the base of the coteau, to avoid the deep coulées of Mouse river,* and its tributary, Rivière des Lacs, the coteau is turned, near the head of the latter river, by the Grande Coulée, and with a grade not exceeding 40 feet per mile, the line passes to the bottom lands of the Missouri, near the mouth of Big Muddy river, about 30 miles west of Fort Union. Steamboats of two-feet draught can at all times, when not obstructed by ice, ascend the Missouri to Fort Union, the trip up from St. Louis occupying 42 days, and back 17 days. The total rise in this distance (about 400 miles) from the prairie of the Bois des Sioux to the Missouri is 700 feet. From Dead Colt Hillock to the valley of Mouse river, 200 miles, the country is in part undulating, rising gradually.

The earth-work from thc Mississippi to the Missouri will be neither heavy nor expensive, and no rock excavation, except in crossing the "divide into the valley of the Missouri. The grades need not exceed 30 feet per mile, and will rarely be so great."

For 400 miles of this portion of the route, wood for building and fuel (if wood be used for it) must be obtained from the Red River of the North, and from the bottom lands of Mouse river. But little stone for masonry is needed. Excellent sandstone can be obtained in the vicinity of the Butte de Maison du Chien, near which the line enters the valley of Mouse river. Materials for good bricks are to be obtained on Red, Bois des Sioux, Shayenne, and Mouse rivers. From Camp Guthrie, on the Shayenne, to the Mouse River valley, (about 150 miles,) nearly one-half the small ponds and lakes are brackish and salt. The fresh-water ponds are, however, constantly interspersed and more abundant, and "occur quite as often as is desirable either for travelling or railroad purposes. With this abundant supply, no unusual construction or expense will be required in establishing watering places."—Governor Stevens's report.

Mr. Lander, the estimating engineer, says, "the portion extending through the salt-water region—the one under consideration—will need particular attention regarding a supply of pure water for the use of engines. The proper mode of overcoming this difficulty will be by extending an aqueduct along the line of the road from the lakes upon the Grand Coteau du Missouri." An estimate for this purpose is made, and, including the cost of planting 640 acres of trees every 20 miles over — miles of the route, amounts to $2,000,000.

Should supplies of water be needed at points where it could not be furnished by the usual means, because of the small quantity of rain that falls, artesian wells might prove more economical, if the geological formations indicate their feasibility.

The position of the northern part of the Grande Coulée, by which the route leaves the valley of Rivière des Lacs and enters that of the Missouri, has been determined from an estimated distance of twenty miles from the odometer line. As represented upon the map, it approaches so close to the 49th parallel (about two miles from it) that, without more accurate determination, it cannot be known whether the route, as here projected, may not pass over British territory.

* Mouse river, next to the Red River of the North, is the most important river on the route between the Mississippi and Missouri. It flows in a deep, wide valley 200 feet below the prairie-level, with a wooded bottom from one-half to two miles wide, its high and steep banks being cut by deep coulées extending ten and fifteen miles into the prairie.

After reaching the Missouri, the line follows the valley of this stream to the mouth of Milk river, 120 miles from Fort Union, then ascends the valley of Milk river, 187 miles, the grades rarely exceeding the river-slopes, (the Missouri being one foot per mile, the Milk three feet per mile,) with an average embankment of eight feet, and with but little rock excavation, and that in soft sandstone. The river bottoms, composed of clay and sand, are soft and sloppy in wet weather, and parched and cracked during the dry season. As the Rocky mountains are approached, the country bordering the Missouri river is rough and broken; nearer the mountains, prairies afford more favorable ground for location.

Having turned the Bear's Paw mountains, lying between the Milk and Missouri rivers, the line leaves the valley of Milk river and rises to the prairie, with a grade of thirty-five feet per mile, taking a southwest direction towards the passes in the Rocky mountains, which lie near the 47th parallel of latitude, crossing in its course the Maria's and Teton rivers with grades of forty feet per mile, and the Sun river without difficulty, the whole distance being about 440 miles.

The cotton-wood of the Missouri and Milk rivers not being suitable for building material, except for a temporary road, by which to build the permanent one, this portion of the route is dependent upon the pine of the Trois Buttes mountain, (sleepers for 300 miles single track from this source,) of the Rocky mountains, and of the mountains south of Fort Benton. Good sandstone is to be found near Fort Union, at the crossing of Milk river, and at the Trois Buttes; lime near Fort Union, the Trois Buttes, and the Rocky mountains; clay, for brick, on the Missouri and Milk rivers; and sand in the beds of the rivers, though not abundant, in a clean state.

If cotton-wood cannot be used as fuel, we have on this route spaces of 100, 200, and 400, or 500 miles between the points of supply; that is, 200 miles from the Red river supply to that of the Mouse river; 400 miles from the Mouse river supply to that of the Bear's Paw, or 500 to that of the Trois Buttes; and from the Trois Buttes to the Rocky mountain supply, not less than 100 miles. The supplies of lumber are the same as for fuel.

At what distances apart large supplies of water can be had from the Red River of the North to Maria's river is not stated. The rivers along which the road runs cannot always be relied upon for it, since the road is immediately under the bluffs of the valley, and the small streams are dry in summer, and so of the ponds on the prairies; both in extreme dry and hot seasons, and in the winter, there would be deficiencies. The high plateaux making back from these rivers, it is thought, will afford the means of securing, by reservoirs, ample supplies. The precise data upon which this opinion is formed are not given; the number, capacity, and position of the ponds or small lakes proposed to be used are not stated, nor the distances at which the reservoirs can be made.

Between the Maria's and Sun rivers, Grizzly Bear lake is indicated as a point of supply. From the Bois des Sioux to Rivière à Jacques is about 120 miles. From Rivière à Jacques to Butte de Maison, where probably the ponds of the Coteau du Missouri could give a large supply of water, is 115 miles. Thence to head of Rivière des Lacs, 120 miles. Thence to mouth of Big Muddy, on the Missouri, 120, &c. There can be no doubt that supplies of water at these distances can be got during all seasons, which may be made to answer for railroad purposes, though not sufficient for working parties.

The line has now reached the base of the Rocky mountains, and an elevation, where it may enter the passes through them, of 4,700 feet above the sea.

In deciding upon the route by which the road should cross this mountain chain, regard must be had, not only to the difficulties of approach to the passes and the difficulties in the passes, but also to the best pass (from every consideration) of the Bitter Root mountains.

This last is a secondary mountain chain lying west of the principal, separating from it in about latitude 45° 30′, and running northward and westward into the British possessions. Flowing in the valley, between these two chains, are the Flathead and St. Mary's or Bitter

Root rivers; the former rising in about latitude 48° 30′, and running south, and the latter rising in about latitude 45° 30′, and running north. As these two streams approach each other a spur from the Rocky mountains turns them towards the west. Their junction forms Clark's fork of the Columbia, a clear, rapid river, from 150 to 200 yards wide, rarely fordable, which has forced a passage through the Bitter Root mountains; this pass was adopted for the railroad route.

Seven passes in the Rocky mountains were examined; they lie between latitude 48° 30′ and latitude 45° 30′.

Beginning at the north, in about latitude 48° 30′, is the Maria's Pass, leading from the Maria's river to the Flathead river. It is not desirable in direction, unless a route leading westward be found north of Clark's fork. The tunnel, at its summit, would be at an elevation of 8,000 or 8,500 feet; about the limit of perpetual snow in that latitude. On the west, the fall in seventeen miles would be 2,170 feet. The great severity of the climate would of itself render this pass almost impracticable. About the 20th of October, Mr. Tinkham found the snow-banks of the previous winter still lying upon the shaded borders of the small lakes or ponds on the eastern slopes at an elevation of about 5,600 feet. The instruments used by Mr. Tinkham were a barometer and pocket-compass.

The next pass is that of Lewis and Clark, connecting the head-waters of Dearborn and Blackfoot rivers—the former a tributary of the Missouri, the latter of the St. Mary's. The summit ridge has an elevation of 6,323 feet, which must be pierced by a tunnel two and a half miles long, through rock, at an elevation of 5,300 feet; grades of approach from the east forty feet to the mile, and of descent to the valley of Blackfoot river, "it is believed," will not exceed fifty feet per mile.

The examination of this pass was made by Mr. Lander; his instruments were a barometer and pocket-compass. He abandoned the examination (the reasons for it are not, to my apprehension, contained in the extracts from his report) seven and a half miles west of the summit, and four and a half miles before reaching the route of the main party that entered the valley of Blackfoot river by Cadotte's Pass. The connexion of Lewis and Clark's Pass with the valley of the Blackfoot river has not, then, been made, though "believed practicable at grades not exceeding fifty feet per mile." This pass should be gone over instrumentally before its practicability can be considered demonstrated. It has been adopted in the railroad estimate, and is probably practicable.

The next pass is Cadotte's, connecting a tributary of Dearborn river with a tributary of the Blackfoot river. The approach to this pass is practicable, though difficult, owing to the numerous deep ravines of the tributaries of Beaver creek, a northern branch of Dearborn river, over which the road must cross in approaching the pass from Sun river. The summit of the pass has an elevation of 6,044 feet; will require a tunnel 4½ miles long (fifty per cent. of cutting in clay slate,) at an elevation of 5,000 feet, with grades of sixty feet approaching from the east, and forty feet per mile from the west. The pass itself is difficult.

The main train of the exploring party passed over this route, the instruments used being a barometer, odometer, and Schmalkalder compass. It follows the valley of Blackfoot river, generally narrow and wooded, to its junction with the Hell-Gate, a distance from the summit of ninety-three miles. For twenty miles before this junction there is a narrow gorge ending in Hell-Gate. From the narrowness of the valley and winding of the stream, it will be necessary to cross frequently from side to side, and the bridging will be expensive from the absence of stone suitable for building material, the nearest point of supply known being in Flathead River valley, seventy miles distant from Hell-Gate. The grades will vary from thirty-five to forty-five feet per mile.

The Blackfoot river joins the Hell-Gate river just before the latter makes the passage of the gorge from which it derives its name, the Hell-Gate river itself being a tributary of the St. Mary's. At the head of the *Little* Blackfoot (another tributary of the Hell-Gate, coming from the east,) two passes in the Rocky mountains, in latitude 46° 30′, were explored. They are sometimes called the Northern and Southern *Little* Blackfoot Passes, but named in Governor Stevens's map as the Hell-Gate Passes. They connect between the waters of the Little Blackfoot and Prickly-Pear creeks.

South of these, in latitude 45° 45′, another pass was examined, called the Hell-Gate Pass. It connects the south fork of Hell-Gate with a branch of Wisdom river. And still further south, in latitude 45° 38′, another pass, called the Big Hole Mountain or St. Mary's Pass, was explored, connecting the waters of St. Mary's river with a fork of Wisdom river. These last four passes are all reported as probably practicable; but as the southern *Little* Blackfoot, Hell-Gate, and St. Mary's Passes received no instrumental examination, as the last-named is out of direction, and the two former involve a considerable detour from the route of the Missouri, are approached with difficulty, and will only become important should a good route or routes be found through the Black Hills to the Mississippi, it is unnecessary to note them further. The profiles of the northern *Little* Blackfoot with its approaches from the Missouri, of the valleys of the *Little* Blackfoot and of part of the Hell-Gate river, were determined by Mr. Tinkham, his instruments consisting of a barometer and pocket-compass.

The approach by this route is over a broken region of country, and a better approach, it is thought, will be found north of the Missouri, nearer the base of the mountains, along the line examined by Lieutenant Mullan. The elevation of the summit is 6,250 feet; a tunnel of two miles will be required. The eastern approach is estimated practicable with grades of fifty or sixty feet per mile, and the western descent with a grade of thirty feet to the mile. A thorough examination of this route is recommended in connexion with the other passes in this vicinity. It is unnecessary, therefore, to consider it further, since the data are still too imperfect to enable us to form certain conclusions.

Three passes through the Bitter Root mountains were explored; a fourth was subsequently examined, but has not yet been reported upon; a fifth pass, the northern Nez Percés, it was not considered necessary to examine.

The passes reported upon are that of Clark's fork, which has been adopted as being the least difficult; the Cœur d'Alene Pass, by the Cœur d'Alene Mission, and the southern Nez Percés trail. Beginning at the south, the southern Nez Percés trail, leading from the head of St. Mary's river to the head of a tributary of the Snake river, (the southern fork of the Columbia) was examined by Mr. Tinkham, in the latter part of November and first half of December; his instruments were a barometer and pocket-compass until the former was cached. From the great height of the summit, 8,000 feet, and the great depth of snow so early in the season, it is not necessary to consider this pass. It is probably impracticable.

The northern Nez Percés trail is reported to be of the same character.

The Cœur d'Alene Pass, leading from the Bitter Root near its junction with the Flathead to the Spokane river, if found to be practicable, would give a route to Wallah-Wallah seventy miles shorter than that by Clark's fork; but as no instruments for measuring vertical or horizontal distances were carried with the party that examined this route, its practicability cannot be considered established, but merely such information gained as serves to show that it is probably practicable, and that an instrumental profile should be taken.

The pass of Clark's fork formed by the passage of the river through the Bitter Root mountains, along which the main party travelled, is practicable.

It will be noticed that the passes of Lewis and Clark, and Cadotte, give the most direct route from the line east of the Rocky mountains to this pass.

We will now return to the line of the main party at Hell-Gate, the termination of the Blackfoot valley. From this point two lines were examined to Clark's fork. One follows the valley of the Bitter Root to Clark's fork; the other crosses a dividing ridge to the valley of Jocko river, keeping along this stream to its junction with the Flathead, which it then follows to Clark's fork.

Of the first, Governor Stevens says: "The route will be long, in consequence of the curves of the river, and will involve curves of the minimum radius, numerous bridge-crossings, considerable side-cutting, and high embankments on the prairie portions, in consequence of the spring freshets (twenty to thirty feet vertical rise.) The rock, in side-cuttings, can be easily quarried. The greater portion of this route has been personally examined by me, and I am satisfied of its practicability, though at great expense."

Mr. Lander, in whose judgment and experience Governor Stevens placed great confidence, says of this portion of the route: "The descent of the Bitter Root is very severe. The general grade of the river-valley for that distance is not great ($11\frac{1}{10}$ feet per mile,) but the changes in level are abrupt, the valley extremely narrow and crooked; sharp curvature and steep gradients will be needed under any system of location, and, by the best mode of conquering these difficulties, the line will be extreme in cost and nearly impracticable."

The only instrument used on this examination was a pocket-compass. Governor Stevens's party left the Bitter Root at the debouche of the Cœur d'Alene Pass, and Mr. Lander at a point several miles before reaching Clark's fork. The topographer of the expedition, Mr. Lambert, describes this unexamined portion of the Bitter Root as a cañon, but in conversation I find that his description was inferred from partial information, and was not intended to mean that the mountain-sides closing in upon the river were vertical walls. Dr. Suckley makes no special mention of it. In respect to this portion of the route, he says: "The numerous very short curves, obliging frequent crossings by strong bridges, the great length of the route if the river is followed, the steep banks, and the high-raised work necessary to prevent the encroachments of the freshets, (which in many places rise from twenty to thirty feet above the common level,) will all render this part of the road exceedingly expensive." In view of the difficulties to be encountered on this line, and of the nature of the reconnaissance of it, it should not be considered practicable until more exact data are obtained upon which to form a correct opinion.

By the second line to Clark's fork: To overcome the summit of the Jocko divide, 852 feet above Hell-Gate, the approach will require a grade of sixty feet, and the descent to the valley of the Jocko a grade of sixty feet, both for short distances, with heavy embankments, and probably a lofty bridge. Lieutenant Donelson is of opinion that these grades may be reduced to forty-five and forty feet. Along the valley of the Jocko and Flathead rivers, on their left banks to Clark's fork, the grade will be twenty feet per mile. Ten or twelve miles before reaching Clark's fork, the mountains close in upon the river with steep slopes and rough projecting rocks. The heavy growth of timber obliged the party to leave the river, returning to it again at Horse Plain on Clark's fork, a few miles below the junction of the Bitter Root and Flathead. This portion of the Flathead, like that of the Bitter Root, is described by Mr. Lambert as a cañon. The distance to Horse Plain from Hell-Gate by the Jocko is 70 miles, by the Bitter Root 95 miles.

A better connection with the Flathead can probably be made by leaving the Blackfoot valley above the defile; further examination is necessary to establish this, however.

Lieutenant Donelson says the average fall of Clark's fork is eleven feet per mile, and he estimates that the railroad could descend with gradients of from fifteen to twenty feet per mile. With the exception of occasional small prairies, marked on the map, its valley throughout is heavily timbered, mainly with pine. At several points on the route the rocky hill-sides crowd upon the river, and all deep-cutting will probably expose the rock, apparently, in general, a species of limestone or trap.

The line crosses the Flathead some miles above its junction with Clark's fork, (or Bitter Root?) continues on the right bank as far as Big Rock; then crosses Clark's fork, following the left bank, and recrosses at the Cabinet mountain. Tunnelling the Cabinet mountain 300 yards through 50 per cent. basaltic rock, it would continue on the right bank of the river to

Lake Pend d'Oreille, and on the western side of the lake to its lower extremity. The river and lake are subject to freshets fifteen feet in height.

The summit separating Clark's fork and Spokane river is about 800 feet above the level at which these two rivers are crossed. The transit could be made, Lieutenant Donelson reports, with gradients not exceeding twenty-five feet per mile, though Governor Stevens says forty feet. The mountain region ends near the crossing of Spokane river. Mr. Lander, in continuation, after reporting upon the Bitter Root, says: "From the junction of the Bitter Root with Clark's fork to the crossing of Clark's fork, below Lake Pend d'Oreille, the line assumes a more favorable character; and, although still severe, may be readily adjusted to reasonable rate of curvature and grade. The crossing of the summit section, between Lake Pend d'Oreille and the valley of the Spokane, is very favorable, and can be made upon gradients of forty feet per mile. All great difficulties of location upon the route cease at the valley of the Spokane."

Regarding the subject of construction west of the Rocky mountain summit, the line passes, in nearly its whole extent, through forests which could furnish an abundance of pine and cedar of fine quality, and of fir and larch. The rafting of lumber cannot be carried on above Horse Plain, though it is probable that logs can be run in the freshets from the heads of the tributaries of Clark's fork. Lieutenant Donelson saw no good stone for building over this space. A locality on the Blackfoot, not far from Hell-Gate, another at Big Rock, (on Clark's fork,) and the mountains on the right of Clark's fork, for some distance below Thompson's prairie, would furnish stone in great abundance, which would answer for ordinary purposes. Mr. Tinkham states that not far from the Hudson Bay Company's post, among the Flatheads, good limestone for building could be obtained. Good granite is found on the Columbia, 140 miles above the mouth of the Yakima. Dr. Evans, geologist, informs me that stone will be found throughout this section at distances sufficiently near to obviate excessive cost. Sand can be obtained from Clark's fork, Pend d'Oreille lake, and elsewhere. The earth excavation and embankment throughout this section (from the east base of the Rocky mountains to the Spokane river) will be large in amount, and expensive. In all the mountain valleys the deep side-hill cuttings will frequently expose rock, and the bulk of the rock excavation in the entire railroad route will be in this section.

It is evident that throughout this section, from the entrance of the Rocky Mountain Pass to the crossing of the Spokane, a distance of 365 miles, the difficulties of construction will be very great; and that even if the two extremities rested upon thickly inhabited districts, the cost would be excessive.

Upon the passes of the Rocky mountains, Governor Stevens says:

"It is not doubted there are other passes in this portion of the Rocky mountain range, even better than those explored; they are indicated by the general depression of the mountain range, with the greater frequency of the streams stretching out to meet each other from the opposite slopes of the mountains; and I consider it important that, in future operations, a whole season should be devoted to their thorough examination, and that instrumental surveys should be made of the pass found to be the most practicable."

The region between the Cœur d'Alene mountains and the Cascade range, a space of 200 miles, is called the Great Plain of Columbia, or the Spokane Plain. It is a table-land, whose central and western portions are of trap formation, and are described on the map as sandy, rocky, and sterile. Its summit, some 800 feet above the level of the crossing of the Spokane, could probably be attained with gradients of 35 feet, the descent to the crossing of the Columbia river (near the junction of the Snake river) with grades of 30 feet, and from thence to Wallah-Wallah, 10 miles further, with grades of 20 feet. From the crossing of the Spokane to the crossing of the Columbia it is about 140 miles, 110 of which are over the treeless plain of the Columbia. The river is here from 400 to 450 yards wide, with good approaches. The earth excavation and embankment will not probably exceed the heaviest work of the prairies east of the mountains. A portion of the excavation on the first part of the Spokane Plain will be rock (basaltic trap.) Its eastern end rests upon the pine, cedar, and larch districts of the Columbia.

Lumber can be brought down the Columbia to its western end, and also from the Yakima, 100 miles above its mouth. Good granite is found on the Columbia, 140 miles above the mouth of the Yakima.

Within our territory, nearly the whole space between the Columbia river (its general course being from north to south) and Puget sound, is occupied by the Cascade mountains, with their secondary chains, spurs, and high, broken table-lands. Through these mountain masses, between the parallels of 45° 30′ and 49° north latitude, there are but two passes reported practicable for a railroad—that of the Columbia river, and that in which the north or main fork of the Yakima (a tributary of the Columbia) heads. This latter pass has been heretofore erroneously called Snoqualme Pass. The Yakima Pass gives the most direct route to Puget sound, the distance by it being 150 or 160 miles shorter than by the Columbia River Pass. The approach to it is by the valley of the Yakima. From the crossing of the Columbia to the commencement of the pine timber, 96 miles, the valley is wide, open, and terraced; the ground is sand, gravel, or loose stones. For 21 miles further, an open pine wood extends, with a light soil, sometimes gravelly. The grades are from 8 to 12½ feet per mile. No difficulties of construction whatever are met with. From this point there are two methods of passing the dividing ridge—one by a tunnel 4,000 yards long, 3,000 feet above the sea; the second by a tunnel of 11,840 yards, 2,400 feet above the sea. For the short tunnel the ascent of 895 feet is made in 18½ miles, giving a grade, supposing it to be uniform, of 48.4 feet per mile, in fifty per cent. rock-cutting. The tunnel 4,000 yards long will pass through solid rock, (silicious conglomerate;) thence to the falls of the Snoqualme, 45 miles from the tunnel, the road will be in side-cutting, (silicious conglomerate) with a grade of 59.8 feet per mile, supposing it to be uniform. The distance to the falls of Snoqualme was travelled over and estimated to be greater by Mr. Tinkham, and the grade proportionately less. From the Snoqualme falls to Seattle, on Puget sound, it is about 30 miles; the first ten will require a grade of not more than 20 feet per mile, and the remaining 20 miles will pass over a level country. If the second tunnel be used, the 18½ miles before reaching it will be with a grade of 15.2 feet per mile, with little side-cutting, through a thickly timbered country. The divide must be pierced by a tunnel 11,840 yards long, of a similar character to the short tunnel; the grade to the Snoqualme falls will then be 46.3 feet per mile, and the total length of the section 240 miles.

But the grades in both cases will be necessarily broken, and higher than the estimate in many places.

The elevations of the different points from the Columbia, to a point about three miles west of the summit, were taken with a barometer; the distances were estimated.

In conclusion, Captain McClellan states: "I am of the opinion that the Yakima Pass is barely practicable, and that only at a high cost of time, labor, and money." The depth of snow upon the summit of this pass has been much discussed. Captain McClellan, who made the reconnaissance, says, that he and his party spared no pains in inquiring of the Indians during the summer, fall, and winter, as to the quantity and nature of the snow in the mountains during the winter. We examined (he says) the snow-marks on the trees, (similar, he informs me, to those made by standing water on trees,) in the passes, &c. All the information obtained was consistent; and the resulting conclusion, that in ordinary winters there could not be less than from 20 to 25 feet of snow in the passes.

For the purpose of examining this point, Mr. Tinkham crossed the mountains from Wallah-Wallah to Seattle, by the Yakima Pass, during the month of January, passing the summit on the 21st of January. "For about six miles on the summit the snow was found to be six feet deep, with an occasional depth of seven, as also of four feet." "The whole breadth of snow, over twelve inches deep, was somewhat less than sixty miles in extent. Of this, about forty-five miles were two feet and upwards; about twenty miles were four feet and upwards; and six miles were six feet and upwards. All the snow was light and dry; it was the accumulated snows of the winter to January 21, deposited in successive layers of a few inches to two feet, which have generally lain undisturbed since their fall; and they present little obstruction to removal, in comparison with the compact drifted snows of the Atlantic States."

From the known effect of abrupt mountains, rising from plains, in increasing the precipitation of rain, it is not probable that less rain falls on the main chain of the Cascade mountains than at Puget sound, but rather more.

The mean amount of the winter rain at Steilacoom, on the sound, is 20.6 inches; the amount is nearly the same each winter. The yearly means of the winter rain, in the table of Governor S.'s report, are erroneous, though the mean for the winter of several years is correct.

Snow occupies from ten to twelve times the bulk of an equal quantity of rain. The snow of the Cascade mountains is reported to be very dry and light, and the proportion between it and rain is probably greater than as 12 to 1. Assuming it to be 12, and supposing the precipitation on these mountains, during December, January, and February, to be in the form of snow, we have at the close of February 20.6 feet of snow.

The mean temperatures at Steilacoom, Puget sound, from observations at the military post there for (four) years, are:

November, 46°.2 Fahr.; December, 38°.3 Fahr.; January, 38°.1 Fahr.; February, 40°.7 Fahr.; March, 41°.8 Fahr.; April, 48°.6 Fahr.

Applying the rule that for every 300 feet of elevation there is a decrease of 1° Fahr., we have for the temperatures of an elevation corresponding to that of the summit of the Snoqualme or Yakima Pass—

November, 36°; December, 28°; January, 28°; February, 30°.7; March, 31°.8; April, 38°.6.

But from the barren and broken character of the mountain masses east of the Cascade crest, the abruptness of the eastern slopes of the main chain, and its great general elevation, 8,000 feet above the sea, with bare rocky peaks projecting above this height, the highest reaching an elevation of 15,000 or 16,000 feet, the temperature of the Yakima Pass must be lower than the rule of decrease of temperature for increase of elevation would give when applied to the temperature of Steilacoom. The influence of these causes is shown in the meteorological report of Lieut. Mowry, by which it will be seen that the climate of the Cascade range and the country east of it is very cold. Lieut. Mowry says, page 404, at Chequoss (a pass in the Cascade chain 4,000 feet above the sea,) on the summit of the Cascade range, August 9th, the thermometer indicated a temperature below the freezing-point, and ice formed to the thickness of half an inch. At the same time and place, strawberries were growing in great luxuriance and abundance. The Indians informed him that the snow fell there as early as November, &c., &c.

Of the 8.69 inches of rain that fell during January at Steilacoom, 5.37 inches fell after the 26th; and of the 20.7 inches rain that fell there during the winter (December, January, and February,) but 7.74 inches had fallen at the time Mr. Tinkham crossed the Yakima Pass, (21st January;) that is, but little more than one-third of the whole quantity that fell during the winter. The above investigation is in accordance, then, with the facts as found by Mr. Tinkham; but one-third of the snow had fallen when he crossed.

Lieut. Grover, in crossing from Clark's fork to the Cœur d'Alene prairie, between the 19th and the 22d of February, found 2½ feet of very hard snow for the most part of the way, the elevation being about 2,000 and 2,500 feet. The country here is very dry, according to Lieut. Mowry.

It seems probable, from the foregoing investigation, that not less than 20 feet of snow is usually to be found on the summit of the Yakima Pass at the close of winter—gradually changing to 12 feet, 6 feet, &c., &c. But the question should not be considered settled until further examinations and an instrumental survey of the Yakima Pass are made.

The terminus of the road should be on Puget sound, and, from the report of Capt. McClellan, the harbor of Seattle would appear to be the most favorable on the eastern shore. To return to the crossing of the Columbia river near the mouth of Snake river.

Capt. McClellan states: "With regard to the Columbia river, I am not prepared to speak so much in detail; the last barometer being broken before we reached there on our return, and for other good reasons, I passed down by water. Mr. Lander, however, travelled the greater part of the distance by land; and as his examination corroborates the opinion I formed at the time, I shall content myself with expressing in general terms the nature of that pass." His conclusion is, that "it is not only practicable, but remarkably favorable;" and, in his opinion, it would be desirable that an instrumental survey should be made of the Yakima Pass and the Columbia River Pass, should any more railroad explorations be made on this line. In conversation Capt. McClellan informed me, that the work on the route along the Columbia river, from the Dalles to near Vancouver, 90 miles, would be similar to that of the Hudson River railroad along the mountain region. Mr. Lander says, "the high floods to which the Columbia river is subject, are serious obstacles to obtaining the best location for cheap construction offered by its valley." From observations made at Fort Vancouver, from May 8 to July 20, 1854, the rise of the river during the flood was 10 feet above spring level, and 17 feet above summer level.

Governor Stevens says: "The pass of the Columbia river, examined personally by myself as well as Captain McClellan and Mr. Lander, is remarkably favorable in its grades, which rarely exceed ten feet, in the ease with which debris from the ledges can be worked to form the embankments required to guard against freshets, and the great facility with which wood and stone, both of good quality, can be transported down the Columbia for purposes of construction. The only serious obstacle is Cape Horn mountain, which, to avoid sharp curvature, may require a tunnel seven hundred feet in length. The grades down the Columbia to near the mouth of the Cowlitz, and thence to Olympia, Steilacoom, or Seattle, will be small, the work light, and abundant materials of all kinds will be found for road-beds and superstructure." The ascents and descents are estimated at 300 and 700 feet. On the Columbia the line is, for the most part of the way, located in the bottom lands of the river, and will rarely be forced from them to the rocky bluffs bordering its intervale. Between Wallah-Wallah and the Dalles Mr. Tinkham found it necessary in only two instances to cross the rocky spurs jutting out from the river bluffs.

The bluffy country bordering the Columbia ceases near Cape Horn. From below the Dalles the woods commence, and continue to the head of Cowlitz river.

"The wide and comparatively flat and wooded valley of the Cowlitz connects with plains, sometimes of prairie and sometimes of woodland, extending to Puget sound, and which, although not fully explored, are sufficiently well known to insure the unusually favorable character of the country for the construction of a railway."

The total length from the crossing of the Columbia to Seattle is about 390 miles. The earth excavation will not probably exceed the heaviest work of the prairies east of the mountains, and is estimated not to exceed an average of seven to eight feet. The material for embankment is almost always of a superior character.

The amount of rock-cutting, with the exception of the portion of the line between the Dalles and Cape Horn, will be very small. The rock is generally a basaltic trap.

In reference to the facilities for construction upon Clark's fork and on the Columbia, Governor Stevens says: "By improvements either in the bed of the river, or in the use of locks at several points on the Columbia and Clark's fork, and by the substitution of rail where such improvement is impracticable, it is not doubted that a continuous communication can be established from the mouth of the Columbia to the mouth of the Spokane, and probably to Colville, and from the Pend d'Oreille lake to Horse Plain. Rails will undoubtedly be required at several of the places, and transfer be made from steamer to steamer."

The total length of the route from St. Paul to Seattle, Puget sound, by the Columbia River Pass, is 2,025 miles, or 2,050 if the Bitter Root river is used instead of the Jocko; by the Yakima Pass, 1,870 and 1,845 miles respectively. The distances just given are taken along the line of location for the proposed railroad. They are nearly the same as those travelled, except on the prairies east of the Rocky mountains, and on the Spokane Plain, where the located line is shorter than that travelled over, there being no serious obstacles to the more direct course. The distances given differ from those used by Governor Stevens, owing to a revision which the maps have undergone since his report was written.

SOIL.

In the absence of the geological report of Dr. Evans, whose field duties in Washington and Oregon Territories have detained him there until recently, the information upon the character of the soil upon the route is not as full, detailed, and satisfactory as could be desired. Previous geological examinations, over portions as far west as about longitude 101° or 102°, show that the uncultivable region begins in about the same longitude on this route as in the latitude of the Arkansas.

From the geological information respecting the region between the meridian of 101° and the Spokane Plain imparted recently by Dr. Evans, from the report of Mr. Gibbs upon the section west of the Spokane, and after a close examination of the reports, the following general conclusions have been arrived at respecting the soil of the region traversed by the northern route.

From the Mississippi to the western border of the Plateau of the Bois des Sioux, in about the meridian of 98° west of Greenwich, the soil is fertile; the upper layer being composed of vegetable mould. Here it begins to be mixed with sand and gravel, the proportion of which ingredients increases as you proceed westward. From Fort Union to the foot of the mountains, (15 or 20 miles east of the crest,) the upper covering of sand, clay, and gravel is from one to three feet thick, and lies upon a coarse sandstone. The grass, luxuriant on the vegetable mould, gradually becomes thinner, until on the sterile soil it is very sparse. Immediately under the mountains it improves again—perhaps from the intermingling of limestone debris, and the comparatively greater fall of rain.

On the Coteau du Missouri the ground is rougher, and the grass thinner, than on the prairie; and west and south of the Missouri it is in many places even yet more rough and sterile, the Mauvaises Terres beginning not far from the mouth of L'Eau-qui-court river.

In fact, the tertiary and cretaceous formations extend from about longitude 97° west of Greenwich to the eastern base of the Rocky mountains; the soil being stiff clay and sandstone, alternating with each other. The former are well constituted for fertility; but, under the present meteorological conditions, (the small yearly amount of rain, and the total absence of it at certain seasons,) they are unsuitable for agricultural purposes. They produce luxuriant grasses in the spring, but in the dry season (the summer) the sun withers the grass; parches, bakes, and cracks the clay surface, and not only gives it a sterile aspect, but renders it uncultivable. The sandstone soils are in themselves sterile. It is thought by some that if the annual burning of the prairies were to cease, forests would grow upon the clay soils, a greater amount of rain in the summer be precipitated by them, and that these clay soils would thus become cultivable.

The river-bottoms in part (where the soils of the different strata become mixed,) and the valleys among the mountains, form exceptions to this general condition of sterility. As, for instance, it is Lieut. Donelson's opinion that upon the Missouri the soil is such that the settlements might be continuous upon its banks up to the mouth of L'Eau-qui-court river, longitude 98°; from that point to Fort Union, about one-fourth could be settled. Above Fort Union, Lieut. Grover says: "On the lower portion of the river (between Fort Benton and Fort Union,) there are many quite extensive bottoms well adapted to agricultural purposes. There is a good deal of arable land, also, in the vicinity of Fort Benton, and in the Sun River valley." The proportion of cultivable bottom lands on this section of the river is much less than one-fourth. The Mouse River valley is represented to be fertile, as its growth of ash, elm, and oak indicates. Describing that portion of the route from Fort Union to Fort Benton, Governor Stevens writes, "The bottom lands, both of the Missouri and Milk rivers, are composed of clay and sand, &c."

The space between the Rocky and Cascade mountain chains is principally occupied, between the parallels of 45° and 49° latitude, with mountain masses and the great elevated plain of the Columbia.

From the main Cascade chain the generally sterile soil extends eastward over the dry region until the rain that falls upon the Cœur d'Alene, Bitter Root, and other mountains, begins to be felt; we then have grazing. The soil improves in quality as the mountains are approached, the valleys of which are represented as fertile, perhaps influenced in some degree by the nature of the mountain debris that have been washed upon them. The Columbia river and its affluents, in their lower courses within the limits above mentioned, are stated to carry gravel and sand, but no fertilizing matter.

It is their upper or mountain valleys (between the Cascade and Rocky mountains) only that are productive; their lower are uncultivable.

The fertile or cultivable areas are most probably the exceptions to the general character of the soil between these two mountain chains, and are of limited extent.

The soil, too, of a large portion described as fertile, is most probably better adapted to grazing than to farming. The valley of St. Mary's, and other mountain valleys in that region, and west of the Bitter Root mountains, are represented to have dark gravelly soils. The prairies on the Columbia river are also more or less gravelly. The middle and western parts of the plain of the Columbia are sandy, rocky, and sterile; here and there are *swales*, having rich mould; bunch-grass, varying in degree of sparseness of growth, is found over a large portion of its surface.

Lieutenant Mullan says of the St. Mary's valley, which has been considered as a kind of standard, "the soil of the valley of the Bitter Root (St. Mary's) is fertile and productive, well timbered with pine and cotton-wood, but whose chief *characteristic* and *capability* is *that of grazing large herds of cattle,* and affording excellent mill-sites along the numerous mountain streams."

Probably about one-fourth of the area of the valley is cultivable, the remainder being suitable for grass-lands only.

Dr. Suckley, referring to the Hell Gate, Bitter Root, Clark and Columbia rivers, and to the Dalles, says, "there are a few pieces of excellent land along these rivers." The valley of Clark's fork is heavily timbered with pine; there is no grass.

Within the limits of Washington Territory, between the Cascade and Rocky mountains, there are 7,356 Indians. Within the same Territory, west of the Cascades, the areas being as 3 to 1 about, there are 6,903 Indians. This may give some indication as to the capabilities of the soil for supporting animal life.

West of the Cascade mountains there are generally prairies, soon exhausted by cultivation, but offering good grazing; clay formations that are arable, and rich river bottoms. The fall of rain in the year is about 47 inches; the temperature is moderate.

Governor Stevens estimates that there are 4,000 square miles of tillable land on the eastern slopes of the Rocky mountains, and that the mountain valleys on the western slopes contain 6,000 square miles of arable land.

The preliminary report of the geologist of the party, made from Washington Territory, where he was still engaged in the field when the report of Governor Stevens was prepared, failed to reach the latter, who thus was not afforded the means of correcting opinions formed from those appearances of fertility presented by the growth of grasses, &c., which are liable to mislead, especially after traversing a region devoid of such verdure. A more thorough examination of the country and soil proves that very little, if any, of the eastern slopes of the Rocky mountains is suitable for cultivation; and that the valleys of the streams east of the mountains, and those west, are capable of sustaining merely small agricultural settlements. The greater portion of these valleys are only suited for grazing lands; and this mountain region, described as containing 10,000 square miles of arable land, admirably adapted by nature for a grazing country, can never sustain a large agricultural population.

There must be some numerical error in the estimate of the area of the grassed lands between the Bitter Root and the Rocky mountains, since careful measurements in the office make it much less than that given above.

It is not probable that the area of cultivable soil within the limits mentioned, east and west of the Rocky mountains, will exceed one-tenth of the area stated—that is, 1,000 square miles.

The character of country along the route from St. Paul to Seattle may be summed up as follows:

From St. Paul to Little Falls, fertile soil	109 miles.
From the Mississippi river at Little Falls to Dead Colt Hillock, the soil is fertile—the distance is about	166 "
From that point to the crossing of Revière à Jacques, near the 99th meridian, the change from fertility to an uncultivable condition takes place	66 "
Thence to the crossing of Sun river, a distance of 752 miles, the prairie is uncultivable; the river bottom of the Missouri in part, those of Jacques river, Mouse river, and of other streams, possessing a cultivable soil	752 "
We then have mountain region of 404 miles, a well-wooded district to the Spokane river, with mountain valleys of partly cultivable soil, and prairies of the same character	404 "
(The sum of the areas of the cultivable soil in the Rocky mountain region being about 1,000 square miles.)	
From the Spokane river to the crossing of the Columbia, 10 miles above Fort Wallah-Wallah, over the barren plain of the Columbia	142 "
Thence to the Cascades, an uncultivable though grazing district, about	192 "
Thence to Seattle, on Puget sound, over cultivable land, about	194 "
Total	2,025 "

So that of the 2,025 miles from St. Paul to Seattle, on Puget sound, we have only a space of about 535 miles of fertile country; the remaining 1,490 miles being over uncultivable prairie soil, or mountain-land producing only lumber, with the limited exception of occasional river-bottoms, mountain-valleys, or prairie.

CLIMATE.

Of the 47 inches of rain that fall yearly at Steilacoom, Puget sound, 15 inches fall during the autumn months, and 20.6 inches during the winter months. At Fort Laramie, on the plain just east of the Rocky mountains, 23.5 inches rain fall during the year. Ten inches of these 23.5 fall during the spring, and only 3.4 inches during the winter. At Fort Snelling about 25 inches fall during the year: of this only 2 inches fall during the winter; 6.8 inches during the spring; 10.2 inches during the summer; and 5.7 inches during the autumn. The excessive autumn and winter rains of Puget sound are converted into spring rains at the eastern base of the Rocky mountains, and into summer rains at Fort Snelling. It is probable that the Bitter Root range has a heavy winter precipitation, and, arresting a large proportion of the moisture from the west, protects the Rocky mountains from it and from heavy winter snows—a circumstance favorable to the construction and working of a railroad through the Rocky mountains in this latitude. It appears probable, too, that the greatest precipitation in this region takes place during the latter part of winter and the early part of spring. Mr. Tinkham, in crossing the Bitter Root range, found two and three feet of snow in the latter part of November; and, before he left the camp on the summit of the pass, (7,250 feet elevation) the snow increased to the depth of six feet.

The evidence adduced by Gov. Stevens shows that no obstruction to a railroad need be apprehended from snow across the plains through the passes of the Rocky mountains, and thence by way of the Columbia River Pass to Puget sound, though the great rise of the Bitter Root and Flathead rivers and Clark's fork, in the spring freshets, indicates a large deposition of snow at their sources. It is reported, that two winters previous to that of Gov. Stevens's party being there, (winter of 1851–2,) a party of Flathead Indians were prevented from returning to their village, in St. Mary's valley, although only two or three days' travel from it, by the passes being blocked up with snow; they were on that account obliged to pass the winter in one of the valleys east of St. Mary's. This does not, however, make it impracticable for a railroad, since it was the accumulation of drift of the whole winter, and on a railroad track it would be removed as fast as it fell. The meteorological observations made at Fort Benton and in St. Mary's valley during the past year, will be interesting. The amount of winter rains converted into snow, give pretty sure indications, in these climates, of the greatest depth that may be encountered, allowing one foot of snow to one inch of rain.

With respect to the temperature of the route: San Francisco, in about latitude 37°, has a winter temperature of 50° Fahrenheit; Fort Moultrie, Charleston harbor, about latitude 33°, has about the same winter temperature, 50° Fahrenheit; Steilacoom, Puget sound, about latitude 47°, has a winter temperature of about 39° Fahrenheit—the same, nearly, as that of Fort Monroe, Old Point Comfort, Chesapeake bay, in latitude about 37°, which is 40° Fahrenheit.

The mean winter temperature of Steilacoom, Puget sound, is 39°; of San Francisco, 50°.4; showing an increase of about 1° of Fahrenheit for 1° of latitude, which is the change generally on that coast within those limits, corresponding nearly with the eastern part of Europe, as given by Humboldt.

On the Atlantic coast, the change from south to north in our territory, as far north as Boston, is about 2°.4 Fahrenheit for 1° of latitude. The meteorological observations that I have access to, those of the Surgeon General's bureau, do not show whether this change of proportion takes place gradually between the shores of the two oceans, or if it be sudden.

Along the Mississippi river the decrease of temperature for increase of latitude is somewhat less than on the Atlantic.

Along the chain of the Rocky mountains the change of temperature in some instances corresponds with the Atlantic, sometimes with the Mississippi; in other cases, the proportionate decrease of temperature going north is greater than either. The observations on the northern route, as given in the report, are too imperfect to enable a satisfactory comparison to be drawn between them and those made at points further south. So far as any conclusions can be deduced from them, they indicate that the law of change of temperature along the Rocky mountain range for change of latitude is nearly the same as that along the Mississippi or the Atlantic coast—the points being reduced to a common elevation by the allowance of 1° Fahrenheit for every 300 feet of elevation. It is supposed, also, that no great modifying influences from local causes exist—such, for instance, as the Great Salt lake. If, then, we find points along the northern route, among the mountains, with winter temperatures not exceeding those many degrees further south, in the same mountain chain, it will be due simply to the low elevation of the former. That the winter climate is severely cold on the prairies between Fort Benton and the mountains, and in the Rocky mountain passes, is inferrible from the reports of Mr. Tinkham and Lieutenant Grover. That the cold is excessive on the prairie over the whole route is evident, from the meteorological information contained in the report. Mr. Tinkham, after crossing the summit of the Marias Pass, (latitude 48° 30′ about,) found, on the 20th of October, at an elevation of 5,600 feet, (300 feet higher than the proposed tunnel in Lewis and Clark's Pass,) the snow-banks of the previous winter still resting on the borders of the shaded ponds or small lakes; and in the prairies, twelve miles from the summit, he found four inches of snow. On the route to Fort Benton, (from this pass,) between the 20th and 27th of October, distance 136 miles, the thermometer was once or twice as low as 3° Fahrenheit.

Lieutenant Grover crossed the Rocky mountains through Cadotte's Pass, in January of 1854, and while in the pass the thermometer descended as low as 21°, 19°, 15°, below zero of Fahrenheit.

The meteorological observations of the Medical department of the army, furnished me from the Surgeon General's office, form the data, in addition to those given in Governor Stevens's report, for the deductions drawn respecting the amount of snow, rain, temperature, &c.

GENERAL REMARKS.

The two principal favorable characteristics of the northern route, are its low profile and low grades; the prairies extending in this latitude from the Mississippi to the base of the mountains, fifteen or twenty miles from the summit, in about longitude 112° and 113°, a distance by the railroad route of 1,000 miles. Its proximity to, and connexion with the Missouri and Columbia rivers and their principal tributaries, is also favorable to its construction.

The road leaves the Mississippi river, at Little Falls, at an elevation above the sea of about 1,100 feet. Between Mouse and Missouri rivers it has attained an elevation of more than 2,000 feet. Its general elevation on the Missouri and Milk rivers is 2,200 feet. Leaving Milk river, it crosses the high prairies towards Lewis and Clark's and Cadotte's Passes; at the distance of 100 miles on the travelled, and 130 on the railroad location from these passes, the elevation is about 3,000 feet. Upon entering the passes it is about 4,600 feet, the summits being respectively 6,300 and 6,044; and the proposed tunnels at elevations of 5,300 and 5,000 feet respectively.

After passing the summit we descend to the elevation of 3,000 feet, at about 100 miles west of it, by following the valley of the Bitter Root, and 130 miles west of it, following the Jocko, making the whole distance on the railroad route, exceeding an elevation of 3,000 feet, to be about 260 miles. At the junction of the Bitter Root and Flathead rivers, which forms the commencement of Clark's fork, the elevation is about 2,500 feet, and at Pend d'Oreille lake about 1,600 feet. In crossing the dividing ridge between Clark's fork and the Spokane river, and the Great Plain of Columbia, between the Spokane and Columbia, the elevation attained is about 2,400 feet. If the mountain district be considered to extend from Sun river to Pend d'Oreille lake, the route runs through 310 miles of it; if to the Spokane river, about 400 miles.

The sum of the ascents in crossing main divides or ridges going from Fort Vancouver, elevation 0, to St. Paul, elevation 828 feet, is about 9,500 feet; from Seattle, on Puget sound, to St. Paul, the sum would be 10,000 feet.

The descents, going west, would be, respectively, above 8,700 and 9,200 feet.

Applying Latrobe and Knight's rule for equating grades, the effect of these ascents and descents, on the working of the road, would be equivalent to 343 miles in the first instance, and 362 in the other.

The distance from St. Paul to Vancouver is 1,864 miles.
" " Seattle 2,025 miles.
The equated distances become (to Vancouver) 2,207 miles.
" " (to Seattle) 2,387 miles.

The numbers just given are not necessarily a measure of the sum of all the ascents on the route, since in making any one of the great ascents the road may and does rise and fall repeatedly. These minor undulations careful instrumental surveys only can measure accurately.

If the prairies give a low profile, they at the same time have the disadvantage of furnishing neither lumber nor fuel, nor a good supply of water, and, at some seasons, none at all over certain distances. The cotton-wood on the river bottoms (of which but a limited supply exists) should not be depended upon for fuel—it is no doubt of small growth; that of large growth, on the rich lands of the Mississippi, is used for fuel on western steamboats, but the small growth will hardly prove fit for use in locomotives. It will not, certainly, be good fuel for that purpose. Opinions differ as to its fitness for ties, even for a temporary track by which to reach supplies of better lumber for a permanent road. By some it is said to be totally unfit for this purpose, as it will not hold a nail.

TIES, LUMBER, &C.

The points of supply of good timber are Little Falls, Mississippi river; Red river, Mouse river, Bear's-Paw mountains, the Three Buttes, and the western slopes of the Rocky mountains.

The distances apart of these points, over which ties and lumber generally must be transported up the Missouri, are—

From Little Falls to Red river, 100 miles;

From Red river to Mouse river, 260 miles;

From Mouse river to Bear's-Paw mountains, 470 miles;

From Bear's-Paw mountains to western slope of Rocky mountains, 170 miles; or,

From Three Buttes to western slope of Rocky mountains, 130 miles.

West of the Rocky mountains the country is well supplied with lumber throughout, except for the space of 110 miles in crossing the plains of the Columbia.

It will cost to transport lumber great distances by the built portions of the road, $4 50 per 1,000 feet per 100 miles.

FUEL.

Supposing the road supplied with fuel, in the districts destitute of it, from the coal-fields of Illinois, the nearest point to St. Paul is Port Byron on the Mississippi, 330 miles from St. Paul, and coal will probably cost at St. Paul from $4 to $6 per ton.

As coal can be transported three and a half times as far as wood, and be equally economical for locomotive use, it may be used over 600 miles of the northern route, beginning 100 miles west of the Mississippi, at an average cost to the road of from $15 to $17 per ton. This estimate is made merely to show what would be the cost over these portions of the route if cotton-wood cannot be used for fuel. The cost of wood per cord, for 200 miles east of the Rocky mountains, would be in the same proportion. The sources of supply of good fuel from Red and Mouse rivers, Bear's-Paw mountains, and the Three Buttes, will of course be availed of, so far as they can be economically.

The navigation of the Missouri river to Fort Union is closed by ice four or five months in the year; that of the Mississippi, at St. Paul, about four and a half months, from the latter part of November to early in April.

TUNNELS.

In forming a judgment upon the practicability and length of time required to execute a tunnel, the only safe guide is the result of well-tried means of excavation.

When the question is the construction of a tunnel of several miles in length through rock, the depth from the surface being so great that shafts cannot be resorted to, the tunnel is only practicable if some machinery can be applied to the excavation so as to bring its time of completion within reasonable limits. The rate at which rock excavation could be made in it, by the only means as yet successfully tried, would be so slow that the project would be considered entirely impracticable. It does not appear that any of the machines invented for this purpose have as yet proved successful, and no tunnel project depending upon their use can be considered practicable until they have proved successful in trials of every kind.

In hard rock, where continual blasting is required, the rate of progress may be taken at 10.5 inches every 12 hours. On the Black Rock tunnel, Reading railroad, through graywacke slate, the progress was but little more than 0.6 of a foot every 24 hours, or 2,387 spaces of 12 hours each, for constructing 1,782.5 feet in length of the tunnel.

In the Blue Ridge tunnel, on the Virginia Central railroad, the progress has been less than two feet per day of 24 hours.

Tunnels two, three, and four miles in length, in rock or partly in rock, at depths exceeding 1,000 feet below the summit, in severely cold climates, at great distances from thickly inhabited districts, form serious objections to any route.

The more southerly passes of the Rocky mountains partly explored, in connexion with this route, have the advantage of not requiring tunnels.

ESTIMATE.

Governor Stevens's estimate of the time required to build the road cannot be founded upon the experience of any great line of railroad built in the United States.

The estimate of 25 per cent. to the cost at eastern prices from the Bois des Sioux to the Rocky mountains, and thence to the Pacific of 40 per cent., is, in my judgment, too small an increase. It would have been safer, probably, to have added 100 per cent. to the cost at eastern prices, from the crossing of Milk river to the Pacific. Under this supposition, the corrected estimates of $105,076,000, of $112,121,000, of $105,091,000, and of $129,806,000, would have added to them $30,690,000, $33,750,000, $30,690,000, and $41,440,000, and would become—

Cost of road to Seattle by the Yakima Pass, using the long tunnel, 1,875 miles..	$135,766,000
Cost of road to Seattle by the Columbia valley and the Cowlitz river, 2,025 miles	145,871,000
Cost of road to Vancouver, 1,864 miles..........	135,781,000
Entire system, St. Paul to the Columbia, with branches down the Columbia and across the Cascades, and a connexion from Seattle direct to the Columbia river, 2,175 miles, at a cost of..........	171,246,000
To the above original sums Governor Stevens adds for engineering and contingencies..........	5,000,000

It does not appear whether equipment is included in the estimate; if it is not, about $3,000,000 should be added to the above sums on that account. If a full equipment has been included, $10,000,000 should be subtracted from each of the preceding sums, to bring the estimate in accordance with those of the other routes; and under this latter supposition the estimate finally becomes—

Cost of road to Seattle by the Yakima Pass, using the long tunnel, 1,875 miles.	$130,766,000
Cost of road to Seattle by the Columbia valley and the Cowlitz river, 2,025 miles	140,871,000
Cost of road to Vancouver, 1,864 miles..........	130,781,000
Entire system..........	166,246,000

CHAPTER II.

ROUTE NEAR THE FORTY-FIRST AND FORY-SECOND PARALLELS OF NORTH LATITUDE.

That portion of this route from the Missouri river to Fort Bridger, on a tributary of Green river, has not been explored with a special reference to the practicability of constructing a railroad, and the reports do not contain all the details necessary to the elucidation of the subject. The information respecting it is to be found in the reports of Colonel Fremont and Captain Stansbury.

From Fort Bridger to the Pacific, the route has been explored and reported upon by Lieutenant E. G. Beckwith.

The accompanying report upon the route east of Fort Bridger, by Lieutenant G. K. Warren, is based upon the reports of Colonel Fremont and Captain Stansbury.

The eastern terminus of the route may be either Council Bluffs or Fort Leavenworth. It ascends the Platte and passes through the eastern chain of the Rocky mountains, (the Black Hills,) either by the North fork and its tributary, the Sweet Water, or the South fork and a tributary called Lodge Pole creek. By the former it enters upon the great elevated table-land in which the headwaters of the Platte and the Colorado of the west are found, by the South Pass, the ascent having been gradual from the first mountain gorge in the Black Hills, 30 miles above Fort Laramie, to the summit of the so-called pass, a distance of nearly 300 miles, bounded, generally, on either side, by mountains. This table-land, including the Laramie plains, extends 300 miles from east to west, and 100 from north to south. Its soil is light and dry; its growth artemisia, with a little scattered grass, a border of the latter being found on the water-courses, and scattered cedars upon the mountains in the western half.

By the second route, the same difference of elevation is overcome by the Cheyenne Pass, probably in about the distance usual in the Rocky Mountain passes, the route thus entering the Laramie plains, which may be considered to form the eastern part of the Great Plateau first mentioned.

From the Missouri river to the entrance of the Black Hills, the route resembles others from the Mississippi to the Rocky mountains, fully discussed elsewhere, and needs no special mention.

It may be estimated to cost $35,000 per mile for construction and equipment, 25 per cent. having been added to cost at eastern prices for one-half the distance.

Following the northern fork of the Platte, 30 miles above Fort Laramie, 520 from Council Bluffs, and 755 from Fort Leavenworth, this line enters the Black Hills through a gorge with vertical walls from 200 to 400 feet high; thence to the Red Buttes, 117 miles, the road must cross many streams coming from the Black Hills, that have cut deep ravines in the earth near their mouths. The construction will be costly.

From the gorge of the Red Buttes to the Hot Spring gorge, 34 miles, the route lies through a valley. Above this point the Platte passes through exceedingly rugged ground, and is walled in by cañons.

The road should leave the river just below the Hot Spring Gate, turn to the north, and cross the hills, the peaks of which are 800 feet above the Platte, giving an average grade of 133 feet to the mile for six miles, but which doubtless will be found steeper than the average near the summit, descend 10 miles, with an average grade of 56 feet to the mile, to the Sweet Water, a branch of the Platte. This stream occasionally cuts through spurs, making cañons, that of the Devil's Gate being through granite; but it is represented to be generally rather open, with abundant grass on the immediate bottoms, though the hills on either side are rocky and bare. At the source of the Sweet Water, the summit of the South Pass is attained, its elevation being 7,490 feet, the distance from the first gorge in the Black mountains being 291 miles, and from Fort Laramie 321 miles.

This whole section, from the first gorge to the summit of the pass, 291 miles, will be expensive, and is assimilated, in amount of work required, to the Baltimore and Ohio railroad, and may be estimated, therefore, to cost, for construction and such equipment as will be required for first use, 50 per cent. being added for increased cost over eastern prices, $75,000 per mile.

The only practicable route known, from the South Pass to the Great Basin, is by Fort Bridger through the passes in the Wahsatch mountains, explored by Lieutenant Beckwith. The route would traverse the Great Plateau, following Sandy creek, a tributary of Green river, to the crossing of the latter, from which point to Fort Bridger no doubt exists of its practicability. The distance is 131 miles; the elevation of Fort Bridger, 7,254 feet.

The amount of work on this section would be considerably less than that on the preceding, and the construction and equipment may be estimated to cost $50,000 or $55,000 per mile; 50 per cent. being added to the cost at eastern prices.

From Council Bluffs to Fort Bridger the distance is 942 miles, and from Fort Leavenworth 1,072 miles.

The points of supply for ties, lumber, &c., will be found only at the eastern extremity, on the Black Hills and on the Wind River mountains, the distances apart being 500 and 300 miles. Fuel for working parties will be found along the Platte; none on the streams of the great plain west of the South Pass. Good building-stone is found on the Sweet Water.

Coal is to be had at the eastern terminus, and extensive beds exist on Green river and its affluents; the distance apart of the points of supply being about 800 miles.

The route along the South fork of the Platte and Lodge Pole creek, by the Cheyenne Pass and Bridger's Pass, is not so well known as the other. Lodge Pole creek has never been continuously explored, and there is no profile of this route. Respecting the Cheyenne Pass, Captain Stansbury says his "examinations fully demonstrate the existence of a route through the Black Hills, not only practicable, but free from any obstructions involving in their removal great or unusual expenditure." He gives no estimated grades, and had no barometer or other instrument for measuring elevations.

From the Cheyenne Pass to Fort Bridger "the country can be crossed in many places, the choice being determined by considerations of fuel and water." That selected crosses the divide between the waters of the North fork of the Platte and Green river, by Bridger's Pass.

The expense of construction on this route, from the Cheyenne Pass to Fort Bridger, would probably be less than that along the Platte. The rock-cutting would be small in amount, and in soft material. It crosses ground much cut up by ravines and gullies, and in many places easily torn up by the torrents, probably requiring care in location, and much masonry, which the absence of good building-stone would render expensive. Captain Stansbury says an extensive embankmentwill be required on Muddy creek, west of Bridger's Pass. The distance from Council Bluffs to Fort Bridger by this route is 897 miles.

A reliable comparison of the cost of the two routes cannot be made with the present information; and in the estimate of the cost of the whole route, I shall adopt that by the South Pass, though Captain Stansbury, who examined both, is positive in his preference of the other.

It is probable that no unusual difficulty may be apprehended from the depth of snow between Fort Laramie and Fort Bridger. The quantity that falls is not exactly known.

The eastern terminus of the exploration of Lieutenant Beckwith upon the route of the 41st parallel is at Fort Bridger, situated on Black's fork, a tributary of Green river, at an elevation of 7,254 feet above the sea. The line ascends the divide between the waters of Green river and those of the Great Salt lake, by the valley of Black's fork or of one of its tributaries, with grades of 69.5 and 40.3 feet per mile. The summit is a broad terrace at the foot of the Uinta mountains, and has an elevation of 8,373 feet. From this point the line descends over the undulating country separating the Uinta and Bear River mountains, crosses the head of Bear river, and, entering the valley of White Clay creek at its head, follows that stream to its junction with Weber river.

The Wahsatch mountains now intervene between this rolling country and the Great Salt lake, and the passage through them may be effected by following Weber river, or by ascending to near the sources of the Timpanogos, and descending that stream—both being affluents, directly or indirectly, of the Great Salt lake. The distances are about the same to their common point on that lake.

There are cañons upon both these streams; that of the Timpanogos is ten miles in length, and narrow, being from 100 to 300 yards in width. It is direct in its general course, but must be bridged at several points to avoid short curves. The sides are of blue limestone, and will require rock-blasting at some points. The river, thirty yards wide, descends with a powerful current, and, when most swollen, is six feet above its ordinary level.

The upper cañon, on Weber river, is rather a gorge, or defile, eight and a half miles long. The mountains rise to a great height above it, and are rocky and precipitous, and much broken by ravines. The river is winding, and it will be necessary to cross it frequently.

The lower cañon, near the borders of the valley of the Great Salt lake, is four miles long, direct, with an average width of 175 yards, the stream being thirty yards wide, and impinging, frequently, with great force against the base of the mountains, which are sufficiently retreating to admit of the practicable passage of a railway.

Entering the valley of Great Salt lake from either this or the Timpanogos cañon, there is no obstacle to the construction of a railway, passing by the south end of the lake, and crossing the Jordan, Tuilla valley, and Spring or Lone-Rock valley, to its west side.

By the valley of the Timpanogos, the distance from near Fort Bridger to the south end of the Great Salt lake, on the western side of the valley of the Jordan, is 182.55 miles—the greatest grade required, eighty-four feet to the mile.

The amount of work required on this section, excepting that along the cañon, will not, in the opinion of Lieutenant Beckwith, be great.

"From the western shore of Great Salt lake to the valley of Humboldt river the country consists alternately of mountains, in more or less isolated ridges, and open, level plains, rising gradually from the level of the lake on the east to the base of the Humboldt mountains on the west—that is, from 4,200 feet to 6,000 feet above the sea." West of the Humboldt mountains the country is of the same character, the plains declining until, at the west shore of Mud lake, usually called the foot of the Sierra Nevada, the elevation is 4,100 feet. Here the ground rises again to the plain, table-land or basin of the Sierra Nevada, whose elevation is 5,200 feet above the sea. It is covered with irregular spurs, ridges, and isolated peaks, rising a few hundred feet, leaving a plain surface in a north and south direction sometimes ten miles, sometimes only a few hundred yards, in width. In an east and west direction this plain is about forty miles in extent, bounded at either end by mountains, the summits of the passes through which are 400 and 500 feet above the plain, and which prevent its drainage into the Great Basin, or into the waters of the Pacific. This plain, or basin of the Sierra Nevada, might properly be called a part of the Great Basin, since it is in every respect similar to it.

The mountains in this space of 500 miles, between the Great Salt lake and the foot of the Sierra Nevada, have a general north and south course; occasionally cross-spurs close the valleys to the north and south, but more frequently this isolation is only apparent. They are sharp, rocky, and inaccessible in many parts, but are low and easily passed in others; their general elevation varies from 1,500 to 3,000 feet above the valleys, and but few of them retain snow upon their highest peaks during the summer. They are liberally supplied with springs and small streams, but the latter seldom extend far into the plains. At the time of melting snows there are many small ponds and lakes, but at other seasons the waters are absorbed by the soil near the base of the mountains. Grass is found in abundance upon nearly every range; but timber is very scarce, a small scattered growth of cedar only being seen upon a few ranges. East of the Humboldt mountains, the growth of cedars is more abundant and the grass better. The valleys rarely have a width east and west of more than five or ten miles, but often have a large extent north and south. They are irregular in form, frequently extending around the ends of mountains, or uniting to succeeding valleys by level passages. The greater part of the surface of these valleys is merely sprinkled by several varieties of sombre artemisia, (wild sage,) presenting the aspect of a dreary waste; though there are spots more thickly covered with this vegetation, yet the soil is seldom half covered with it for a few acres, and is nowhere suitable for settlement and cultivation. Immediately west of Great Salt lake there is a desert plain of mud, clay, and sand, impregnated with salt, seventy miles in width from east to west by its longest line, and forty at a narrower part further south—thirty miles of which must be piled for the passage of a railroad across it.

A railroad may be carried over this series of plains, and around the mountain masses, at nearly the general level of the valleys. The route in this manner reaches the foot of the Humboldt mountains—a narrow but elevated ridge, containing much snow during most of the year—and crosses them by a pass nine miles long, about three of which are occupied by a narrow, rocky ravine, above which the road should be carried on the sloping spurs of the mountains on the western descent. Elevation of summit, 6,579 feet above the sea. At the time when passed, 21st May, snow covered the high peaks above it, and a few drifts extended into the ravines down to the level of its summit.

The descent is now made to the open valley of Humboldt river, which is followed for about 190 miles. The steepest grade proposed in the pass of Humboldt mountain is eighty-nine feet per mile for eight miles, but this can be reduced by gaining distance to any desirable extent.

The Humboldt river, as described by Colonel Fremont, is formed by two streams rising in mountains west of the Great Salt lake—the Humboldt mountains. Its general direction is from east to west, coursing among broken ranges of mountains; its length about three hundred miles. It is without affluents, and terminates near the foot of the Sierra Nevada in a marshy lake. It has a moderate current, is from two to six feet deep in the dry season, and probably not fordable anywhere below the junction of the two streams during the melting of the snows. The valley varies in width from a few miles to twenty, and, excepting the immediate river-banks, is a dry, sandy plain, without grass, wood, or arable soil. Its own immediate valley (bottom) is a rich alluvion covered with blue grass, herdsgrass, clover and other nutritious grasses, and its course is marked through the plain by a line of willow, serving for fuel.

Of the three lines from the Humboldt river to the foot of the Sierra Nevada, the best is that by the Noble's Pass road, as it avoids the principal range of mountains crossed on the line followed a few miles south. The line followed crosses two ranges of the general character of the Basin mountains, and reaches the foot of the Madelin Pass of the Sierra Nevada, on the west shore of Mud lake, in a distance of 119 miles, and at an elevation of 4,079 feet above the sea. The topographical features of the Great Basin present extraordinary facilities for the construction of a railroad across it. By the route followed, the distance is more than 600 miles from the debouche of the Timpanogos river to the west shore of Mud lake.

In this latitude, the Sierra Nevada was found to be a plateau about 5,200 feet above the sea, forty miles in width from east to west, enclosed at these limits by low mountains, the summits of the passes through which are four and five hundred feet above its surface. The plain is covered with irregular spurs, ridges, and isolated peaks, rising a few hundred feet, limiting it in a north and south direction sometimes to a space of a few hundred yards, and in others to that of ten miles. These spurs, &c., on the eastern portion of the plateau are sparsely covered with cedar; on the western, heavily covered with pine.

There is no drainage from this plain, the waters of a few small streams and springs forming grassy ponds upon its surface. In its general features it is similar to the Great Basin, excepting that as more rain falls upon it, the vegetation is comparatively luxuriant.

The two routes by which this plain is reached from the Great Basin, and the descent afterwards made to the Sacramento river, are described in detail in the concluding chapter of Lieutenant Beckwith's report.

That called the Madelin Pass, the more northern, is most probably the better of the two, and is the only one necessary to be considered. Leaving Mud lake, it ascends by the valley of Smoky creek, for three miles through a narrow gorge (from 100 to 150 yards wide) in an outlying spur of the Sierra Nevada. The sides, formed of coarse, crumbling, metamorphic rock, much broken by side ravines, rise abruptly to the height of from fifty to two hundred feet on the south, and to a much greater elevation on the north side. The course of the gorge is direct, and can be followed without difficulty by a railroad. Above the gorge, the valley expands to the width of half a mile and a mile, and again becomes narrow; being enclosed on the north by retreating mountain spurs, the means of ascending by a very uniform grade is afforded. Near the summit the grassy ascent is but 200 yards wide, with rocky hills rising gently two or three hundred feet above it. The pass is, thus far, of a very favorable character; the length of the ascent is 22.89 miles, the difference of elevation 1,172 feet, the altitude of the summit 5,667 feet, and the steepest slope 75 feet per mile.

By a gentle descent for five miles the plateau is gained, and then crossed to the low ridge enclosing it to the west, the summit elevation of which, 5,736 feet, is attained by following a ravine valley, sometimes a mile, at others a quarter of a mile wide, bounded by ridges rising gently on either side. The descent is commenced by a narrow ravine, and is at first rapid, 420 feet in 2.4 miles; but the ravine soon widens, and a creek descends from it with a free current, a tributary of the Sacramento river. A cut is proposed at the summit 120 feet deep, running out to the surface at either end, making a length in all of four miles, and a grade of 124 feet per mile for 2.4 miles. It may be preferable to tunnel instead of cutting, or to cut only one-half the depth proposed.

The open plain of Round valley, on the Sacramento, is reached 15 miles from the summit, (difference of elevation 1,300 feet,) over one-half of which distance the road must be located along the mountain on the northeast side of the stream. Although the greater number of ravines is found on that side, there are no cañon walls, two of which exist on the southwestern side.

From this point the route lies over the smooth plain of Round valley to the head of the first cañon on the Sacramento, a distance of 15 miles.

This cañon is a formidable obstacle to be overcome. Its entire length is nearly 14 miles, succeeded by an open valley of similar extent, which is followed by a second cañon nine miles in length, of the same character as the first. From the mouth of Canoe creek, four miles below the foot of the second cañon, for the space of 96 miles the course of the Sacramento lies entirely through heavily timbered mountains, which rise precipitously from the river-banks to the height of from 1,500 to 2,000 feet above the stream. Its course is very sinuous, with all varieties of curves greater than a right-angle, and is seldom entirely straight for two miles consecutively. The construction of this portion of the route, 136 miles in length, would be one of no ordinary difficulty or expense under the most favorable circumstances of dense population, and the facilities of railroad construction which it would afford. It is impossible, with the data presented, to form a reliable opinion of its probable cost. To set down the amount of labor required at that of the Hudson river railroad, will be, it appears to me, to under-estimate it, since only a portion of that railroad, 144 miles long, runs through the mountainous district, whereas the whole of this is of that character.

As an intelligible description of these portions of the river cannot be more brief than that of Lieut. Beckwith, I make the following extract from his resumé of the route:

EXTRACT FROM THE REPORT OF LIEUTENANT BECKWITH.

"Round valley, through which the Sacramento river descends from the northeast, and through which a road can be carried at pleasure, extends for fifteen miles below this point to the head of the first cañon of the Sacramento. This cañon is a formidable obstacle to be overcome. Its entire length is 13.74 miles, succeeded by an open valley of similar extent, which is followed by another cañon, 8.95 miles in length, of the same character as the first. The river, as it enters the first cañon, is from thirty to forty feet wide, flowing with a rapid current over a bed of rocks, and it is sixty feet wide as it enters the second cañon just below the junction of Fall river, and flows over a similar bed with an equally swift current. At their heads these cañons are vertical, metamorphic rocks, eighty feet high, with large masses of fallen rocks accumulated at the bases of the walls. The first is cut through a high plain for six miles; the plain then rises somewhat, and is surmounted by high sloping ridges, rising five or six hundred feet above it, and the cañon becomes much broader and its walls more elevated for two miles, to where it makes a large bend to the north; below this the walls gradually decrease, and in two miles the cañon opens to the width of half a mile, which it preserves for three miles to the succeeding valley. The highest portions of the walls rise two hundred feet above the stream, with an accumulation of fallen rocks extending half way to the top. For eight miles the course of the cañon is direct. It then makes a long bend to the north, and is followed by two or three short curves, but with a generally direct course. Its open part is timbered and its walls less abrupt, and on the right bank of the stream the mountains, followed by the river, extend considerably into the plain of Fall river. The most favorable line for the passage of a railway leads along the plain on the north side of the river, and descends the sides of the rocky hills which surmount it, and continues on the side of the mountain until it enters the plain of Fall river. The second cañon is only less formidable than the first because of its less extent. Its character is entirely the same, except that it is surmounted near its head by sloping mountain ridges of a similar altitude to the former. But on the south side, a few miles distant, the ridge subsides into rocky volcanic hills and plains. It will require a minute survey to determine the most practicable line by which to pass it; but it is probable that the best line will be found to leave the river a few miles above Fall river, and to pass around the ridge extending southward, and again return to the Sacramento at the mouth of Canoe creek, four miles below the foot of the cañon, avoiding short curves which must be encountered in it, and diminishing the amount of rocky cutting; for, in the passage of each of these cañons the expense will be very heavy from this cause, and can only be estimated after an extensive and complete survey.

"For ninety-six miles below the mouth of Canoe creek to seventeen miles above Fort Reading the course of the Sacramento lies entirely through heavily-timbered mountains, which rise precipitously from the river-banks to the height of from 1,500 to 2,000 feet above the stream. Its course is winding, with all varieties of curves greater than a right-angle, and it is seldom entirely straight for two miles consecutively; but its general courses are more uniform.

"The foot of the mountains along the stream is often obstructed by fallen rocks to such an extent as to prevent its passage on horseback, and it is also obstructed by fallen timber and dense thickets of bushes; but the obstructions from fallen rocks are favorable rather than otherwise, for the construction of a railroad, as they will serve to form its sub-structure. At many points, but for short distances only, the way is obstructed by rocks in place. The road will require to be carried on the side of the mountains, a few feet above the stream at high water, throughout this entire section to the open valley of the Sacramento, whence it can be continued on the open plain."

The estimate of cost may be set down at not less than from $150,000 to $200,000 per mile; 100 per cent. to the cost at eastern prices having been added.

Seventeen miles above Fort Reading the open valley of the Sacramento is attained, over which a railroad may be carried to the Bay of San Francisco, 250 or 300 miles distant.

The distance from Fort Bridger to Fort Reading, by the line of Lieutenant Beckwith's profile, is 1,012 miles; from Fort Leavenworth to Fort Bridger, 1,072 miles; making the whole distance from Fort Leavenworth to Fort Reading, on the Sacramento, 2,084 miles, and to Benicia 2,264 miles.

The distance from Council Bluffs to Benicia, by the above route, is 2,134 miles.

Using the line along which the route can be located in the Great Basin, about 103 miles shorter than that travelled, the distances become, from Fort Bridger to Fort Reading, 909 miles; from Fort Leavenworth to Fort Reading, 1,980 miles; and to Benicia, 2,161 miles.

The distance from Council Bluffs to Benicia becomes 2,031 miles.

TIMBER, BUILDING MATERIALS, &C.

Pine and fir are found on the Uinta mountains and terrace, and pine upon the Wahsatch mountains. Dense forests, furnishing timber of the best quality, cover the western slopes of the Sierra Nevada; the distance between these points of supply being about 700 miles. Lieutenant Beckwith is of opinion that the scattered growth of cedar upon the Basin mountains, between the Great Salt lake and the Sierra Nevada, is su ciently large for ties, and "although it will require transporting for long distances, it is believed to be sufficiently abundant for the construction of the road."

Should this growth be found unsuitable for ties—and it has been so considered by me, in the review of the route near the 35th parallel—ties, as well as other lumber required for his portion of the route, must come from the Wahsatch or Uinta mountains on the east, and the western slope of the Sierra Nevada—the distances apart of these points being, as above stated, about 700 miles.

FUEL.

Should the coal beds in the Great Plain of Green river prove to be of such quality and extent as to admit of their being profitably worked, they will supply fuel for the use of the road for 600 miles west of that plain, or for as much more of the remaining 230 miles to the western slope of the Sierra Nevada as may be found economical. The cedar growth of the Great Basin could furnish but a very small supply of fuel.

The distance between the supply of coal near Fort Leavenworth and that of Green river may be set down at 800 miles, and to the cost of mining must be added that of transportation for a mean distance of 200 miles over the railroad, for the mean cost of the coal throughout this distance of 800 miles.

This estimate does not take into account the changes in the physical condition of the country that the construction of a railroad would effect on this as upon all other routes. When the annual burning of the prairies ceases, it is thought that trees will be found in many places now destitute of them—that a greater amount of precipitation will then take place, the forest growth be extended, and thus not only supplies of lumber, fuel, &c., be found where none now exist, but a gradual amelioration of soil likewise take place.

SNOW—CLIMATE.

The information respecting the amount of snow to be met with in the ravines of the mountain passes, and cañons, and respecting the winter climate of these portions of the route, is meagre. Apparently, Lieutenant Beckwith does not apprehend unusual difficulties in the working of a railroad on the route from this cause. That the winter is long and severe on the most elevated portions, especially on the great plateau and divide between the waters of Green river and the Great Salt lake, is to be inferred from the fact that when Lieutenant Beckwith's party was on this divide, about the 10th of April, the streams were not swollen, and they could not discover that the depth of snow (from 12 to 16 inches) was less than in winter; that is, the sun had not yet begun to melt it; on the northeast slopes of the hills and ravines it had accumulated in deep drifts. The spring freshets of Weber and Timpanogos rivers are six feet in height.

Captain Stansbury says that the Uinta mountains were covered with snow for a considerable distance from their summits on the 19th of August, 1849. The following extracts from his report may give an idea of the severity of the winter in the mountains east of the Great Basin.

Of the winter of 1849–50, he says: "I had hoped, from the representations which had been made to me of the mildness of the two previous winters, that we should be able to keep the field the greater part, if not the whole of the season; but, in the latter part of November, the winter set in with great and unusual severity, accompanied by deep snows, which rendered any further prosecution of the work impracticable."—(Page 120 of Report.)

"The winter season in the valley was long and severe. The vicinity of so many high mountains rendered the weather extremely variable; snows fell constantly upon them, and frequently to the depth of ten inches in the plains. In many of the cañons it accumulated to the depth of fifty feet, filling up the passes so rapidly that, in more than one instance, emigrants who had been belated in starting from the States were overtaken by the storms in the mountain gorges, and forced to abandon everything, and escape on foot, leaving even their animals to perish in the snows. All communication with the world beyond was thus effectually cut off; and, as the winter advanced, the gorges became more and more impassable, owing to the drifting of the snow into them from the projecting peaks.

"We remained thus shut up until the 3d of April."—(Page 122.)

The Uinta terrace and the great plain of Green river no doubt possess the usual attributes of elevated table-lands, dryness of atmosphere, and great difference between the temperature of day and night, increased by their great elevation of 8,000 and 7,000 feet. But the precipitation on the mountains is very much greater.

The winter temperature of the vicinity of the Great Salt lake is generally mild, tempered, no doubt, by the large body of salt water. That of the Great Basin generally, I should infer to be more severe.

Dr. Wozencraft, of California, visited the plateau of the Sierra Nevada about the 10th January, 1854, and found the snow on the route of Lieutenant Beckwith to average six inches in depth, and nowhere reaching eight or ten inches in its average fall; but encountered one drift of snow on the eastern slope of the Sierra Nevada, in a ravine, extending a mile, averaging two feet or two feet and a half in depth.

From the observations of the Surgeon General's department, the results of which are tabulated below, it appears that of the 6.18 inches of rain that fell during December, 1853, January and February, 1854, at Fort Reading, on the Sacramento, in lat. 40° 28′, 1.18 inch had fallen previous to the 10th January, and this fell during December; that is, about one-fifth of the whole winter precipitation of that year had fallen previous to the 12th January. On that day, 1.30 inch of rain fell.

The plateau of the Sierra Nevada partakes of the character of mountain and table-land. It is probable that on the western portion, at least as much rain falls as at Fort Reading; on the eastern portion, probably much less. Should the winter precipitation be in the form of snow, it is probable, then, that 7.6 feet of snow falls on the western part of the plateau during December, January, and February—the mean winter fall of rain at Fort Reading being 7.6 inches. The mean winter temperature of this portion of the plateau is not, probably, higher than 30°.2 Fahrenheit, that of Fort Reading being 47°.2 Fahrenheit. The temperature of the eastern portion is probably lower.

Yearly precipitation and temperature at Fort Reading, Sacramento river, California, latitude 40° 28′.

Year.	January.	February.	March.	April.	May.	June.	u y.	August.	September.	October.	November.	December.	Spring.	Summer.	Autumn.	Winter.	Year.
1853............	4.66	3.18	7.11	4.57	0.70	0.00	0.00	0.24	0.02	0.02	2.52	1.18	12.38	0.24	2.56	7.84	23.02
1854............	2.90	2.10	8.00	3.07	2.40	0.00	0.00	0.00	0.00	2.26	0.87	....	13.47	0.00	3.13	6.18	22.78
Mean........	3.78	2.64	7.55	3.82	1.55	0.00	0.00	0.12	0.01	1.14	1.69	1.18	12.92	0.12	2.84	7.60	23.48

Observations for December, 1854, have not yet been received. For the mean of the two years the rain for that month has been supposed to be the same as in 1853.

Mean temperature of Fahrenheit from two years' observations.

	°		°		°		°
December............	47.0	March..............	53.74	June................	75.30	September............	71.84
January............	44.25	April..............	60.02	July................	84.40	October............	64.03
February............	50.55	May..............	66.71	August................	78.95	November............	54.72
Winter..........	47.2	Spring..........	60.16	Summer.........	79.55	Autumn..........	63.53

Abundant supplies of water were found by Lieut. Beckwith on the mountains of the Basin. The season of the year when he crossed it, the spring, was the most favorable. In the dry season, the supply is, no doubt, much less abundant.

SOIL.

The only large body of cultivable soil found on this route west of the 99th meridian, is that occupied by the Mormons on the western foot-slopes of the Wahsatch mountains, forming the eastern border of the Great Basin. The following description of this fertile tract is taken from Lieut. Beckwith's report upon the route near the 38th and 39th parallels of north latitude:

"The western range of the Wahsatch mountains, standing on the eastern border of the Great Basin, is continuous, extending north and south over five degrees of latitude, from the vicinity of Little Salt lake to north of Bear river, broken only by the passage of the Sevier, Timpanogos, Weber, and Bear rivers. Its altitude at 3,000 feet above the general level of the country is quite uniform; but it occasionally falls down to 2,000, and at a few points rises to 4,000 and 4,500 feet. Its western slope is very steep—often inaccessible—presenting generally a formidable barrier to the entrance of a railroad into the Basin from the east. Many small streams descend from it; and as far as its disintegrations have been deposited at its base upon the alkaline plains of the Basin, it forms a rich soil. This line of deposite is narrow, and not continuous, but varying in width, where it is found, from two or three miles to ten or twelve at a few points, as opposite Utah and Great Salt lakes, where it occupies the entire space from the mountain to the lake shores. It is to this narrow belt of land that the Mormon settlements are almost exclusively confined, the isolated settlements being upon similar deposites in small valleys at the base of other mountains, the small mountain streams, upon which these deposites are the richest, and chiefly exist, being used for irrigation. Respectable crops of wheat and oats are produced, and barley has been cultivated to some extent; but corn does not flourish well. The grass of this district and of the higher mountain valleys is excellent; and potatoes and other roots are produced in abundance, and of a superior quality."

The area of this body of fertile soil, susceptible of irrigation by the construction of suitable works, is estimated by Lieutenant Beckwith at 1,108 square miles.

The areas of the different localities are estimated as follows:

	Square miles.
Eastern shore of Great Salt lake, from Bear river to Great Salt Lake City	350
Valley of the Jordan river	374
Valley of Tuilla, west of Oquirrh mountains and east of Cedar mountains	204
Total on Great Salt lake proper	928
Upon the borders of Utah lake	180
Total (as above)	1,108

About one-tenth of this area is susceptible of irrigation without the construction of costly works, and is tilled by the Mormons, 27,000 in number, who eagerly seek for, and occupy, small tracts of cultivable soil, if sufficiently large to support a few families, even though at great distances from the main settlement.

On this route, as on others, from the 98° or 99° meridian westward to the western slopes of the Sierra Nevada, a distance of about 1,400 miles, the soil is generally uncultivable, the exception being the comparatively limited area of the Mormon settlement, and an occasional river-bottom and mountain-valley of small extent.

East of the Rocky mountains, the plains are of the same character as those described for the route of the 38th and 39th parallels, uncultivable west of the 99th meridian. West of the first chain of these mountains the plains are covered with artemisia, rarely furnishing any grazing, except along the water-courses. The mountains, however, are generally covered, to a greater or less extent, with grass—the soil of those north, south, and west of the route between Fort Bridger and the headwaters of the Timpanogos river being of superior quality.

The absence of the geological report prevents my referring to the geological structure, which together with the climatological conditions, serve to corroborate or disprove opinions formed on appearances of sterility or fertility.

The indications given of the character of both, however, from the report, are sufficient to establish the general correctness of the opinions expressed.

ESTIMATE OF PROBABLE COST.

This estimate is made to show the probable relative cost of this route, as compared with others. That portion of it for the difficult and costly section of the Sacramento river, 136 miles in length, and for the cañon on the Timpanogos river, I have less confidence in than in the estimates generally. The estimate includes an equipment suitable for the first working of the road, about one-fifth that requisite for the development of its full power.

From Council Bluffs to the first gorge of the Black Hills, 520 miles, 25 per cent. being added to cost at eastern prices for one-half the distance, $35,000 per mile	$18,200,000
From the first gorge of the Black Hills to the summit of the South Pass, 291 miles, at $75,000 per mile, 50 per cent. having been added to cost at eastern prices	$21,825,000
From the South Pass to Fort Bridger, 131 miles, at $50,000 per mile, 50 per cent. having been added to cost at eastern prices	$6,550,000
From Fort Bridger to the Pacific, 100 per cent. has been added to the cost at eastern prices.	
From Fort Bridger, Green River valley, to foot of Oquirrh mountains, south end of the Great Salt lake, deducting ten miles for the length of the cañon on the Timpanogos river, 173 miles, at $60,000 per mile	$10,380,000

Ten miles of cañon on the Timpanogos river, at $150,000 per mile..................	$1,500,000
From the Oquirrh mountains, Great Salt lake, to the head of the first cañon on the Sacramento river, deducting ten miles of the length of the pass in the eastern ridge of the Sierra Nevada, and seventeen miles of the length of the pass in the western ridge of the Sierra Nevada, 547 miles, at $45,000 per mile..	$24,615,000
Portion of the pass of the western ridge of the Sierra Nevada, seventeen miles, $100,000 per mile......	$2,700,000
From the head of the first cañon on the Sacramento river to the termination of the mountain passage of the river, seventeen miles above Fort Reading, 135.5 miles, at $150,000 per mile..	$20,325,000
Thence to Fort Reading, on the Sacramento river, seventeen miles, and thence to Benicia, 180 miles; being about 200 miles, at $50,000 per mile.....................	$10,000,000
Total..	$116,095,000

GENERAL REMARKS.

The characteristic features of this route consist in the table-land character of the two great mountain systems of the continent, the Rocky mountains and the Sierra Nevada, in the latitude where crossed by it, in the distance from the eastern foot of the Rocky mountains to the Great Basin (350 miles,) being the least, and in the width of the Great Basin, whose topographical features (those technically called *movements* of ground) are so highly favorable to the construction of a railroad, being here the greatest, 500 miles.

These elevated table-lands of the Rocky mountains and the Sierra Nevada bear some general resemblance, in their topographical features, independent of vegetation, to one of the elementary or small basins of the Great Basin; they are bounded on the east and west by ridges, whose crests are at no great height above the general plateau, but several thousand feet above the plains from which the mountain systems rise. In the Rocky mountain plateau, this difference of elevation is upwards of 4,000 feet; in the Sierra Nevada upwards of 3,000 feet on the east, the mountain slopes on the west descending to nearly the level of the sea. The Sierra Nevada assumes this table-land character again in latitude 35°.

The South Pass cannot be considered favorable, since it requires expensive construction for nearly 300 miles. The route by the Cheyenne Pass may be found more favorable, but there is not sufficient known of it to determine this.

The unfavorable feature of the passes in the Wahsatch mountains consists in their cañons, where the expense of construction will be great.

The two cañons of the Sacramento, fourteen and nine miles in length, and the very sinuous course of the river for the space of ninety-six miles, through heavily timbered mountains, rising precipitously from the stream, form the principal characteristic unfavorable features of the route, the cost of constructing a railroad along which cannot be properly estimated until minute surveys are made.

It partakes of the character of the route near the 47th parallel, in the long and severe winters on the plains east of the Rocky mountains and westward to the Great Basin.

The profiles compiled in the office show the route, near the 41st parallel, by the South fork of the Platte, the Cheyenne and Bridger's Pass. The estimate is made for the route by the South Pass.

SUPPLEMENT TO ROUTE NEAR THE FORTY-FIRST AND FORTY-SECOND PARALLELS; PREPARED BY LIEUTENANT G. K. WARREN, TOPOGRAPHICAL ENGINEERS.

The great South Pass, one of the key-points of this route, has in its character nothing of a mountain gap, being merely a depression in the line of intersection of two gently inclined plains sloping east and west. A few miles to the north of it commences the elevated range called the Wind River chain, (a portion of the Rocky mountains,) while an extensive table-land, dotted here and there with isolated hills, stretches away to the south. This elevated plateau is in latitude 42° north, and, viewed as a whole, may be said to extend east and west from the Black Hills to the Bear mountains; and from the Wind River mountains and Black Hills in the north, to the Park and Uinta mountains in the south, having a length from east to west of about 290 miles, and breadth north and south of 100 miles. Its general elevation is about 7,500 feet, though in portions it has been reduced to 6,000 feet by the action of streams.

The direction taken by the waters of its surface, divide this great plateau into three distinct parts,—one drained by the Laramie river, one by the North fork of the Platte and Sweet Water river, and the other by the Green river and other branches of the great Colorado of the west. The divides between each of these portions are slight, and such, perhaps, as have been produced by the action of the waters alone. Small lake basins exist in several parts, which contain only pools of brackish water, proving in themselves the dryness of the climate, since the accumulated waters have never been sufficient to force an outlet or form a continuous lake. The waters that traverse the other portions come mainly from the mountains.

The amount of snow that falls is not exactly known, but it must be small; and there is reason to think that, probably, the accumulations of the winter will rarely exceed one foot in depth.

During certain seasons of the year, (the spring,) parts of this plateau are well watered, and abound with buffalo and other game. Captain Stansbury saw abundant signs of the buffalo having been in immense numbers just west of Bridger's Pass; but at the time, (September,) they had all disappeared in search of water. He also encountered slight rains and fog in this vicinity; but the character of the soil was such as promised fertility, had there been a sufficiency of moisture, the absence of which is the *curse* of all this region. Excepting the immediate banks of the streams, some of which produce grass and trees of cotton-wood, willow, and aspen, it is one vast sage or artemisia desert. All reports concur in giving it this character.

The rocks and soil in the western part are soft and easily crumbled, and, under the action of its torrent-like streams during spring freshets, are much abraded and torn away; and the debris scattered over the bottoms have, in many cases, destroyed every particle of vegetation, and reduced these to the most perfect desolation.

The valley of the North fork of the Platte is narrow and well timbered with magnificent cotton-wood, but west of this Captain Stansbury says he saw nothing deserving the name of tree, only a few stunted cedars being found between the Platte and Green rivers, 175 miles.

The Wind River mountains are clothed with excellent pine and other trees, but the immediate hills on either side of the Sweet Water are naked. Wood is found in the Black Hills and Park mountains, (of the amount I cannot speak positively,) and also in the Bear, Wahsatch, and Uinta mountains.

Coal is found in quantity in various localities on branches of Green river; it is bituminous, and thought to belong to the oölitic period.* Captain Stansbury found seams of it ten feet in thickness, and he says the quantity is, apparently, unlimited. We have to regret, that after all the explorations in this belt of country, and after having so long been a highway to Oregon, Salt lake, and California, little is positively known about its geology.

Of the great section of country lying *east* of the extended plateau of which we have been speaking, and which, beginning at the foot of the Black Hills at an elevation of about 5,000 feet, reaches to the Mississippi, there is little to be said which is peculiar to the route under consideration. It has the same general features as in the other latitudes. In the eastern part it is a beautiful and fertile prairie, with wood upon the banks of the streams, and coal

* See remarks of Professor James Hall, attached to Fremont's report, 1842-'3-'4, p. 298.

beneath its surface. As we go west it loses this character, and about the 99th and 100th meridians becomes, for the most part, dry and almost barren. The islands of the Platte are well wooded as far west as the 99th meridian. From the 100th meridian to the base of the Black Hills, it is in summer hot and arid, and the summer winds, in many places, as they come from the hills, seem to have just left a furnace. Wood and grass in this portion (250 miles) are very scarce.

The favorite feature of the great section east of the mountains is the almost direct flow of the Platte and its branches from west to east, enabling us to obtain a location along the foot of the bluffs, which will give for the most a continuously ascending grade, and avoid the rolling country. Wood, water, and grass will also be found here more abundant than on the divides between the streams. This location, however, will no doubt involve much cutting and embankment, with frequent culverts.

There are two routes proposed for crossing the great plateau west of the Black Hills: one by the South Pass, in latitude 42° 20′, longitude 113°; and the other by Bridger's Pass, in latitude 41° 13′, longitude 110° 48′. If we begin at Council Bluffs, a route through either pass would have a common location in the valley of the Platte, to the junction of the North and South forks. Here they would separate; the one by the South Pass taking the North fork and Sweet Water, and the one by Bridger's Pass taking the South fork and Lodge Pole creek. The elevation at Council Bluffs is 1,300 feet; at the junction of the forks of the Platte, 2,900 feet; distance, 300 miles; average grade, 2 feet per mile.

As regards a connexion with Great Salt Lake City, the latter would be the more direct; but it is still a question as to which would be the better route for a railroad, though Captain Stansbury, who was over both, is positive in his preference for Bridger's Pass. Unfortunately he had no barometer or means of measuring elevations, and much is left to be inferred. The following facts concerning the two routes are extracted from Fremont's and Stansbury's reports:

By the South Pass.—The Platte river, 30 miles above Fort Laramie, and 220 miles above the junction of the forks, comes through a gorge with vertical walls, 200 to 400 feet high, formed by spurs from the Black Hills, and changes its character from a mountain stream to a river of the plains. Thence to the Red Buttes, 117 miles, there are numerous streams coming into the Platte from the Black Hills, which have made deep cuts in the earth near their mouths. The railroad would probably, through this portion, keep near the present wagon-road some miles to the south of the Platte, where the greatest obstruction Fremont found to his wagons was the strong growth of artemisia. A road along this section would be expensive, though the grades would probably not be difficult. At the gorge of the Red Buttes "the river is not much pent up, there being a bank of considerable though variable breadth on either side." A road could be located through this. Thence to the Hot Spring Gate, 34 miles, is an open valley. Above this point, the Platte is "exceedingly rugged and walled in by cañons." The road just below the Hot Spring Gate should turn off to the north, up the sandy bed of a dry creek to the summit of the Hills, the peaks of which are only 800 feet above the Platte; grade, 133 feet per mile for 6 miles. Then a gradual slope, 56 feet per mile, for 10 miles, conducts to the Sweet Water, at an elevation of about 5,640 feet; distance from Red Buttes, 50 miles. The Sweet Water occasionally cuts through spurs, making cañons, (that of the Devil's Gate being through granite;) but generally it is represented as rather open, and the immediate bottoms abound in soft grasses. The hills on either side are "rocky and bare." At one of the head-branches of the Sweet Water we reach the South Pass, (elevation 7,490 feet,) 124 miles from where we first struck the Sweet Water; average grade for the first 12 miles east of the summit, 22.5 feet, and the remaining 112 miles 14.7 feet per mile. The grades between these points would probably be somewhat undulating, but the present surveys do not afford the means of judging their extent. From the Red Buttes to the South Pass would be an expensive road, but it does not involve any difficult problem of engineering. Little need be apprehended from snows. The necessary fuel for working-parties could no doubt be obtained from the Platte, and ties from the Wind River chain, and excellent building-stone on the Sweet Water.

The sum of the known ascents to be overcome from Council Bluffs to the South Pass is 6,650 feet, including 460 feet at the Hot Spring Gate, to avoid which it was gained and lost.

The Bear River mountains, lying due west from the South Pass, forbid any direct passage in that direction. As yet, we know of no practicable way of reaching Salt lake but by Fort Bridger, through the pass explored by Lieut. Beckwith. This would carry us down the Sandy creek, a tributary of Green river, with coal in its banks, to the crossing of the latter stream: elevation 6,238 feet; distance 81 miles; average grade for the first four miles west of the South Pass, 70 feet; and for the remaining 77, 13 feet per mile. The width of Green river is here 400 feet, and the ford excellent, (Aug. 16, 1843.) No doubt exists as to the practicability of connecting with Lieut. Beckwith's survey in the neighborhood of Fort Bridger, elevation 7,254 feet; distance from Green river 50 miles: we thus have, from Council Bluffs to Fort Bridger, by the South Pass route, a total of ascents and descents of 9,386 feet, and a total distance of 943 miles.

By Bridger's Pass.—This proposed route is not so well known as the other. It keeps the South fork of the Platte (100 miles) to the mouth of Lodge Pole creek, which it is then proposed to take. This creek has never been continuously explored. Frémont crossed it near its mouth, and represents it as a clear, handsome stream, running through a broad valley, having a uniform width of 22 feet and depth of 6 inches, (July 6, 1842,) a few green willows on its banks forming a pleasing contrast to the surrounding barrenness. The timber appeared to have been formerly more abundant. He crossed this creek again, as near as he could ascertain from his "uncertain means of information," about 120 miles from its mouth, the elevation being about 4,800 feet: the banks were here about 700 feet above the stream; average slope about four feet per mile.

From this point to the Cheyenne Pass, in the Black Hills, is about 60 miles. The Black Hills act here much like the sustaining walls of a terrace, the plain at their east base being much lower than at the west. Capt. Stansbury says, speaking of this pass, that his "examinations fully demonstrate the existence of a route through the 'Black Hills' not only practicable, but free from any obstructions involving, in their removal, great or unusual expenditure."

The elevation of the east base of the mountains must be about 5,000 feet; the elevation of Laramie plain is 7,500 feet; the most favorable supposition is, that the pass is no higher. Not knowing in what distance this elevation is gained, it is impossible to speak of the grades. In crossing the divide between Laramie and Medicine Bow rivers, the elevation is given by Frémont at 7,994 feet; but there is such a confusion between Frémont's and Stansbury's maps, that its distance from the Cheyenne Pass cannot be ascertained. At the crossing, the North fork of the Platte has a width of 160 feet, depth 2 feet, (Sept. 6, 1850;) elevation, by Frémont, 6,820; distance from Cheyenne Pass, by Stansbury, 102 miles; thence to the summit of Bridger's Pass 30 miles. Capt. S. says the slope either way from the summit is so gentle as scarcely to be perceptible. In the table of distances we find it stated, that "the champaign country continues north to the Wind River mountains, and can be crossed in many places, the choice being determined by considerations of fuel and water."

It is altogether probable this pass does not differ much in elevation from the South Pass, and may be supposed the same, viz: 7,490 feet.

From the summit west the line descends Muddy creek a few miles, then crosses a rolling divide, (height not known,) between it and Bitter creek, both tributaries of Green river, and down the latter to Green river, elevation about 6,200 feet; distance from Bridger's Pass 135 miles; (the Green river is here 800 feet wide; the deepest water found, September 13, was 3 feet, but in high stages it is a formidable stream, and will have to be ferried;) thence to Fort Bridger, 50 miles. One important feature of this route, from the Cheyenne Pass to

Bridger's Fort, is the small amount of rock-cutting, and even that in very soft material. It, however, crosses ground much cut up by ravines and gullies, and many places easily torn up by the torrents, probably requiring great caution in location and much masonry, which the absence of good building-stone would render exceedingly expensive. An extensive embankment will be required on Muddy creek. It is probably very deficient in wood, for nowhere contiguous to it are large supplies reported to exist. Coal is abundant on the Green River section. From Council Bluffs to Fort Bridger, by this route, is 897 miles. If my reasoning as to elevations is correct, the sums of the ascents and descents are at least 12,082 feet. Applying the equation of grade, this would give an increased length of 229 miles—making the total equivalent horizontal distance 1,126 miles.

For the route by the South Pass we have, in the same way, an increased length of 178 miles, and an equivalent horizontal line 1,120 miles. I do not think it possible to make a correct comparison as to cost of constructing the two routes. It could only be done after careful examination on the ground with that object in view.

Should any route to Oregon be found practicable, leading along the foot of the Wind River mountains up the head-streams of Green river, and across the mountains between them and the headwaters of the Snake or Lewis river, the South Pass would gain additional importance as a point from which branches could be sent both to Salt lake and California, and to the Columbia.

There are reasons to believe that this latter route may be practicable; and it is, at least, worthy of a careful examination. The straight line from the South Pass to Fort Hall is 175 miles, while by the route surveyed by Frémont it is 444 miles, being the one usually travelled by emigrants. The known abundance of grass and water in the beautiful valley of Bear river has justified this great detour, to enjoy its plenty and repose, recruit the energies exhausted by the long journey already performed, and prepare for the desert of the Snake River valley. It is said by Mr. Lander, that the more direct northern route to Oregon is about to be opened for emigrants. If a feasible route be found between the headwaters of Green and Snake rivers, the exploration should be continued to Wallah-Wallah, as the passage of the Blue mountains is not yet demonstrated to be wholly practicable, either by the way of the Grande Ronde or the cañons of Snake river. The profiles will show the present emigrant route to Oregon, as surveyed by Frémont, and give all the facts necessary to be considered. Enough is there shown to demonstrate its impracticability for a railroad. The pass over the Bear River mountains might, however, be avoided by going south of Fort Bridger.

CHAPTER III.

ROUTE NEAR THE THIRTY-EIGHTH AND THIRTY-NINTH PARALLELS OF NORTH LATITUDE.

The general consideration that determined the position of the route to be examined near the 38th and 39th parallels of latitude, was its central position geographically—it being about midway between the northern and southern boundary lines of the United States—which is likewise the position, nearly, of the Bay of San Francisco, the two termini of the route, St. Louis and San Francisco, being respectively in latitudes 39° and 38°, nearly.

A route near these parallels would probably give the shortest road from the Bay of San Francisco to the navigable waters of the Mississippi.

But, since the only passes in the Sierra Nevada practicable for a railroad, yet made known, are found in latitudes 41° and 35°, this advantage of centrality of position is lost upon entering the Great Basin, in longitude 112° or 113°.

Neither do the features of the country, from and including the Rocky mountains to the Great Basin, favor the construction of a railroad along this line, recommended by considerations connected with its central geographical position, for the elevation of the two passes through the Rocky mountains, the Sangre de Cristo and Coo-che-to-pa, 9,200 feet and 10,000 feet, are the highest known practicable for a railroad, exceeding by 4,000 feet and 5,000 feet the highest mountain pass on the route near the 32d parallel, and by 3,000 feet and 4,000 feet the elevation of the passes on the route near the 47th parallel; and from the Rocky mountains westward to the Great Basin, 500 miles, the country is so broken, and the difficulties of construction so great, and the expense would be so enormous, that the building of a railroad over this portion may be pronounced impracticable.

In neither soil, climate, productions, nor population, nor from any other cause, does it possess advantages superior to other routes, favoring the construction and working of a railroad.

The concluding chapter of Lieutenant Beckwith's report upon the route from Westport to Sevier lake recapitulates so clearly and forcibly the characteristics of the country through which it passes, the nature of the soil, climate, and topographical features, the amount and quality of timber, fuel, stone, &c., with their bearing upon the construction and working of a railroad, that nothing remains to be added to it.

It appears that from the western frontier of the State of Missouri to the Sangre de Christo Pass, 650 miles, no *timber* suitable for railroad purposes will be found upon the route upon which reliance can be placed; that from the Coo-che-to-pa Pass to the Great Basin, more than 500 miles, there is no growth of timber on the route, and that such as exists in the mountains north and south of the line is too difficult of access to be available; nor is any to be found in the Great Basin on the route as far as followed towards Sevier lake, the nearest known supplies being in the mountains to the north, in latitude 40° or 41°. With building stone generally, it is, like the other routes, sufficiently well supplied. Of water, there is a sufficient supply on the whole route, except between Grand and Green rivers, a distance of 70 miles, over which at certain periods of the year it is probable little or none can be obtained.

The soil west of the meridian of 99° is, under the present meteorological conditions, uncultivable, except in limited portions of river bottoms and small mountain valleys; these latter, from their great elevation, being better adapted to grazing than agricultural purposes. This description is completely in accordance with the geological formation and meteorological condition, the former from the meridian of 99° west being apparently tertiary, excepting in the high mountain passes.

The great coal field of Missouri lies at the eastern extremity of the road, and could supply fuel on the route as far as the Rocky mountains—and still further west, should the coal formations on Grand river not yield an abundant supply. The existence of a seam one foot thick, though not sufficient for profitable working, is a good indication that others accompany it that would admit of mining.

In regard to grade and construction, it would appear that the Sangre de Cristo and Coo-che-to-pa passes are practicable; the latter with a tunnel nearly two miles long; their greatest grades are 103 and 124 feet per mile; their elevations are 9,200 and 10,000 feet above the sea, the general elevation of the mountain chains being 2,000 and 2,500 feet higher than this.

The construction of the road through the Coo-che-to-pa Pass and the western approach to it would be costly under favorable circumstances of population, &c., not only on account of the tunnel, but of the numerous ravines that are crossed west of the pass, and the cañon that follows.

From the head of the cañon on Grand river, not far below the mouth of Coo-che-to-pa creek, to the Uncompahgra river, a distance of 70 miles, the ground is cut up with deep, wide, precipitous ravines, (the largest several hundred feet deep,) over which the construction of a railroad is utterly impracticable. These ravines cannot be turned near the mountains without encountering similar difficulties, and at a cost greater than that of a route along the river.

Thus the route is forced upon Grand river, and along its cañon, 60 miles in length, broken and interrupted by the deep ravines already mentioned, and numerous smaller gulleys. The road-way throughout the greater part of this distance must be blasted out of solid rock, and these wide ravines, from 100 to 200 feet deep, where they cut through the cañon, crossed by viaducts or filling. Then follow 50 miles to the mouth of Blue river, the construction still of a difficult and costly character from the cañons of the river and broken nature of the ground. From Blue to Green river is 100 miles, over which the road will require numerous bridges and culverts, and a costly road-bed foundation of broken stone or piling over a clayey soil, in which, in wet weather, animals sink half-leg deep. From Green river to the Wahsatch Pass, about 80 miles, the construction would still be of a costly character, the country being of the same ravine and chasm-like nature as that between the mouth of Coo-che-to-pa creek and Uncompahgra river, though on a smaller scale. Next follows the Wahsatch Pass, the work in which is difficult and expensive; the greatest grade is 131 feet per mile; a tunnel not quite three-quarters of a mile long is requisite; and finally a cañon 16 miles long on Salt creek, the walls of which are frequently broken by lateral streams, gives the only route along which the road can be brought, by cutting in solid rock at very great expense.

The difficulties of engineering, and the cost of construction of this portion of the route from the Coochetopa Pass to Sevier river, in the Great Basin, a distance of about 500 miles, would be so great that it may be pronounced impracticable; and it is evident, from the report of Lieutenant Beckwith, that, to use his own language, "no other line exists in the immediate vicinity of this worthy of any attention in connexion with the construction of a railroad from the Mississippi river to the Great Basin."

It is unnecessary, therefore, to consider the route further, or to enter into any discussion connected with the probable practicability and cost of constructing and working a railroad over other portions of the route, where not one counterbalancing advantage is to be found to compensate, in any degree, for the enormous cost of that under consideration.

Laying aside the utter impracticability of this route, the following considerations will show its disadvantages as regards expenses of working, supposing it constructed.

From Westport to the west base of the Un-kuk-oo-ap mountains is 1,323 miles; sum of ascents, 23,190 feet; of descents, 19,050 feet; length of equivalent horizontal line for the route, 2,123 miles.

Of the direct route from the point at the western base of the Un-kuk-oo-ap mountains—elevation 5,131 feet, distance from Westport 1,323 miles, where the survey under Captain Gunnison terminated—to the Tay-ee-chay-pah Pass, there is no positive information or survey. Colonel Frémont says, page 270 of his report for 1842, '43, '44, that from the time he descended from Walker's Pass and began "to skirt" the desert, till he reached the vegas of Santa Clara, "*he had travelled* 550 *miles, occupying* 27 *days in that inhospitable region;*" and that "*in passing before the great caravan, he had the advantage of finding more grass,*" &c. And again, he speaks of the journey as "a month's suffering in the hot and sterile desert." This, in connexion with Colonel Frémont's description of other parts of the Great Basin, gives every reason to believe that from Sevier lake to the Tay-ee-chay-pah Pass it is, for the most part, a desert of the same general character as other portions of the Great Basin. Supposing the route to be a straight line, with uniform descent from the Un-kuk-oo-ap mountains to the entrance of the Tay-ee-chay-pah Pass, in latitude 35° 7′, (no pass being known to be practicable to the north of it, in this portion of the Sierra Nevada,) the distance will be 430 miles, and the descent 1,830 feet; the equated horizontal distance, 464 miles.

From the entrance of the Tay-ee-chay-pah Pass to San Francisco is 326 miles; sum of ascents, 1,308 feet; sum of descents, 4,608 feet; equated length, 438 miles. Adding these together with the equated distance from the mouth of the Kansas to the west base of Un-kuk-oo-ap mountains, we have the total equated distance from Westport to San Francisco—3,025 miles; the length of the straight horizontal line, which supposes no obstacle to be avoided, being only 1,500 miles.

The straight line from St. Louis to San Francisco is 1,740 miles long; it crosses the Rocky mountains in about latitude 39° 13′, the Wahsatch in about latitude 39°, the Sierra Nevada in about latitude 38° 6′; it is 110 miles north of the Sandy Hill Pass, 75 miles north of Coo-che-to-pa, and about coincides with the north bend of Grand river; is 20 miles north of the Wahsatch Gap, and 225 miles north of Tay-ee-chay-pah Pass.

From the Sevier river a practicable connection can be made with the route surveyed by Lieut. Beckwith, near the forty-first parallel, through the Great Basin.

The distance from Sevier river, at the crossing of the Mormon road to Salt lake, is 120 miles, sum of ascents and descents 1,600 feet, and equated distance 150 miles; thence to Benicia is 872 miles, sum of ascents and descents 15,200 feet, and equated distance 1,160 miles; from Westport to Sevier river 1,298 miles, the sum of the ascents and descents are 39,714 feet, and equated distance 2,050 miles. Taking the sum of these three portions, we have from Westport to Benicia, via Coo-che-to-pa Pass, Great Salt lake, and Madelin Pass, a distance of 2,290 miles, sum of ascents and descents of 56,514 feet, and an equated distance of 3,360 miles.

NOTE.—This line could, perhaps, be considerably shortened by taking a direct route from Sevier river to the pass of the Humboldt mountains; but it has not been explored. The straight-line distance between these points is 200 miles, while by the route surveyed it is 280 miles.

CHAPTER IV.

ROUTE NEAR THE THIRTY-FIFTH PARALLEL OF NORTH LATITUDE.

The report of Lieut. Whipple upon the route explored by him, near the thirty-fifth parallel of latitude, with its accompanying sub-reports, being brief, it is unnecessary to recapitulate the details given in them. Some remarks upon the general direction of the route, and upon the points which characterize it, and in which it differs from that of the thirty-second parallel, may be necessary.

From the general description that follows, it will be seen that the features of the ground which have determined the direction of the route are the extension west and east of the interlocking tributaries of the Mississippi, the Rio Grande, and the Colorado of the West.

The route may be said to commence at Fort Smith, on the Arkansas, in about longitude 94° 26′, latitude 35° 23′; elevation above the sea 460 feet; the connexions of which point with Little Rock, Memphis, St. Louis, and other centres of trade, are clearly stated. From Little Rock to the Antelope Hills, on the Canadian, elevation 2,100 feet, in about longitude 100°, a distance of near 400 miles, the route may follow either the valleys of the Arkansas and Canadian, or a shorter line, perhaps, but over more broken ground south of the Canadian—this latter route branching again and following either the valley of the Washita, or the dividing ridge between it and the Canadian.

From the Antelope Hills the route continues along the bottom of the Canadian, on the right bank, to the mouth of Tecumcari creek, about 250 miles, and ascends by the valley of Tecumcari, or by that of Pajarito creek, to the dividing ridge between the Canadian and the Pecos rivers, elevation about 5,543 feet, and enters the valley of the latter. It follows this valley until, by means of a tributary, it rises to the high table-land, or basin, lying east of the Rocky mountains, elevation about 7,000 feet, crosses the elevated Salinas basin, 30 miles wide, the lowest point being 6,471 feet, and gains the divide in the Rocky mountains, elevation about 7,000 feet; from which point it descends to Albuquerque, or Isleta, on the Rio Grande, through the San Pedro Pass; or it may descend to the Rio Grande by the valley of the Galisteo river, north of Sandia mountain. A third route is indicated along the valley of the Pecos to its headwaters; thence to an affluent of the Galisteo; and thence, as before, to the Rio Grande.

Isleta, on the Rio Grande, is 854 miles from Fort Smith, and 4,945 feet above the sea.

Crossing the ridge separating the Rio Grande from the Puerco, the route follows the valley of its tributary, the San José, to one of its sources in a pass of the Sierra Madre, called the Camino del Obispo. At the summit (elevation 8,250 feet) a tunnel three-fourths of a mile long, at an elevation not less than 8,000 feet, is required, when the descent is made to the Zuñi river and near the Pueblo of Zuñi; the route then crosses over undulating ground to the Puerco of the West, at the Navajo spring. Another route across the Sierra Madre, about 20 miles further north, was examined by Mr. Campbell, which is, apparently, far more favorable. The profile is not from reliable instrumental examination. The height of the summit is about 7,750 feet above the sea. The Puerco of the West heads in this pass, and the route follows the valley of this stream to its junction with the Colorado Chiquito, then the valley of that stream to the foot of the southeastern slopes of the San Francisco mountains, (elevation 4,775 feet;) distance from Fort Smith 1,182 miles, and from the crossing of the Rio Grande 328 miles. Here it ascends to the dividing ridge between the waters of the Gila on the south, and of the Colorado of the West on the north, and continues (or nearly so) upon it for about 200 miles, to the Aztec Pass, (elevation 6,281 feet;) distance from Fort Smith 1,350 miles. The highest point reached upon this undulating ridge is 7,472 feet at Leroux's spring, at the foot of the San Francisco mountain. From the Aztec Pass the descent to the Colorado of the West is made by a circuitous route northward along valleys of its tributaries, the largest and last being Bill Williams fork, the mouth of which, on the Colorado, is 1,522 miles from Fort Smith, and at an elevation above the sea of about 208 feet.

The Colorado is now ascended thirty-four miles, the route leaving it at the Needles. The supposed mouth of the Mojave river was examined: by the valley of this stream it was expected to ascend to the Cajon Pass in the Sierra Nevada. This proved, however, to be the valley of a stream, dry at the time, whose source was in an elevated ridge which, probably, divides the Great Basin from the waters of the Colorado. It is not yet ascertained that the valley of the Mohave river is continuous to the Colorado, though Lieutenant Whipple is sanguine that it will be found to be so. From the summit, 5,262 feet (cut thirty feet) above the sea, the descent is made to Soda lake, the recipient, at some seasons, of the waters of the Mohave river, 1,117 feet above the sea, at an average grade of 100 feet to the mile for forty-one miles, the steepest grade yet required on this route. The ascent to the summit of the tunnel, elevation 4,179 feet, in the Cajon Pass in the Sierra Nevada, is made by following the valley of the Mojave river. The summit of this pass, by the line of location, is 1,798 miles from Fort Smith, and 242 from the point of crossing the Colorado. Here, according to Lieutenant Whipple, a tunnel of $2\frac{1}{2}$ miles, through white conglomerated sandstone, is required. But, according to Lieutenant Williamson, who spent more time upon it, it would be $3\frac{4}{10}$ miles. The tunnel descends to the west with an inclination of 100 feet per mile, which grade will be the average for twenty-two miles, into the valley of Los Angeles, by side location, and thence to the port of San Pedro, 1,892 miles distant from Fort Smith.

Lieutenant Williamson reports upon the Cajon Pass, that, in his opinion, the natural grades, varying between 90 and 171 feet per mile, cannot be much reduced by side-location, on account of the broken character of the hills.

Should it be desired to reach San Francisco by the Tulares and San Joaquin valleys, the route should leave the Mojave valley some thirty miles before reaching the entrance to the Cajon Pass, 1,768 miles from Fort Smith, elevation about 2,555 feet, and proceed across the southwest corner of the Great Basin, towards the Tah-ee-chay-pah Pass, reaching its entrance at an elevation of 3,300 feet, in a distance of about eighty miles, and without crossing ridges that would increase the ascents more than 500 feet beyond the difference of elevation of the two points. The route is then coincident with that described for the 32d parallel.

The general features of the country indicated lines for examination at more than one point, which will, probably, greatly improve the route by reducing the ascents and shortening distances. The party was, however, unable to examine them.

An examination of the profile of this route shows that, in respect to grade, it is not only practicable, but that the heaviest grades that will probably be required do not equal those in use on the Baltimore and Ohio railroad.

SOIL.

Grama grass being found on the north bank of the Canadian, in longitude 96°, and extending westward in greater or less abundance to the Sierra Nevada, indicates that the change from fertility to barrenness begins in that longitude, at least north of the Canadian. Cactaceæ also make their appearance with grama grass. South of it, however, the geological formation is that of a good soil to about longitude $98\frac{1}{2}$. At this point the change to uncultivable land is complete, excepting in the river-bottoms, which are more or less fertile, but not the great body of the land. Not far south of the route good soil extends westward to the termination of the Witchita mountains. Some portions of the upper valley of the Canadian, the upper valley of the Pecos, the valleys of the Rio Grande, Zuñi, Colorado Chiquito, San Francisco, Colorado of the West, and its tributaries, possess a fertile soil, requiring, generally, irrigation to make it productive. That portion of the southwest corner of the Great Basin traversed by this route, and over which the explorations of Lieutenant Williamson extended, is well constituted for fertility, its barrenness resulting from the absence of rain. Generally the uncultivable plains have an abundance of nutritious grass, though there are extensive tracts where little or none is found—the two greatest being from the Antelope Hills to Tecumcari creek on the Canadian, 250 or 260 miles, and from the lower part of Santa Maria river to the Mohave river, 200 miles.

The country north of the Colorado Chiquito and west of the Sierra Madre as far as the eastern slope of the San Francisco mountain, is represented to be a remarkably fine grazing country; from that point westward to about the meridian of 113½° (sixty or seventy miles east of the Colorado,) it is well wooded, the whole presenting an attractive appearance to the traveller, who would, no doubt, from its strong contrast to other portions, describe it as a highly fertile region, though, with the exception of the valleys of the streams, it would prove upon trial to be uncultivable.

The land now cultivated in New Mexico is estimated at 200 square miles, and the land cultivable now vacant, exclusive of the vast region occupied by the Navajoes, Moquis, Tanians, and wilder tribes of Indians, at about 490 square miles, giving a total of about 700 square miles.

Only one-fifth of the bottom land of the Rio Grande capable of irrigation and cultivation, is now under culture.

The valley of the Colorado between its mouth and the 35th parallel, contains 1,600 square miles of fertile soil capable of irrigation.

BUILDING MATERIALS, TIES, LUMBER, &C.

The geologist, Mr. Marcou, describes the Trias and Jurassic formations, extending from Delaware mountain on the Canadian, to the Rocky mountains, 600 miles, as generally soft and friable; but as Lieutenant Whipple, and Mr. Campbell, the assistant railroad engineer, report the existence in these formations of good sandstones, suitable for the bridge-building required, this portion of the route may be considered well supplied with good building-stone. Over other portions of the route it would be found at intervals not too great for economical transportation.

TIES, LUMBER, &C.

Timber of size suitable for ties, and lumber generally for railroad uses in large quantities, is found in the following localities: Continuously on the route east of longitude 97°; in or near the Pecos valley; in the Rocky mountains and Sierra Madre; in the Mogoyon mountains, (south of the route) in which the Colorado Chiquito and some of its tributaries rise; on the slopes of the San Francisco mountain, and continuously with short intervals for more than 120 miles, and on the Sierra Nevada. The distances apart of these points of supply are, respectively, 540 miles, 100 miles, 150 miles; from the Sierra Madre to San Francisco mountain, 250 miles; then for a space of about 120 miles the supply may be considered continuous; thence to the Sierra Nevada, 420 miles. The road being built from the two termini, the greatest spaces over which ties, lumber, &c., must be brought by it, are 400 and 500 miles. The route, therefore, in comparison with others, is favorably circumstanced in this respect.

FUEL.

From longitude 97° to the Pecos valley, 540 miles, there will probably be sufficient fuel for working parties, and perhaps for 200 miles of this distance sufficient for railroad use might be found, but not for the remaining 350 miles. Between the Pecos and the Rocky mountains, 100 miles; across the valley of the Rio Grande, 150 miles; from the Sierra Madre to San Francisco mountain, 250 miles, sufficient fuel for working parties will probably be found without excessive cost. As it can be brought from the Mogoyon mountains to various points on the Colorado Chiquito, and exists at the extremities of these spaces, this portion of the route may be considered amply provided with fuel. Over the space of 120 miles from San Francisco mountain to the Aztec Pass, a sufficiency for railroad purposes will be found at convenient distances. From the Aztec Pass to the Sierra Nevada, 420 miles, no fuel for railroad purposes will be found, and that for working-parties will be scanty in some places. From the point of leaving the Colorado to the Mohave river, 115 miles, no fuel is to be had.

It is reported that coal exists in several localities in the Rocky mountains, both east and west of the Rio Grande, near this route, but there is no positive and reliable information that it has been found in sufficient quantities for profitable mining.

As coal for locomotive uses will bear transportation 3.5 times as far as wood, the supplies of fuel for the 350 miles east of the Rio Grande can be had from the coal-fields of Delaware mountain; that for the space of 540 miles east of the Sierra Nevada, from the Pacific ports, the mean distance to which it must be transported in the latter case being 260 or 270 miles. These are the only two portions of the route which cannot be readily supplied from convenient distances on the route.

Fuel forms about one-fifth the yearly expense of maintaining and working a railroad.

WATER.

The exact distances over which water is not found at certain seasons, or permanently, are not stated. It does not appear, however, that a resort to unusual means will be necessary east of 100° longitude. Between that and the Pacific there are spaces destitute of it, where, from the known character of the geological structure, there is no doubt that sufficient supplies can be obtained either by deep common wells, artesian wells, or reservoirs. It is better supplied with water than the route of the 32d parallel, and from the Rio Grande to Santa Maria river there are supplies of timber and fuel on the line, which the other route is deficient in. These larger supplies of timber and water west of the Rio Grande are attained at the expense of great elevation and somewhat rugged ground.

The Galesteo Pass in the rocky mountains and the passes in the Sierre Madre being wide openings, or valleys, rather than mountain passes, no difficulty need be apprehended from snows, even if it fell to greater depths than those known. Over the remainder of the route no difficulty from this cause is to be met with.

ELEVATIONS, &C.

The line rises gradually from the eastern terminus, and on Pajarito creek, 705 miles from Fort Smith, has attained an elevation of 5,000 feet above the sea, which elevation it does not descend to again (except for a short distance) for a space of over 600 miles, and until on the descent to the Colorado of the West. It passes the Rocky mountains at an elevation of 7,000 feet, the Sierra Madre at 8,000 feet, the foot of San Francisco mountain at 7,450 feet, the Aztec Pass at about 6,000 feet, the divide between the Great Basin and the Colorado at 5,300 feet, and the Cajon Pass by a tunnel 4,000 feet above the sea.

The sum of the ascents from San Pedro to Fort Smith is 24,641 feet, of descents 24,171 feet—equivalent, in the cost of working the road, to an increased horizontal distance of 924, which added to the length of the line of location, 1,892 miles, gives for length of equated distance 2,816 miles.

The sum of ascents from San Francisco to Fort Smith by the route from Mohave river to Tah-ee-chay-pah Pass is 25,570 feet, of descents 25,100 feet; the equivalent in miles of horizontal road is 963 miles, which added to the location distance between these two points, 2,174 miles, gives for equated length of road 3,137 miles.

ESTIMATE.

The description of the topographical features of the route is not sufficiently minute to enable one to form a satisfactory opinion of the difficulties of ground to be encountered, and consequently of the probable cost of the formation of the road-bed. Upon this point we must rest satisfied with the opinion of Lieutenant Whipple, who assimilates the several portions of the route to roads already built possessing as nearly as possible similar features and difficulties. The impression, however, conveyed by the report, as to the nature of the ground passed over, together with that formed from the description by others of some portions of it, induced me to think that the ground was more favorable than the comparison of Lieutenant Whipple shows it to be, and that the amount of work in forming the road-bed would have been less than that of the roads mentioned.

Four hundred and eighty miles of the route are assimilated to the Hudson River railroad; 151 miles to the Worcester and Albany railroad, (Western railroad;) and 374 miles to the Baltimore and Ohio railroad; making 1,005 miles assimilated to railroads among the most difficult and costly that have been constructed in the United States.

It is probable that, from the Rio Grande to the Colorado, the additional cost to eastern prices should have been rather 100 per cent., than 40, 50, and 60 per cent.—the increased cost allowed by Lieutenant Whipple. For the remaining distance, from the Colorado to the Pacific, 100 per cent. has been added by Lieutenant Whipple to the cost at eastern prices. This estimate includes the cost of equipment. This, on the roads used as standards of comparison, amounts to $6,000 or $7,000 per mile, four-fifths of which should be deducted, as the cost per mile from this source may be one-fifth of the cost on the eastern roads. This would diminish the estimate about $12,000,000, but at the same time the increased per-centage would increase it about $19,381,000. The difference between these sums, $7,381,000, (about,) should be added to the corrected estimate, $161,829,265, and the total estimate under this supposition becomes $169,210,265.

CHAPTER V.

ROUTE NEAR THE THIRTY-SECOND PARALLEL OF NORTH LATITUDE.

As the information respecting this route is to be found in several separate reports, and as those upon that portion of it between the Rio Grande and the Pacific ocean do not discuss the railroad practicability and mode of construction with the minuteness necessary, and as there is no railroad report upon the whole route, I have been obliged to enter minutely into details which, on the other routes, are found in the reports of the exploring officer.

1. FROM FULTON TO THE RIO GRANDE.

The report of Captain Pope is methodically arranged; and being brief, yet sufficiently full, it is unnecessary to make a synopsis of it. The portion of the route near the thirty-second parallel examined by him is that from the Red river to the Rio Grande, a distance of 646 miles. It is naturally divided into three distinct belts, which are clearly described by Captain Pope.

The first division, from the Red river to the eastern border of the Llano Estacado, 352 miles, gives generally easy grades, except where, in crossing streams, we have probably to descend from the bluffs to near the level of the stream, and ascend again; but which can be reduced, by lengthening the line, to the grade found suitable to the other portions of the route. This part of his line has an abundant supply of water and fuel, of wood for cross-ties, and lumber for two-thirds of the distance.

The important characteristic feature of Captain Pope's route, dwelt upon with so much force by him, is the extension westward of fertile land to near the headwaters of the Colorado. It is to be remarked that, from the geological indications, it is probable that a line drawn from Red river at the termination of the fertile soil, *in its basin*, in a general parallel direction with the Gulf coast, from the mouth of the Sabine to the Nueces river, will mark the boundary between the cultivable and barren soil. The influence of the moist winds of the Gulf of Mexico may also aid in giving this westward extension to the fertile land near the parallels of 32° and 34°. North of the Canadian, this boundary line between fertility and barrenness takes the direction of the meridian, and extends along it northward into the British possessions.

The evidence adduced in support of this western extension of fertile soil is not sufficiently full or conclusive.

The specimens of soils, of which the analysis is given, were gathered from the Upper Cross Timbers westward; but it is not stated whether those which belong to the section, from that point to the Llano Estacado, were intended to represent the condition of the most fertile portions, or the average condition of the whole surface.

Even if their analysis exhibited fertile constituents, it is well known that many extensive areas of tertiary soil well constituted for fertility are uncultivable, from the meteorological conditions of the district in which they are found. Additional facts are, in my opinion, required to establish the existence of the westwardly extension of fertile soil in this latitude.

The second belt described is the Llano Estacado, 125 miles across. Upon this it is only necessary to remark, that its geological formation is such as to render the success of artesian wells, in obtaining large supplies of water, certain. To build a railroad across it, commencing at the eastern border, at the last point of abundant supply of water, parties should be pushed forward to dig tanks wherever the ground favors their construction, and to sink artesian wells at distances of 20 miles apart, or less, should water be readily procured by this process. Supposing it even necessary to bore an artesian well at every 10 miles, and that the cost should be $10,000 each well, which is double that of an excessive estimate of the cost of a series of these wells, we should have $1,000 per mile for cost of road from this cause. By these two means, abundant supplies of water can be got at points a few miles apart, where the camps of the working parties, which need not be large, can be established. The dwarf mezquite, found on the Llano, will furnish sufficient fuel for these parties.

Railroad trains having engines of twenty-two tons, on four drivers, can carry sufficient water from the headwaters of the Colorado to the mouth of Delaware creek or the Pecos, 125 miles, without adding to the expense of running the trains; and can, from either end of this line, supply all the intermediate stations necessary for the superintendence, repair, and supply of the road.

Ties can be brought from the country east, and from the Guadalupe mountains, at reasonable cost. Fuel, also, can be supplied from the Brazos, or from the Colorado of Texas. Fortunately, over these plains, destitute of water, but very little excavation or embankment will be required, and the rails can soon be laid. Probably it would be most convenient to bring ties, sleepers, and lumber generally, by the road itself, from the route east of the Llano. In fact, from the east border of the Llano westward, and from the Pacific eastward, a distance of 1,200 miles, the road must be made, as it were, to build itself, carrying its lumber, iron, rails, provisions, and sometimes water, so far as a proper adjustment of economy of time with that of expenditure admits of its doing so. Its progress, from this cause, will be slow; but as the surface is very smooth, and the inclinations gentle, over these plains, its construction will be proportionately more rapid, aiding to balance the slow progress from the other cause.

The third section, from the Pecos river to the Rio Grande, presents no unusual difficulties in grade or construction, so far as dependent upon the topographical features of the country. The Guadalupe mountains are passed without a tunnel, and with a grade of 108 feet to the mile; a grade not exceeding those found on roads now built, as on the Baltimore and Ohio, and other railroads. Other routes through or around these mountains are recommended for examination, which, it is thought, will give easier grades. Sufficient supplies of water can be had at convenient distances apart, fuel for working parties from the dwarf mezquite on the plains, and cross-ties and lumber can be had from the Guadalupe mountains immediately on the line of the road, and from the Waco mountains, 30 miles distant from it, and also by means of the built portions of the road, from the supplies on the Brazos and Red rivers.

BUILDING-STONE, &C.

In regard to good building-stone the report of the geologist, Jules Marcou, on the specimens procured by Captain Pope—see Chapter 13, Captain Pope's Report—is not sufficiently explicit respecting all the formations. The cretaceous from Red river to the lower line of the Upper Cross Timbers, 70 miles, is probably too soft; but thence to the Clear fork of the Brazos, 120 miles, it is undoubtedly good. From the Clear fork to the Guadalupe mountains, 340 miles, the route is over formations called by the geologist Trias and Jurassic. From his description it is possible they may be found too soft, though good building-stone is found in the Trias, as, for instance, the new red sandstone of the Connecticut. The geologist says: "For the construction of a railroad the rocks of the Trias present great facilities. They furnish sandstone, plaster or gypsum, excellent hydraulic lime from the magnesian limestone, and, finally, they are very easy to work, and at the same time firm enough to form excavations or embankments." The sentence is somewhat inexact in its language. The detailed geological report will remove any uncertainty upon this point. Lieutenant Whipple passed over the same formations on the route of the 35th parallel, and, with the assistant railroad engineer, reports the existence of good building-stone there. From the Guadalupe mountains to the Rio Grande excellent building-stone is found.

The existence of coal upon the Brazos is of importance to this route. Fuel for working the road, as well as lumber, will be considered separately for the whole route.

In general it may be remarked on this section of the route near the 32d parallel, from the Red river to the Rio Grande, 780 miles, that the topographical features of the ground present no unusual difficulties and many favorable circumstances; that supplies of building material can be obtained throughout the line without excessive cost; and that the supply of fuel and water, throughout those portions destitute of it, can be had without greatly increasing the cost of construction and transportation.

The elevations are:

From Preston, on Red river, 641 feet above the level of the sea, the ground rises in six miles to the level of about	1,200 feet.
At the Upper Cross Timbers	1,782 feet.
At the West fork of Trinity	1,524 feet.
At the Brazos river	1,700 feet.
At the divide of the Brazos and Colorado rivers	4,237 feet.
At the Colorado	3,989 feet.
At the border of the Llano Estacado	4,278 feet.
The greatest elevation of the Llano Estacado is	4,707 feet.
The general elevation of the Llano Estacado is about	4,500 feet.
The elevation of the Pecos, where crossed	4,070 feet.
The elevation of the summit of the Guadalupe Pass	5,717 feet.
The elevation of the summit of the Hueco Pass	4,812 feet.
The general elevation of the table-lands between the Pecos and the Rio Grande, is from	4,000 to 4,500 feet.
The elevation of the Rio Grande valley, at Molino, is	3,830 feet.

ESTIMATE.

The estimate for cost of construction is, perhaps, in excess; the cost per mile from Fulton, on Red river, to the Rio Grande, a distance of 780 miles, being at the rate of $50,000 per mile. On the northern route, the estimated mean cost of the first 780 miles is about $35,400 per mile, (240 miles at $25,000 per mile—next, 712 miles at $40,000 per mile;) yet, from the description of these portions of the two routes, it is evident the difference in cost per mile of constructing the two will not be great. This is mentioned to show what different judgments are formed in making these estimates, and what caution should be used in being guided by estimates in figures of the costs of routes that have not been subjected to the same judgment or same standard. The difference of estimated cost in this distance of 780 miles on roads that would not probably vary greatly in their actual cost of construction, is $11,700,000; and if the same difference should exist throughout the entire distance, it would sum up to about $35,000,000.

2. FROM THE RIO GRANDE TO THE MOUTH OF THE GILA.

After ascending from the bottom lands of the Rio Grande, in traversing the region examined by Lieutenant Parke between these two rivers, from Doña Ana to the Pimas villages, one appears to be travelling on a great plain, interrupted irregularly and confusedly by bare, rugged, abrupt, isolated mountain masses, or short ranges, seemingly, though not in reality, without system. Winding around these isolated or lost mountains, or using a few passes through them, a railroad may be constructed with easy grades. The instrumental profile, however, shows that what to the eye appears to be a plain, is really an undulating surface, constantly rising and falling, rarely horizontal, and that the plain is converted into a series of basins, the steepest parts of which are found in passing around the lost mountains, or through the passes in them. The summits of these basin-rims or passes are generally about 400 feet above the lowest parts of the basins, though in two instances 850 and 1,200 feet respectively; the mean elevation of the basins above the level of the sea being about 4,100 feet, decreasing from near the Rio Grande, where it is 4,350 feet, towards the Gila. The mean elevation of the lowest points of the dividing rims is 4,700 feet, the highest of them, the pass through the Chiricahui range, being 5,180 feet. Seven basins are crossed, the eighth continuing or conducting to the Gila. Except through the mountain passes, the surface is so smooth as to require but little preparation to receive the superstructure of a railroad; and even in the two most difficult of the passes, (where, in one case, deep cutting or a tunnel at the summit, near the surface, in rock, with heavy side-cutting and high embankments for short distances, and in the other a short cut of 60 feet—probably through rock—are proposed by Lieutenant Parke, to attain grades of 46 feet and 90 feet per mile, or less by increasing distance,) the natural slope of the ground may be used for a railroad for temporary purposes, and until the road itself can reduce the cost of materials and supplies to the lowest rates.

The following table of distances and grades over the natural slopes, is given to show this. These two most difficult parts of the road are from 25 to 30 miles apart. In the Chiricahui Pass, the steepest natural slope is 194 feet to the mile for a distance of 2¼ miles. A twenty-four ton engine, on six drivers, can carry a load of 76 tons (200 passengers with 100 pounds baggage each) up a grade of 221 feet to a mile in the worst condition of the rail.

In the pass through the ridge east of the Valle de Sauz, the steepest natural slope is 240 feet to the mile for a distance of three-quarters of a mile. A thirty-ton engine, on six drivers, will carry a load of 76 tons (200 passengers with 100 pounds baggage each) up a grade of 281 feet per mile. But the tunnel of three-quarters of a mile through rock near the surface, or cutting, may be preferable to using this steep slope. This natural slope of 240 feet to the mile for the distance of three-quarters of a mile, may be reduced to one of 200 feet to the mile, by a short cutting of 30 feet depth. The natural slope in the steepest part of the Chiricahui Pass being nearly 200 feet to the mile, this cut would reduce these two passes to the same condition. These two points have been referred to not as presenting very great difficulties in construction, but merely from their being the only points on the line that appear to require any excavation and embankment, except of a trifling kind, to obtain grades generally in use on railroads, and to show that even here the natural slopes were such as might be used with but little preparation for the superstructure.

It is probable that further examination will show that the pass of Puerto del Dado may be avoided by passing to the north of the Chiricahui mountains.

The elevation of the camp near Fort Fillmore is 3,938 feet above the sea. The river between this and El Paso is about 300 yards wide when confined to one channel, and presents no serious difficulty to bridging. The elevation at Molino, the terminus of Captain Pope's survey, is 3,830 feet; the distance between them 32 or 35 miles.

Parke's grades.

From the Gila, 10 miles, 28.6 feet per mile, ascending.
60 " 7 " "
12 " 23 " "
19 " 50 " "
3 " level.

18 miles,	38	feet per mile ascending.
6½ "	61	feet per mile, descending.
6½ "		level.
16½ "	62	feet per mile, ascending.
8½ "	54	feet per mile, descending.
5 "		level.

In the Puerto del Dado of the Chiricahui range, instead of the 60 feet cutting, heavy embankment, and side-cutting, and the grades used by Lieut. Parke, 46 feet the greatest, we may use temporarily the surface grades, which are as follows:

21½	miles,	48 feet per mile, ascending.	
0.65	"	180	" "
2¼	"	194 feet per mile, descending.	
3½	"	94	" "
6	"	19	" "
14	"	23	" "

In the gap in the ridge east of the Valle de Sauz, instead of the cutting of 60 feet, or tunnelling, and a grade of 90 feet, or less, by increasing distance, we may use, temporarily, the surface grades, which are as follows:

Camp 24, to station 1.—	1.55 mile,	150	feet per mile, ascending.
	2.45 miles,	104	" "
	0.7 mile,	240	" "
	0.5 "	30	feet per mile, descending.
	2.25 miles,	57	" "
Station 6	1.45 miles,	72	" "
	4 "	21	" "
	3 "	4	feet per mile, ascending.
	5.5 "	75	" "
	8 "	46	feet per mile, descending.
B....................	16.5 "	51	feet per mile, ascending.
	11 "		level.
	34 "	25	feet per mile, descending.
	11 "	11	feet per mile, ascending.
	12 "	5	feet per mile, descending.
	4½ "	44	feet per mile, ascending.
	11½ "	22	feet per mile, descending.
	3 "	123	" "

WATER AND FUEL.

This region, then, presents great advantages in the construction of a railroad at small cost, so far as the grading and preparing the road-bed for the superstructure is concerned; but in two elements for cheap construction and working of a road, it is now very deficient, viz: water and fuel. For the first, the distances apart of the permanent streams affording large supplies, in the dryest season of the year, and therefore under the most unfavorable circumstances, are as follows:

From the Rio Grande to the Rio Mimbres, 71 miles.

From the Rio Grande to Cook's Spring, 61 miles, it being 53 miles from the Rio Grande, and 8 miles north of the track.

From the Rio Mimbres to the Rio San Pedro, 152.5 miles.

Intermediate is Valle de Sauz, 72 miles, where water is always found; 25 miles further on, is a spring in the Puerto del Dado.

From the San Pedro to Tuczon, 53 miles.

From Tuczon to the Gila, 79 miles.

There are springs between some of these points which it is not necessary to particularize.

For the working of a railroad after construction, the greatest even of these distances, 152.5 miles, is not too great to be overcome by special arrangements. But for the working parties engaged in building the road, supplies of water must be had at every few miles. Fortunately, the formation of these basins is such as to afford, at comparatively small cost, sufficient supplies of water at distances convenient for the construction of the road. During certain portions of the year, the bottoms of some of these basins are converted into lakes, which may be drained into tanks.

The following description of these basins by Dr. C. C. Parry, geologist upon the Mexican boundary survey, shows that artesian wells, of no great depth, can be resorted to successfully:

"All the so-called '*mesa formations*' and '*jornadas*' of this district belong to a distinct system of basin deposites, tertiary, or post-tertiary, in age, and still showing in outlines of greater or less extent the original areas in which these depositions were made. These basins exhibit, quite uniformly, central depressions, and margins gently rising to the limit of the mountain boundaries. The '*mesa*,' or table-land character, is exhibited only along the line of river-valleys, as high bluffs, the result of denuding forces subsequent to the original basin depositions.

"These deposites are characterized, as a whole, by a great preponderance of porous materials, consisting of gravel, sands, marls, and clays.

"The natural supplies of fresh water for these open wastes are derived from uncertain accumulations of rain products in small reservoirs, or occasional permanent springs, the latter generally occupying situations in close proximity to mountain ranges.

"All these basins not directly connected with the Rio Grande valley receive and absorb the drainage of their respective mountain boundaries, except in the higher elevations, rarely showing running water, unless as the temporary result of local rains.

"The above indications are favorable to the formation of aqueous substrata, which may be reached by sufficiently deep boring, and when located at the lower depressions of these basin areas, the water would necessarily be brought to the surface."

Nearly all the rain that falls upon the scattered mountains probably passes underneath the surface before reaching the foot-slopes, since the coarse angular debris of the moun ains extend high up their sides, permitting the water to percolate through and descend into the permeable strata.

It will be noticed that nearly all the mountain streams and drains sink before reaching the plains, and others sink on the plains when they reach a porous soil. Where a deep vertical cut has been made in the strata, as, for instance, in the valleys of large rivers, they reappear, running under the permeable and above the impermeable strata. From these facts and considerations it appears that this country, at times almost destitute of water on its surface, has subterranean ponds, and streams, at no great depth below, which can be made to furnish water at the surface, in some instances by artesian wells, and in others by ordinary wells.

This opinion is confirmed by that of Mr. Blake, geologist of the party commanded by Lieutenant Williamson, whose description of the series of small basins lying in the Great Basin applies strictly to those under consideration. The formations are identical. Mr. Blake has detected the existence of regularly stratified tertiary formations in these basins, in which the success of artesian wells is certain. This question will, however, be satisfactorily solved by boring, as the economy of construction is involved to some degree by the facilities of finding water sufficient for working parties during the construction of the road.

The most unfavorable condition, towards the termination of the dry season, has been presented above. At other seasons lakes and springs will furnish water at much shorter intervals; but the first step in the construction of the road will be building wells between the points of abundant supply. It is supposed that the two ends of the road from the Mississippi and Pacific will reach the Rio Grande and the point of departure from the Gila at the same time, and that the road across the intervening space will be commenced at the two ends.

FUEL.

The report of Lieutenant Parke is not very positive upon the subject of fuel; but it is probable that a very scanty supply for the working parties will be found between the Rio Grande and Tuczon. Should the dwarf mezquite be found in the usual quantity, with grama grass, west of the Rio Grande as east of it, fuel for the working parties will be had along the route without great expense; should it not be, however, the supply will be very scanty. From Tuczon to the Gila there is no fuel whatever, but little or no grass, and at certain portions of the year no water. The deficiency must be supplied from the Rio Grande and the Gila, and, if necessary, by the portions of the road already built, from the Guadalupe mountains, and from the forests on the mountains at the sources of the Rio Mimbres, some 30 miles distant from the route near Cook's spring, and from the Mogoyon and other mountains at the sources of the Gila, San Francisco and Salinas rivers.

The climate is so mild as to require but little more fuel than is necessary for culinary purposes, and the trace so favorable as to require but small working parties. Should the line along the San Pedro be found practicable, the desert between Tuczon and the Gila will be avoided, and the expense of supplying fuel to working parties from the Gila to the point of leaving the San Pedro be saved.

TIES—LUMBER.

For ties, the lumber of the Sacramento and Guadalupe mountains, and, if necessary, from the eastern portion of the route, must first supply them; then the mountains at the sources of the Rio Mimbres, should it be found economical to resort to them, and the source of supply for the road along the Gila, which will be pointed out presently. Lumber will come from the same points.

GENERAL REMARKS.

A party under Lieut. Parke has been directed to make further examinations and surveys in this region, and to give especial attention to the geological structure, with a view to the location and construction of artesian wells.

If the cost per mile of making wells and supplying fuel for culinary purposes from distances unusually great on railroad routes, will add to the usual expense of construction, the regularity, smoothness, and hardness of surface, mildness of climate, and absence of heavy rains, which will dispense with the usual precautions taken against frost, will so far obviate the necessity of the most costly item of construction of a railroad, as to make the construction over this and similar regions of country a positively economical one. The road must be made, as far as practicable, and, as before remarked, as far as consistent with a good adjustment of economy of time with economy of means, to transport its own material. Short sections should be built at a time, so as to have railroad transportation near the working parties. Building-stone, lime, sand, &c., are found at various convenient points along the route.

The further examination of this region, to be made by Lieut. Parke, will no doubt develop more favorable lines even than that gone over. The labors of the Mexican boundary survey, now in progress, will also furnish further information respecting this country.

To resume the route: We have now reached the Gila, seven miles above the Pimas villages, the elevation above the sea being 1,365 feet. From this point to its junction with the Colorado, the valley of the river is highly favorable to the construction of a railroad. There will be no necessity for embankments against freshets, but trifling occasional cutting and filling; and in those instances where the hills close in upon the river, there is ample space for the road without heavy cutting. The elevation at the mouth of the river being 108 feet, and the distance between the two points 223 miles, we have a general slope of 5.6 feet per mile, which, from the favorable character of the ground, may be assumed as the grade of the road.

Water and fuel for working parties are sufficient, though no grass. Logs may be driven down the Gila from the Mogoyon mountains at its source, from the Pinal Lleno, and down the San Francisco and Salinas rivers, from the pine forests on the former, and the mountains at the sources of the latter. But it may be found more economical to receive all the supplies of lumber needed from the western portion of the road, either from the San Bernardino mountains and pass, or from the harbors of San Pedro or Diego, or, should it be found desirable to establish one, from the depot near the mouth of the Gila.

3. FROM THE MOUTH OF THE GILA TO SAN FRANCISCO.

The most favorable point for crossing the Colorado is at the junction of the Gila where the river is narrowest, 650 feet wide, and has bluffs on both banks.

The direction that the road should take across the desert intervening between it and the foot of the Coast range, depends in part upon the position of the pass by which it crosses this mountain chain. There are two passes known and explored. Warner's, the more southerly of the two, will require five miles of excavation in granite and mica-slate for the full width of the road, the grades varying from 130 to 190 feet per mile. Thence to San Diego by the San Luis river there is a practicable route, but at great cost of cutting on the river to San Luis Rey; thence along the seacoast numerous gullies will require bridging. The distance from the mouth of the Gila, over the desert, to the entrance of this pass, is 80 miles; thence to San Diego is 150 miles. The San Gorgonio or San Bernardino Pass, on the contrary, is remarkably favorable. It is an open valley, from two to five miles wide, the surface, smooth and unbroken, affording in its form and inclination every facility and no obstruction to the building of a railroad. Leaving the Colorado, it would be better to keep upon the alluvial soil, passing to the south of the sand-hills, and thus avoid the hard gravelly plain, where it would be necessary to bore considerable depths for water, and where the success of artesian wells is not certain; and it is also desirable to avoid the drifting sand of the gravel plain. But this obliges the road to pass over Mexican territory. The entrance of the San Gorgonio Pass is 133 miles from the mouth of the Gila in a straight line, over a smooth and nearly horizontal plain, which requires scarcely any preparation for the superstructure of a railroad. Thirty or thirty-five miles of this lies upon the gravel plain; the remainder passes over alluvial soil, which only needs irrigation to be fruitful. The first work is to construct wells at every few miles for the use of the working parties. On the alluvial soil, water will, no doubt, be found at a depth of 30 feet; and should deep or artesian wells fail to give a supply on the gravel plain, the expense of hauling it to the working parties for that distance will not be serious. Sufficient fuel for culinary purposes will, perhaps, be found on the alluvial plain—none on the gravel plain; but it can be supplied from the mountains at about double the cost in the eastern States.

The elevation of the mouth of the Gila is 108 feet, and the grade across the plain nearly horizontal. Approaching the pass, we have for 10½ miles an ascending slope of 40 feet per mile; then for 6 miles, one of 89 feet per mile. We are now at the point 133 miles from the mouth of the Gila. The natural slopes along the line of survey are—

13 miles, at	60 feet per mile,	
2 "	132	"
7 "	75	"

to the summit, 2,808 feet above the sea. Descending to the town of San Bernardino, we have—

8⅓ miles, at	72 feet per mile.	
2.7 "	79	"
2 "	77	"
1.3 "	127	"
4 "	75	"
6¼ "	41	"

near the town of San Bernardino, at an elevation of 1,120 feet above the sea.

The above enumeration is made to show that practicable grades can be had by following the natural slopes of the ground without cutting and filling, or side location, and therefore without great expense. The greatest grade is 132 feet per mile, for a distance of 3⅓ miles. They can be modified, however, and reduced, without rock-cutting, so as not to exceed, perhaps, 80 feet per mile. Abundance of water can be got by digging wells, either on the pass or on the Pacific slopes. The San Bernardino and San Gorgonio mountains, north and south of the pass, 9,000 and 6,000 feet high, afford pine and fir timber at about one quarter the distance up their slopes. On these two mountains the growth of timber is thick, consisting mostly of pine and fir.

Should it be considered necessary to connect the harbor of San Diego (distant about 120 miles) with this pass, the general features of the country between it and San Luis Rey (about 75 miles) are favorable to the construction of a railroad. It may be described as a great plain, with numerous hills from 500 to 1,000 feet in height, irregularly distributed on its surface, sometimes assuming the form of a range several miles in extent, between and around which a road may be carried with favorable grades without expensive cutting and filling. It is plentifully supplied with water and fuel and good building-stone. From San Luis Rey to San Diego (about 40 or 45 miles) the unfavorable topographical feature along the coast is the numerous, intricate, deep gullies cut into the plain by its drainage, and which it would be necessary to bridge—the average width to be bridged being between 100 feet and 200 feet; the bridging might amount to one-fifth or one-tenth of the whole distance.

We have now reached the Pacific slopes and harbors which will at least afford great facilities in the construction of the road eastward, and which should be connected with it. The harbor of San Diego is excellent, but not capacious. The harbor of San Pedro is entirely open to the south and southeast, the quarter from which the sudden storms and dangerous winds of the winter come. Should it be selected as the depot from which the materials and supplies for the construction of the road eastward to the Rio Grande are to be drawn, the question of constructing a breakwater for protection against the winter southeast storms should be considered. It would be in a depth of 30 feet.

But the great object of the Pacific railroad will not be accomplished unless a connected line can be had to the best harbor on its coast, that of San Francisco.

If a practicable pass exists leading from the plains of Los Angeles to the valley of the Salinas river, it will give the most direct route, and that which will probably require the least ascent. A party is now making the explorations and surveys to solve this question. With the present information, San Francisco must be reached by crossing the Coast range to the Great Basin, passing over its southwestern extremity, (a nearly horizontal plain,) then crossing the Sierra Nevada and descending into the Tulares valley. From the western extremity of the San Gorgonio Pass two routes present themselves by which we may cross the Coast range and reach the Great Basin. The nearest is the Cajon Pass, which, beginning at the Pacific side, has, over the distance of 11½ miles, natural slopes varying from 90 to 100, 117, 142, 159, 171 feet per mile; then a tunnel is requisite, 3 or 4 miles long, ascending constantly 100 feet per mile, the ground at the highest point being 1,600 feet above the tunnel. Lieut. Williamson is of opinion that these high grades cannot be much reduced by location on the side-hills. Lieut. Whipple thinks that they can.

The "New Pass," made known by Lieutenant Williamson's explorations, is more favorable than the Cajon. It is along the headwaters of the Santa Clara river, to reach which it is necessary to cross the divide between one of its tributaries and one of the Los Angeles river, through the San Fernando Pass, near the mission of San Fernando. From San Bernardino to the mission of San Fernando, 78 miles, the road may pass over a country requiring gently undulating grades, and in other respects presenting features highly favorable to its construction. There is good building-stone and plenty of water and fuel. Ties and lumber can be brought from the mountains. The soil is fertile and well watered, excepting on the divides and in some elevated places where irrigation must be resorted to. This promises to be a highly cultivated, populous, and rich region of country. A branch road about 25 miles long to San Pedro from near Los Angeles, over ground favorable to cheap construction, will enable that port to be used for lumber, iron, coal, and all the materials and supplies for the construction of the road eastwardly.

In the San Fernando Pass the natural slopes on the south side must probably be followed, as deep ravines cut up the hills on either side. Rising from the mission of San Fernando 600 feet in 4.4 miles, at the rate of about 155 feet per mile, we reach a point where a tunnel must be cut through soft sandstone, one-third of a mile long, at an elevation of 1,746 feet. We then have a descending grade for 4 miles of 115 feet per mile. This part of the pass is narrow, and will require side and other heavy cutting in earth. Hence to the point where the grades of the New Pass are given on the profile of Lieutenant Williamson is 7 miles, with an ascending grade of 55 feet per mile.

In the new pass an excavation in drift, (clay, gravel, &c.,) 40 or 50 feet in depth, for a short distance at the summit, and a side location which will not require much cutting, will give an average grade of 67 feet per mile; the natural grades without side location are 55, 37, 58, 73, 62, 70, 105, and 77 feet per mile for 22 miles to the summit. In a portion of the approach, about one mile in length, where the mountains close in precipitously and the stream winds abruptly, it may be necessary to cut two or three short tunnels 100 or 300 feet long through slaty granite. The summit of the pass is 3,164 feet above the sea. East of it for a distance of 1.35 mile the direct natural slope is steep, 240 and 218 feet per mile, and the ground will require cutting and filling to adjust the grade for a distance of at least three miles to that west of the summit. It must probably be 100 feet per mile. From this point to the elevation which will probably be maintained in the Great Basin, about 2,900 feet, the grade may be any that is desirable, and the ground will require little or no preparation for the superstructure.

The San Francisquito Pass (on one of the main tributaries of the Santa Clara river) is more direct than the New Pass, but, if not positively impracticable, is at least difficult, and the grades are excessive.

Having now reached the Great Basin, we have several passes by which to enter the Tulares valley.

In the *Cañada de las Uvas* Pass, elevation of summit 4,256 feet, the average slope for 5¼ miles from the summit to the Tulares valley is 302 feet per mile, the maximum being 348 feet per mile, and the minimum 229 feet per mile. But the bounding hills are so cut up with deep ravines, that the average grade cannot be had, and the natural slope must be used.

In the *Tejon* Pass, elevation of summit 5,285 feet, beginning at the western entrance, for 2.83 miles the slope is 173 feet per mile; for 11.4 miles the average slope is 234 feet per mile, supposing a side location; then a tunnel 1.15 mile long; then a descending slope towards the Great Basin of 205 feet per mile for 6.4 miles, supposing a side location.

The next the Tah-ee-chay-pah Pass, elevation of summit 4,020 feet; ascending to it from the Tulares valley in 15½ miles with natural slopes, varying through 153, 176, 192, (for 1½ mile,) 119, and 157 feet, and eight feet per mile, and descending towards the Great Basin nine miles, at 80 feet per mile, the remaining distance being with gentle grades.

Walker's Pass, elevation of summit 5,302 feet, requires a tunnel of four miles, has a slope in ascending to the summit from the Great Basin of 265 feet per mile for six miles, of 272 feet per mile descending for 6½ miles; and just before the Kern river debouches into the Tulares valley, there is an impracticable cañon of five miles.

It is very evident that the most favorable of these passes is the Tah-ee-chay-pah. From the summit to the Tulares valley a side location in earth-cutting can be made, giving an average grade of 144 feet per mile for 17 miles. The steep grade can be extended four miles further, entering the Tulares valley at a lower elevation than that of 1,489 feet. The New Pass and Tah-ee-chay-pah Pass may be connected by an almost horizontal grade around the border of the Great Basin, keeping along the foot of the eastern slopes for about 25 miles, where supplies of water can be had either from springs, small streams, or common wells or artesian wells; then crossing in a nearly straight line to the entrance of the Tah-ee-chay-pah Pass, descending to a fine spring of water, elevation 2,668 feet, and ascending to the entrance, elevation 3,300 feet, and at a distance from New Pass of about 60 miles. The whole of this surface is prepared by nature to receive the superstructure of a railroad. It has two intervals of 13 and 17 miles where there is no water; but it can be supplied either by hauling or by digging or boring wells. Fuel, ties, lumber, stone, &c., over this distance of 60 miles, as well as for an additional distance at both ends, must come from the adjoining mountains, where it is abundant. The working parties over this part will be small.

Having entered the pass at an elevation of 3,300 feet, there will be 12 miles of grade at the rate of 22 feet per mile; then, as before stated, nine miles at 80 feet per mile. The ground admits of these grades being arranged to suit those descending to the Tulares valley, which commence after a nearly horizontal grade at the summit for 7½ miles. From the manner in which these two passes are connected by an almost horizontal line after descending about 500 feet from the summit of New Pass, they have, combined, the disadvantages attending only one pass, with a summit elevation of 4,300 feet; and after descending the Pacific slopes through the San Gorgonio Pass to an elevation of 1,118 feet, we have reached the Tulares valley by ascending 3,900 feet; and descending again to an elevation of about 1,500 feet above the mean level of the ocean. From the head of the Tulares valley, the waters of the Bay of San Francisco, navigable for sea-going vessels of large draught, may be attained in several ways.

The eastern side of the Tulares and San Joaquin valleys is intersected by numerous streams from the Sierra Nevada. The western is bounded by the coast chain, and has few streams. That part of the Tulares valley between Kern and San Joaquin rivers, a space of 150 miles having a soft alluvial soil, is at certain seasons miry. A road, therefore, extending though it, should keep near the foot-slopes of the mountains. From the Tah-ee-chay-pah Pass to the best point of crossing Kern river, 21½ miles, the route passes over a dry dusty plain, destitute of water and fuel, the soil of which is not well constituted for fertility. The elevation at the crossing being about 500 feet, the general grade will be, for the first ten miles, 78 feet per mile, and for the remaining eleven and a half miles, 18 feet per mile.

From the crossing of Kern river to the second crossing of the San Joaquin, at or near Grayson's, the distance is (the route keeping near the foot of the mountains) 258 or 260 miles—the general descending grade two and a third feet per mile. The numerous river-beds or bottoms should be crossed on piles, the spaces varying from 50 to 300 feet, the greatest width of the portions to be spanned not exceeding 100 feet. This is not proposed as the route for a railroad, but merely to give a general idea of the distance and character of country which separates the head of the Tulares valley from the navigable waters of the Bay of San Francisco. The total distance from the Tah-ee-chay-pah Pass to the Straits of Martinez is 354 miles, following the route travelled by Lieutenant Williamson; but the location distance of a railroad would be 288 miles.

The most direct route to San Francisco from the Tah-ee-chay-pah Pass, will be found through one of the passes known to exist in the mountain range separating the San Joaquin valley from those of the Salinas river and San José river. The distance through them is about ten miles; the elevation of their summits about 600 feet. They may be reached from the Tah-ee-chay-pah Pass by passing around the head of the Tulares valley to its western side, or by keeping on the eastern side of the Tulares valley fifteen or twenty miles after crossing Kern river; then crossing the valley, in doing which it will be necessary to use piling for the distance of ten miles, to make a sufficiently firm road-bed over the soft, miry, alluvial soil. The distance to the port of San Francisco, by this route, from the Tah-ee-chay-pah Pass, is about 288 miles. The average grades, except through the short pass, will be two or three feet per mile.

The soil of the Tulares and San Joaquin valleys is well constituted for fertility, and needs merely the proper amount of water to be highly productive. There are settlements along the eastern side of these valleys under the mountains. The San José valley is one of the best cultivated and most populous districts of California.

Sufficient water and fuel for working parties can be found at convenient distances on this section, and lumber and good building-stone at various points along the line in the mountains, fifteen or twenty miles from the foot of their western slopes.

The sum of ascents, therefore, between the summit of the San Bernardino Pass and the port of San Francisco is 4,516 feet, (supposing the height of the pass through the coast mountains 600 feet,) the distance 521 miles.

This portion of the route is generally of a different character from that east of the Sierra Nevada and Coast ranges. Its topographical features, except the mountain passes, are favorable to the cheap construction of a railroad. The comparative proximity throughout the line of forests of pine and other trees, of good building-stone, and other materials for construction; of supplies of water and fuel for the working parties; the fertility of the soil along large portions of the route, which by irrigation from unemployed mountain streams may be made productive,—these circumstances, together with the population already occupying certain portions of the route, afford the means of estimating how far the cost of the construction, and working of the road, will exceed that under nearly similar topographical circumstances in the eastern States, so far as similarity of topographical features can exist between countries of such different formations.

The mountain passes are of a favorable character, their only objectionable feature being their high grades. Excepting at a few points, and for short distances not exceeding a mile or two at a time, they do not require heavy embankments, or difficult bridging, or heavy side-cutting in rock or even in earth. The only rock-cutting needed is that at the summit of the San Fernando Pass, through soft sandstone one-third of a mile, and in the New Pass, where, for the space of a mile, two or three tunnels, 100 and 300 feet in length, through slaty granite, will probably be required, with a cutting of 43 feet in clay, granite, &c., at the summit, for no great distance.

The construction, however, will cost more per mile in this distance of 521 miles, than between the Sierra Nevada and the Rio Grande. In regard to the grades, there is on the Baltimore and Ohio railroad a grade of 117 feet per mile for a length of 17 miles. A 24-ton engine, on six drivers, can draw a train containing two hundred passengers, with 100 pounds of baggage each, in the worst condition of the rail, up a grade of 221 feet per mile, and a train of three hundred passengers and baggage up a grade of 150 feet per mile.

The maximum loads are rarely carried over long roads. Even supposing twenty-ton engines used, with maximum loads for the grades over other portions of the road, it would merely be necessary to divide the load into three parts to pass a grade of 150 feet to the mile, over the distances through which they extend, supposing the load previously adjusted to a grade of 40 feet per mile: in other words, to reduce a grading of 150 feet to the mile, to one of 40 feet to the mile, the expense of two additional engines, and the cost of working them through the pass, must be added.

For more detailed information in regard to this, I refer to the memoranda and tables prepared by Capt. McClellan, Corps of Engineers, and the following extract from the report of Allan Campbell, Esq., an able American engineer, upon the railroad from Valparaiso to Santiago.

EXTRACT FROM THE REPORT OF ALLAN CAMPBELL, ESQ., CHIEF ENGINEER OF THE VALPARAISO AND SANTIAGO RAILROAD.

"From the known topography of Chili, and particularly from the facts stated in the preceding pages, it will naturally be inferred that a railroad route from Valparaiso to Santiago is only to be obtained by resorting to gradients of extreme acclivity.

In no country where railroads have yet been constructed are more gigantic physical obstacles encountered. I refer particularly to the elevations to be overcome, and not to the labor or cost of constructing the road, because in this respect it presents a very favorable aspect. The only alpine region where this species of improvement has yet been extensively introduced, is that of the eastern part of North America. There the Alleghany mountains, stretching along the Atlantic coast from two to three hundred miles inland, separate that ocean from the rich and extensive valley of the Mississippi.

The trade and commerce of this vast western region has long been the aim of the principal cities situated on the Atlantic. In the various works of canals and railroads constructed for the purpose, nearly two hundred millions of dollars have been expended. Stimulated by the great prize held out, the resources of States and cities have been bountifully applied; private capital has been unsparingly devoted, while the genius and skill of engineers have been developed in the noble rivalry.

Boston, New York, Philadelphia, Baltimore, Charleston, and Savannah, have all engaged in the construction of railroads leading westward. Some of these lines are now completed, and others are approaching their termination. As these works pass over a country bearing a strong resemblance in its topography to that part of Chili now under consideration, some notice of their principal features will not be uninteresting.

Without entering into minutiæ, it may be stated, that the several routes are from three hundred to five hundred miles in length, amounting in the aggregate to about twenty-five hundred miles; and, wonderful to relate, this vast extent of road is carried over such an elevated region without a single inclined plane, worked by stationary power. Some of the lines were originally operated in this manner, but they have been made to give place to gradients suited to the locomotive engine. This fact will show the great importance attached to this consideration in a country where routes affording the cheapest and most rapid method of transport are aimed at.

The route from Boston passes over a summit 1,500 feet above the ocean, with a maximum gradient of 83 feet per mile. Two roads lead from the city of New York to the western waters; one through the valley of the Hudson river, with a summit of only 650 feet above tide, and a maximum grade of 30 feet per mile; and another, (the Erie railroad) whose highest point is 1,700 feet above the Atlantic, on which grades of 70 feet per mile are adopted.

Proceeding southerly, the mountains attain a higher elevation, and the routes from Philadelphia and Baltimore are carried over very elevated summits; that of the former being 2,400 feet, with gradients of 95 feet per mile, and the latter about 2,600 or 2,700 feet, with a maximum gradient of 116 feet. As this latter work so closely resembles the Santiago road, I shall have occasion, presently, more particularly to speak of it.

Proceeding still farther south, the mountains again decline, and the Charleston and Savannah routes cross them at an elevation of 1,500 feet with very moderate grades, not exceeding 40 feet per mile.

Except the Baltimore and Ohio railroad, (one of the lines above mentioned) the exact height of whose summit I cannot state, none of these great thoroughfares pass over ground so much elevated above the sea as the Santiago route; and as all, in this respect, far exceed the works of other countries, it may safely be said that the route described in these pages overcomes a greater elevation than has yet been surmounted by railroad, (except perhaps in one instance,) throughout the world. But the Santiago route is superior to most of the American roads above enumerated in one respect. In approaching to, and departing from their main summits, those roads cross over numerous secondary ranges and deep intervening valleys, which makes the aggregate rise and fall much greater than the Santiago road, as will be seen by the following table:

Road.	Length in miles.	Elevation of summit above the sea.	Total rise and fall.	Maximum grade per mile.	Remarks.
Boston route	500	1,440	4,700	83	
New York route, (Central)	440	650	2,100	30	
New York route, (Erie)	460	1,720	6,500	70	
Philadelphia route	340	2,400	5,600	95	
Baltimore route	390	2,600 or 2,700	7,000	116	Rise and fall, and summit, supposed.
Charleston route	490	1,400	5,000	40	Rise and fall, supposed.
Savannah route	440	1,400	5,000	40	Do. do.
Santiago railroad	110	2,640	4,340	119	

Although the total elevation surmounted by European railroads is much less than in the cases above cited, yet even there, in some instances, inclinations equal to the maximum gradient of the Santiago road are now introduced, and overcome by locomotive power. Two or three instances may be mentioned.

In a work entitled "The Practical Railway Engineer," published at London, in the year 1847, is the following description of the Edinburgh and Glasgow railroad:

"The gradients vary from one in 880 (six feet per mile,) to one in 5,456 (about one foot per mile,) except one incline of one mile, fourteen chains in length, which descends from the Cowlairs towards the Glasgow station, at the rate of one in forty-three (123 feet per mile,) and has hitherto been worked by stationary steam-engines, which are now, or are about to be, replaced by American locomotive engines."

Dr. Lardner, a distinguished writer on various scientific and practical subjects, in a late work entitled "Railway Economy in Europe and America," after giving a table of the German railways, says: "In the first and third columns of this table are given the characteristic or prevailing gradients and radii; and in the second and fourth columns are given those which occur only exceptionally, when the character of the ground rendered them inevitable. In some cases—as, for example, in the section of the railway constructed from Brunswick to Harburgh, on the left bank of the Elbe, facing Hamburgh—the prevailing gradient is 1 in 166 (32 feet per mile;) but in one section of this line, extending over a distance of about five miles, being the section between Hamburgh and the station of Weinenburgh, there is a series of gradients which vary from 1 in 100 (53 feet per mile,) to 1 in 50 (106 feet per mile.) No practical difficulty, however, is encountered in the regular working of this part of the line by locomotives without assistant engines. Trains of an average gross weight of sixty or seventy tons are drawn over this section by locomotives whose weight does not exceed eighteen tons, having six coupled wheels of four feet nine inches in diameter."

In the table mentioned, the maximum gradient of the Brunswick and Harburgh railway is stated at 1 in 43 (123 feet per mile,) and those of Wurtemburgh at 1 in 45 (117 feet per mile.)

* * * * * * * * * * *

The grades of the Santiago railroad, though heavy, are, in comparison with others which have been cited, not unfavorable; and we find on analyzing the expense of operating a railroad, that the cost of motive power is only a fractional part of the whole. It is sufficient for our present purpose to know that important railroads in other countries, with gradients equal to those of the Santiago route, have been, and now are, successfully and profitably conducted. One important fact in this connexion is, that the line now under consideration will be free from the evils resulting from snow and ice, which diminish the adhesion of the engine to the rails, and reduce its effective power. Snow rarely lies even at the highest level over which this route is conducted.

* * * * * * * * * * *

It will naturally occur to many that the descent of trains on gradients of such great declivity, with perfect security to the lives and limbs of passengers, is quite as important a consideration as their ascent with profitable loads. The accounts which follow, founded on fact and official information, afford the most satisfactory evidence on this point.

A branch of the Baltimore and Ohio railroad, in the United States, has gradients of 135 feet per mile, which are worked entirely by locomotive engines. The descent is made with heavy loads in perfect safety, and a single engine takes up regularly a gross load of 66 tons, exclusive of the engine and tender. On one road in the State of New York a short gradient of 175 feet per mile is descended daily with passenger trains.

The superintendent of the Baltimore and Susquehanna railroad, an important line both for freight and passengers, writes as follows: "We have one grade of eighty-four feet per mile, three miles in length. Over this grade a locomotive weighing 26 tons hauls, at the rate of twelve miles an hour, forty (four-wheel) cars, each containing three tons of produce—the cars themselves weighing 114 tons—making a gross load of 234 tons."

The most interesting and analogous case, however, to which I can refer, is that of the Baltimore and Ohio railroad, one of the great lines of the United States alluded to in a previous part of this article, as connecting the sea-board with the valley of the Mississippi across the Alleghany mountains.

In the year 1850, 477,000 tons of merchandise and 180,000 passengers were transported on this road, the receipts amounting to $1,343,000, the road being only about half completed. When finished to the Ohio river, its receipts are expected to amount to $3,000,000. On this road are heavy gradients, with several curves of six hundred feet radius, and some of four hundred feet. It is to the mountain district of the road just opened that I wish particularly to invite attention; and for this purpose an extract is made from the official report of the chief engineer, Mr. Latrobe, one of the most distinguished engineers of North America, in which he describes the route and grades over the Alleghany mountains:

"At about a mile below this last point, the high grade of 116 feet per mile begins and continues about 11½ miles, crossing the Potomac from Virginia into Maryland near the beginning of the grade, and thence ascending the steep side-slopes of Savage river and Crab Tree creek to the summit at the head of the latter, a total distance of about fifteen miles, upon the last three and a half of which the grade is reduced to about 100 feet per mile. From the summit the line passes for about nineteen miles through the level and beautiful tract of country so well known as the Glades, and near their western border the route crosses the Maryland boundary at a point about sixty miles from Cumberland, and passes into the State of Virginia, in whose territory it continues thence to the terminus on the Ohio. From the Glades the line descends by a grade of 116 feet per mile for eight and a half miles, and over very rugged ground, and thence three miles further to Cheat river, which it crosses at the mouth of Salt Lick creek. The route, immediately after crossing this river, ascends along the broken slopes of the Laurel Hill by a grade of 105 feet per mile for five miles, to the next summit, passing the dividing ridge by a tunnel of 4,100 feet in length, and whence, after three miles of light grade, a descent by the grade of 105 feet per mile for five miles is made to the valley of Racoon creek, by which, and the valley of the Three Forks creek, the Tygart's Valley river is reached in fourteen miles more, at the Turnpike bridge above described, and 103½ miles from Cumberland."

The foregoing extract exhibits in a few words the physical obstacles to be overcome. It will be seen that a gradient of 116 feet per mile, both ascending and descending, is required—in the aggregate amounting to twenty miles—and that in both directions there are also thirteen miles more with gradients exceeding 100 feet per mile."

Two important remarks upon the characteristics of the railroad from Valparaiso to Santiago, which will be found in the preceding extract from the report of Allan Campbell, Esq., are equally applicable to the route of the 32d parallel. The first is the favorable character of the approaches to the mountains, by which no numerous secondary ranges and deep intervening valleys are to be crossed, as in the railroads crossing the Alleghany mountains; and the second is, that the line will be free from the evils resulting from snow and ice, which diminish the adhesion of the engine to the rails, and reduce its effective power. Not only are these two remarks fully applicable to the route of the 32d parallel, but the features of the mountain passes are even more favorable than those of the route discussed by Mr. Campbell.

There will be more snow and ice in the Tah-ee-chay-pah Pass than in any other on the route of the 32d parallel; but there is no probability of their being found in sufficient quantity to obstruct in the least the working of the road. In the absence of positive information upon this point, the examination which follows may give some general indication of the climate there.

The absence of snow and ice in these passes is especially important with the high grades proposed to be used. These can in every instance, except one, (the San Fernando Pass, over four and perhaps eight miles,) be reduced by side location to grades in use on several principal railroads. But cars are carried safely over grades nearly double the greatest here proposed for temporary use, and the increased cost of employing additional engines over these portions of the road is not in the least serious, compared with the additional expense and loss of time required to secure easier gradients.

The winter temperature of San Francisco is 50° Fahrenheit. The Tah-ee-chay-pah Pass is about 3° south of San Francisco, and at the same level would have a winter temperature of 53°. The elevation being 4,000 feet, would give, by the usual rule, a temperature from 13° to 15° lower, or a mean winter temperature of 40° or 38°. It is probable, however, that it is somewhat lower than this, which is about the mean winter temperature of Fort Monroe, Old Point Comfort, Chesapeake bay. The mean winter temperature of Charleston is 50°, and that of the summit elevation of the railroad route westward to the Mississippi, 1,400 feet above the sea, is about 45°.

The mean winter temperature of Fort McHenry, Baltimore harbor, is 32°.7; that of the summit elevation of the Baltimore and Ohio railroad, 2,600 feet above the sea, should be about 24°, which is 14° or 16° lower than that obtained for the Tah-ee-chay-pah Pass.

There is deep snow in the Tejon Pass, but from the open character of the Tah-ee-chay-pah Pass, and its greater distance from the junction of the two chains of mountains, the snow and ice found there will not probably be seriously disadvantageous.

GENERAL REVIEW.

Among the general considerations which determine the position of the route near the 32d parallel, the most prominent are the low elevation of the mountain passes, and their favorable topographical features, as well as those of the table-lands, embracing over 1,000 miles of the route; the favorable character of the surface generally, by which the most costly item of construction in railroads, the formation of the road-bed, is in a great measure avoided; the shortness of the line, 1,600 miles, from the navigable waters of the Mississippi to the Pacific, and the temperate climate on the elevated portions in this southern latitude.

The principal characteristic of this route is the great extent of high, arid, smooth, and nearly horizontal table-lands which it traverses, reaching an elevation of 4,000 feet upon the dividing ridge between the Brazos and Colorado rivers of Texas, near which elevation it continues until it descends from the pass of the Sierra de Santa Catarina to the Gila river, a space of nearly 600 miles.

The elevation at the summit of the Llano Estacado is 4,700 feet, and in the passes of the Guadalupe and Hueco mountains, east of the Rio Grande, 5,700 and 4,800 feet respectively. Between the Rio Grande and the Gila, the greatest elevation, which is twice attained, is 5,200 feet; the mean elevation before the descent to the Gila is commenced being 4,100 feet.

From the eastern edge of the Llano Estacado to the pass of San Gorgonio, 1,052 miles, the route crosses three rivers—the Pecos, the Rio Grande, and the Great Colorado of the West.

The peculiar features of the arid region over which the route lies, from the eastern edge of the Llano Estacado to the summit of the San Gorgonio Pass, have been sufficiently explained in the detailed topographical review already given of each portion of this route. Those very characteristics which were thought to offer the greatest obstacles to the construction of a railroad, prove, when closely examined, the most favorable, since they have obviated the necessity of much of that most costly item in railroad construction, the preparation of the road-bed for the superstructure. Throughout the distance of 1,052 miles, with few and limited exceptions, this preparation is already made by nature, and quite as perfectly as, if not better than, it could be done by the hand of man. This item alone usually amounts to from one-half to two-thirds and sometimes three-fourths of the whole cost of a railroad.

The mode and probable cost of obtaining supplies of water over these dry regions have been pointed out and will be subjected to practical tests. Even if these should fail (of which there is no probability) in bringing the required supplies to the surface, the permanent streams and large springs already existing are at distances sufficiently near for the purposes of a railroad, special arrangements having been made to meet the difficulty.

For a 20-ton engine, on four drivers, wood and water, if carried with the train for 25 miles, weigh about $\frac{1}{84}$th of the maximum load on a level, and for 100 miles $\frac{1}{22}$d part; with coal and water the proportions are, for 25 and 100 miles $\frac{1}{105}$th and $\frac{1}{26}$th; but as the load usually carried on freight and passenger trains is much below the maximum, we may safely assume that the trains (freight and passenger) can carry fuel and water sufficient for 100 miles over grades not exceeding 30 or 40 feet without additional cost, the maximum load of this engine on grades of 40 feet, in the best condition of rail, being 252 tons, and in the worst condition 180 tons.

That required for the use of the working parties can be hauled without seriously enhancing the cost of the road, for it must be remembered that the working parties will be small over those portions of the route where the road-bed has been already prepared by nature. We have seen, too, that fuel for culinary purposes for the working parties will probably be found over the greater part of these regions; and where it cannot be found conveniently, that it can be supplied from points so near to the work that its cost will not exceed double that of fuel for the same purposes in the eastern States.

From the eastern limit of the Llano Estacado to the Pacific, 1,200 miles, the plan of building the road has been indicated so as to secure the greatest economy of time and means. Three points remain to be considered: the mode and cost of supplying ties and lumber generally; the mode and cost of supplying fuel; and the manner in which the daily examination of the road can be made and the rails adjusted and protected.

TIES—LUMBER.

Let us assume the most unfavorable case for supplies of ties and lumber over that portion of the route between the eastern limit of the Llano Estacado and the summit of the San Gorgonio Pass, 1,052 miles—that is, that they must be brought from either end of the road, say 300 miles from the eastern limit of the Llano Estacado and from the port of San Pedro on the Pacific, 100 miles from the summit of the San Gorgonio Pass, making the points of supply 1,400 miles apart: the greatest distance to which they must be transported from each end is, therefore, 700 miles by the road, the point of junction of supplies from the east and west being about 110 miles west of the Rio Grande. Lumber can, undoubtedly, be procured in the Red River district for $30 per 1,000 feet. The additional cost for transportation to the Llano, 300 miles by the railroad, at three cents per ton per mile, (double the usual cost on eastern railroads) is $13½, and its cost there $43½ per 1,000 feet; the cost per 1,000 feet for 450 miles additional transportation is $20, and hence the cost per 1,000 feet at this extreme point will be $63½. The mean cost over these 400 or 450 miles from the eastern limit of the Llano Estacado will be $52½ per 1,000 feet. From Fulton to the Llano it is unnecessary to estimate its cost.

Lumber may be delivered at San Pedro or San Diego from Oregon for $30 per 1,000 feet. Abundance of it can be got out from the San Bernardino and other mountains near the line of the road at that cost, and it may be assumed, therefore, to be supplied at San Pedro or San Diego at that price, and at a mean cost over the road (the road supplying itself, as it must do, sections of 40 or 50 miles being built at a time) of $46 per 1,000 feet. The ties should be sawed to the smallest dimensions, if they must be transported to the distances stated. The dimensions may be six inches by eight inches, and their mean cost over these 1,200 miles will be about $34 per 1,000 feet, or the cost of ties per mile $1,760. It may be found desirable to return to the use of stone chairs, or to resort to cast-iron ties over this portion of the route. The latter would cost at eastern prices about $2 per tie.

The mean cost of rails, iron, &c., over this route will not exceed, if it equals, $30 per ton more than their usual cost in the eastern States. Haulage from temporary termini of railroad to unfinished line of road will be about double that in the eastern States; and, indeed, this appears to be about the mean proportion of increase on these great table-lands.

The worst case having been discussed, it remains to be said, that good ties and lumber can be obtained from the Guadalupe and Hueco mountains, from the headwaters of the Rio Mimbres, from the Pinal Lleno, Salinas river and headwaters of the San Francisco, and from the San Bernardino mountains of the Sierra Nevada or Coast range, which sources of supply may be found to materially obviate the necessity of transporting lumber from the two ends of the road.

FUEL.

Bituminous coal is abundant on the Brazos. The coal of Vancouver's island, and also of Puge sound, is excellent. Last summer a cargo was brought to San Francisco from Puget sound at a cost of $11 per ton; $4 per ton being for freight, and $7 per ton for mining and handling. It costs at present prices $5 per ton to mine it. This at no distant period will, doubtless, be reduced to $1 or $2 per ton, and it can be delivered at San Pedro or San Diego at $7 per ton. On the Brazos it can be mined and prepared for transportation at $1 per ton. From the Brazos to San Pedro is 1,400 miles. At three cents per ton per mile, (double the usual cost,) we have it at the foot of the Llano at $7 per ton, and the mean cost per ton over the 1,200 miles, $16.

In regard to transporting wood for fuel for locomotives, as 1,300 pounds of coal make as much steam as 4,500 pounds of pine wood, coal can be transported three and a half times as far as wood, other things being equal.

The cost of fuel on railroads is about one-fifth of the yearly expense of maintaining and working the road.

GENERAL REMARKS.

It may be found desirable to establish a depôt of supplies at the mouth of the Gila, 255 miles distant from San Pedro. The report of a reconnaissance near the mouth of the Colorado of the West, with a view to its navigation, by Lieutenant Derby, topographical engineers, shows that the navigation of this river to the head of tide-water, 40 miles from its mouth, is difficult and dangerous from the rapid rise of the tide called bore. Arnold's Point, 35 miles above the mouth of the river, by the windings of the stream, is the head of navigation in low water (January, February, and March) for vessels drawing nine feet. Above that point, to the mouth of the Gila, the least water is three feet, and the river may be navigated at any season by steamers drawing 2½ feet water. The channel is narrow, and the current, obstructed with small snags and sawyers, is always rapid. The distance from Arnold's Point to the mouth of the Gila is between 70 and 100 miles. The rise of the ordinary spring tides at the mouth of the Colorado is 12 feet. In freshets the river at Arnold's Point rises 15 feet above low water. The velocity of the current, independent of that caused by the tide, is ordinarily from one to three miles per hour, and in freshets nearly double that. Could the work of construction be commenced at the mouth of the Gila at the same time as at San Pedro and the other terminus, and extended east and west, it would hasten the completion of the work.

DAILY INSPECTION OF THE ROAD, &C.

Each portion of a railroad is thoroughly examined every day, and such adjustment and slight repair made as can be done by a single hand. One man attends to from two to three miles of road. From 1,000 to 1,300 miles of the country along this proposed route is uninhabited, except by Indians. Here it will probably be found necessary to establish stations at every 20 or 25 miles distance, capable of accommodating 40 men. As a party of seven or eight men on any portion of the route, with the facilities of a hand railroad car, may be considered perfectly secure against Indians, a party of three men with a guard of five will be able to inspect and adjust 10 miles of a single track; this would require a station for a guard of 25 or 30 men, and for eight or ten employés of the road, every 20 miles. Should the supplies of water be even 100 or 150 miles apart, sufficient could be carried to these parties without extra cost. This guard would not be required at every station; but supposing it necessary over the Indian country of 1,000 miles, it would amount to 1,500 men. As on many of the European railroads the average number of men employed solely for the purpose of preventing access to the railroad from the cross-roads of the country, and for attending to signals, &c., independent of those employed for switches, daily inspection and adjustment, and at the depots, is at least one per mile, their number would amount on a road of 2,000 miles in length, to 2,000 men; exceeding that required for *guarding* the road. Supposing this guard employed by the railroad authorities, it would not be in addition to the usual number of employés, but merely a change of their duties to suit new circumstances.

It is desirable to have stations with relays of engines, cars, &c., at every 100 miles; and favorable sites for those will be found on this route at about the required distance apart, with but two exceptions—one being the table lands west of the Rio Grande, and the other the Colorado desert—where the distances are about 150 miles.

But considerations of this kind, within certain limits, belong rather to questions of nice economy than to greater or less difficulty of working the road.

SOIL, &C.

The table-lands, extending from the cultivable soil of Texas westward, have generally a growth of grama grass. The principal exceptions are a large portion of the Llano Estacado, and for 70 miles of the descent to the Gila; nor is grass found in that portion of the valley of the Gila traversed by the route, although the soil is fertile; nor is it found on the Colorado desert, or on the crossing of the southwest corner of the Great Basin, &c.

The soil of the river valleys is fertile, but for cultivation needs irrigation. After leaving, for the first time, the body of the productive soil of Texas, we have the valleys of the Pecos, Rio Grande, Gila, and Colorado, portions of whose areas possess a fertile soil; the sum of these exceeds 2,300 square miles. That portion of California west and south of the coast range has a soil and climate which will admit of a dense population.

GENERAL ADVANTAGES OF THE ROUTE.

The mineral wealth of the countries near the 32d parallel has been indicated by others, and needs no other mention.

The proposed road passes near the northern borders of the Mexican States, or departments of Chihuahua and Sonora. They extend northward from latitude 27° or 28° to our boundary. The surface is generally table-lands, affording good grazing; the climate is agreeable. The soil of the river valleys is fertile, capable of producing, when irrigated, wheat, cotton, &c. Their wealth is principally in cattle farms and mines of gold and silver. The area is 280,000 square miles. The population exceeds 300,000.

Although this route passes near the frontier of Mexico, yet it is not liable to objection from this circumstance, since we control the frontier, and the construction of the road would probably break the power of the Indian tribes.

It passes through or near territories having already large populations; that of New Mexico, according to the report of Captain Pope, being 50,000; and that of Chihuahua and Sonora, as above stated, being more than 300,000.

The chief advantage of this route is, that for the space of 1,100 or 1,200 miles, the usual item of great expense in railroads is in a great measure avoided, there being no necessity to prepare an expensive road-bed except in a few instances in the passage of the mountain chains. Draining and ballasting are also dispensed with at the same time. Over the remaining portions of the route—418 miles if to San Pedro, and 839 miles if to San Francisco—the ground is generally favorable to the construction of the road-bed.

The mountain passes of the route are generally favorable; those west of the Rio Grande requiring no difficult engineering for location through them, and but little rock excavation or expensive embankment and side cutting. The Guadalupe and Hueco passes are more difficult. The short tunnel on the San Fernando Pass, and those that may be needed in the New Pass, will not be found difficult in their execution.

The climate throughout the route is salubrious, the heat due its southern latitude being moderated by the elevation of the table-lands. On the Colorado desert it is torrid, but not unhealthy, and west of the Sierra Nevada and coast range is celebrated for health and agreeableness.

From a consideration of these favorable circumstances, and after a close examination of all the sources of increased cost of construction, from the peculiarities of situation, climate, and geological and topographical formation, I am of opinion that the road may be built as a first class road, in regard to superstructure, rail, &c., and equipped sufficiently for the business that may be reasonably expected, for a sum that will not probably exceed $45,000 per mile.

The following estimate is submitted, including depots and equipment:

ESTIMATE.

From Fulton, on the Red river, to the Llano Estacado, 449 miles, at $35,000 per mile, 25 per cent. being added to the cost at eastern prices for one-half the distance; over the Llano Estacado, 125 miles, at $35,000 per mile, peculiarities of construction having been considered, and 50 per cent. at cost at eastern

prices having been added; the sum of the two distances being 624 miles, at $35,000 per mile		$21,840,000
From the Pecos to the Rio Grande, the cost being assimilated to that of the Baltimore and Ohio railroad for 80 miles, and 50 per cent. being added to the cost—80 miles, at $75,000 per mile	$6,000,000	
The remaining 83 miles, at $45,000 per mile	$3,735,000	
		$9,735,000
From the Rio Grande to San Pedro, on the Pacific, 831 miles, at $45,000 per mile		$37,395,000
Total from Fulton, on Red river, to San Pedro, being 1,618 miles		$68,970,000
In continuation to San Francisco, the distance from the Rio Grande at El Paso to San Fernando may be considered the same as to San Pedro, and the amount of estimate as above may be adopted. The remaining distance from San Fernando to San Francisco is about 421 miles, of which about 75 miles is of a highly favorable character of mountain passes, which may be estimated at $90,000 per mile		$6,750,000
The remaining 346 miles being estimated at $50,000 per mile		$17,400,000
Total distance from Fulton, on Red river, to San Francisco being 2,039 miles, and the total estimated cost		$93,120,000

This estimate supposes the final condition of the passes in the Sierra Nevada and the coast range. Should the steeper grades be used a reduction of nearly $3,000,000 may be made from the estimate.

The equipment for the first business of the road, included in the preceding estimate, may be estimated for 200 passengers daily each way, and a light freight business. The cost of this would amount, at eastern prices, to $1,000 or $1,200 per mile, less than one fifth of that of the six principal Massachusetts roads out of Boston, the average cost of equipment of which per mile is $6,147; total length of roads 381 miles. The amount of work performed by these roads in 1853 was—

Number of passengers carried one mile	111,075,121
Number of tons of freight carried one mile	61,858,964

Adding 50 per cent. for cost of freight, &c., we may estimate the first equipment of the Pacific road at $3,000,000, and the cost of depots, stations, &c., at from $2,500,000 to $3,000,000; total, equipment and depots, $6,000,000. Should the road be finally worked to its full power, the cost of equipment and depots would exceed $20,000,000.

The length of this route from Fulton to San Pedro is	1,618 miles.
The sum of the ascents and descents 32,784 feet, which is equivalent to 621 miles, and the equated length of the road is	2,239 miles.
The estimated cost is	$68,970,000
From Fulton to San Francisco the distance is	2,039 miles.
The sum of the ascents and descents 42,008 feet, which is equivalent to 795 miles, and the equated length of the road is	2,834 miles.
The estimated cost is	$93,120,000

BUSINESS OF THE ROAD.

It may be desirable to consider the sources of business for a railroad to San Francisco when constructed.

The value of the Santa Fé trade is stated by Captain Pope to be yearly $6,000,000.

The number of passengers to and from California is now 50,000 yearly. It will not be extravagant to assume that the road will double this number at once. This, at $200 per passenger from Fulton to San Francisco, 2,000 miles, will give $20,000,000, or, at $150 per passenger, will give $15,000,000, of which two-thirds may be assumed as profit. It is doubtful whether the present overland emigration can be counted upon as furnishing business for the road.

The light freight which is now carried by the Isthmus route, costing $394 per ton, and which, when the Isthmus railroad is completed, is to cost $169 per ton, would take the Pacific railroad route, since, allowing five cents per ton per mile for this road, the cost per ton from Fulton to San Francisco will be $105, and thence to New Orleans or Memphis, by railroad, $10 per ton additional.

Fifty millions of dollars in gold are sent annually to the Atlantic States from California. It is doubtful, owing to the nature of the risks, if the per-centage on this would accrue to the road. Two per cent., the present cost of transportation, is $1,000,000, three-fourths of which would, if carried, be the earnings of the Pacific road, $750,000.

The transportation of the mails may be set down at from $500,000 to $1,000,000.

In the year 1852–'53, 22,320,417 pounds of tea were imported into the United States, valued at $8,174,670, at a freight cost probably of $15 per ton measurement, (one-half ton weight of tea.) To supply the country west of the Mississippi we have an interior transportation, by railroad, canal, or river, of at least 1,000 miles. Freight from China to San Francisco may be assumed not to exceed $10 per ton. From San Francisco to the Mississippi river the freight on tea would be $50 per ton measurement, and the total cost of transportation would be $60 per ton measurement, against $30, brought from the eastern ports, (freight from China to Boston $15 per ton;) this, in the first instance, is six cents per pound, and in the second three cents per pound. The tea imported into the United States is of inferior quality, and, in the opinion of those familiar with the trade, would not be less injured by transportation by the railroad route than by that now used; nor would the more delicate teas, should there be a demand for them. The earnings from this source, supposing it carried 22,000,000 pounds, would be $1,000,000.

Imports of silks from China in 1852 were valued at $1,567,912.

With the same rates of transportation as cattle are carried on the Baltimore and Ohio railroad, it would cost $36 per head to transport cattle, and $40 per head to transport horses and mules, from Fulton to San Francisco. This mode of taking cattle, horses, and mules across the continent would be only partially resorted to, and for those portions where the grazing is not good, say 500 or 600 miles, or about one fourth of the distance. Cattle driven to New Mexico or California are sold for about double the cost in Missouri and Texas, costing about $36 per head and selling for $72 per head.

To transport a barrel of flour from Fulton to San Francisco would cost from $8 to $10 per barrel, or from four to five cents per pound, (about double the cost now paid by sea to San Francisco;) and a barrel of pork from $12 to $15, or from six to seven and a half cents per pound, and the same for provisions generally.

In the war of 1812 the transportation of all supplies cost from 50 cents to $1 per ton per mile from Albany to the frontier, say 300 miles, or from $150 to $300 per ton—the average being $225 per ton—and required from 15 to 30 days for the journey. We would be nearer therefore to our California coast, in time, by from 7 to 20 days, and at less than half the cost, were this railroad built, than we were to our northern frontier in 1812–'14.

The transportation of troops to California by the isthmus route has cost $225 for each commissioned officer and $150 for each enlisted soldier, &c., with 100 pounds of baggage each, except across the isthmus, where 25 pounds are allowed—the excess being paid for at 15 cents per pound. At present the price is $300 for each officer and $150 for each enlisted soldier.

The cost to the railroad of transporting troops from Fulton to San Francisco would be about $60 per man.

The cost to the road for freight will be about $60 per ton. The cost of transporting ordnance and ordnance stores by Cape Horn has been about $40 per ton.

The cost of transporting military stores to the posts of New Mexico from Fort Leavenworth varies from $8 to $14 per 100 pounds, or from $160 to $180 per ton. By the railroad it would cost from Fulton from $24 to $30 per ton. The cost of transporting baggage and subsistence of troops marching from Fort Leavenworth to New Mexico is about $15 per man; the time consumed about three months—the expense of the soldier during that time being from $17 to $20 per month, or $60; the cost of transportation by railroad in three days would be $50, or cost to the road from $24 to $30.

The question as to what portion of the trade between the United States and Europe, on the one side, and the empires of Japan, China, and India, on the other, together with the islands of the Pacific and Indian oceans, and the South American Pacific States, of the trade between our Atlantic and Pacific territories, and of our whale fisheries, amounting probably to $300,000,000 yearly, would be carried by the railroad from the Pacific to the Mississippi, has been so often discussed, that it is not necessary here to enter upon it. The cost of carriage of some articles has been merely touched upon to give an idea of the value of the road for military purposes. The information respecting the former and present cost of transportation of troops and military stores has been obtained from the letter of Major General Jesup, Quartermaster General of the army, to the War Department.

Whether the saving of interest on outlay of capital in trade by shortening the time of passage would be sufficient to divert a large freight business to the Pacific railroad in the most valuable articles of the trade with Asia, those more familiar with commerce than I am can determine.

The length of the road from Fulton to San Francisco may be put down at 2,000 miles; its cost at $90,000,000; its yearly earnings at $17,000,000, independent of any considerations connected with the trade of Asia, the islands of the Pacific, South America, or the whale trade.

The railroads of Massachusetts are 1,280 miles in length; have cost $60,000,000, and earn yearly $7,713,208. The yearly expense of working them is $4,541,468; their net earnings $3,211,198.

If the earnings of the Pacific railroad should be in proportion to the Massachusetts roads for outlay of capital, we should have $13,000,000 instead of $17,000,000.

But, as the equipment of the Pacific road for this business, yielding $17,000,000 yearly, is merely one-fifth that of the Massachusetts roads, the expense of working the road would be nearly in that proportion; but, as we have supposed it to be worked at double the proportionate cost of eastern railroads, (east of the Mississippi,) we have now the proportion of two-fifths, or about one-half the actual cost per mile of working the Massachusetts roads, for the probable cost per mile of working the Pacific railroad; the equipment in the latter case being one-fifth of what it is in the former. And, by this proportion, the yearly expense of working the Pacific railroad would be about $4,000,000, leaving $13,000,000 for the net earnings. This supposes 100,000 passengers yearly to and from California. Should the present number, 50,000, not increase, the yearly earnings of the road, supposing it to carry all, would be, under the suppositions expressed in the preceding page, about $10,000,000, leaving $6,000,000 for net earnings.

1. On the New York railroads, in 1853, the average cost for maintenance of way was—

For passengers	$455	per mile of road.
For freight	323	" "
Total, about	778	" "

2. The average cost of repair of machinery for each passenger carried one mile was .... 2.11 mills.

The average cost of repairs of machinery for each ton of freight carried one mile was .... 2.60 "

3. The average cost of operating the road for each passenger carried one mile was.......... 5.56 mills.

The average cost of operating the road for each ton of freight carried one mile was.......... 9.20 "

4. The average receipts from each passenger carried one mile was.......... 1¾ cents.
5. The average receipts per ton of freight carried one mile was.......... $2\frac{8}{10}$ "

Applying the above results to the Pacific railroad, the work upon which we have supposed to be at the first but one-fifth of that done on these roads, we have—

1. For passenger travel: for maintenance of roadway, if we estimate $500 per mile, it will be, under the circumstances, an estimate largely in excess, and will cover that for a light freight business. This, for 2,000 miles, is....... $1,000,000
2. The average cost for repairs of machinery, and operating the New York roads, for each passenger carried one mile, is, as above, 7.67 mills. As we have estimated the cost on the Pacific railroad at double that at eastern prices, we shall have for cost of carrying 100,000 passengers 2,000 miles......... $3,068,000

Total.......... $4,068,000

The receipts from these passengers we have put down at.......... $15,000,000

Supposing the yearly number of passengers should be only 50,000, we have from this source.......... $7,500,000
For carrying the mails.......... $1,000,000
And for transportation of troops, arms, public stores, &c., and light freight....... $1,500,000

Total.......... $10,000,000

Supposing, then, the cost of maintenance of way, repairs of machinery, and operating the road, to be, as before estimated, for double the number of passengers actually carried, we have for net earnings about $6,000,000.

The cost of carrying freight cannot be estimated at much less than three cents per ton per mile—that adopted in the previous pages.

The yearly cost of maintenance of way for freight on New York roads was $323 per mile.

The cost of repairs of machinery and operating the road for each ton of freight carried one mile, was 12 mills. Estimating the cost on the Pacific railroad at double, we have about 2½ cents for cost per mile per ton for repairs of machinery and operating the road, besides which there is the cost of maintenance of roadway.

At a railroad convention "held in New York, embracing the officers of the four great lines between the Atlantic and the West, a joint report was submitted by the superintendents of the several roads, in which they state that 'experience has proved that the lowest rates at which ordinary freight (in freight trains at a speed of 10 or 12 miles per hour, and in large quantities) can be carried to pay interest and expenses, will average about 2 cents per ton per mile for heavy agricultural products, 3 cents for groceries, and 4 cents for dry goods.' * * * Sufficient information has been elicited from the railroads of this and other States, from the action of conventions, and from other sources of information, to warrant the belief that a considerable portion of the freighting business now done by our railroads yields no profit at the present rates, when due allowance is made for the increase of capital which it requires, for the increased wear and depreciation of the works, and for the occupation of the track to the injury of the other business."—(*Report of the State Engineer, New York, January* 23, 1855.)

It appears probable, from the foregoing, that the net earnings of the road would pay a reasonable interest upon the sum required to build it. Yet, as the business of the road is to be a through business, to be found only at the two extremities, with but little way business, the capital required must be idle an average time equal to half that required for construction, which latter will not probably be less than 10 years, and the interest during that time would add from twenty-five to thirty millions to the capital. If, in consideration of the great national benefits which the construction of the road would confer, the government of the United States could lend its aid to the road so as to relieve it from the payment of interest upon the cost of the road during the time of its construction, it would seem probable from the foregoing that it might be built by private means. Without this much aid from the government, the road will probably never be built.

A donation of land, such as has been generally proposed, will be of little comparative value.

I regret that there is not time to enter a little more into these discussions.

The following extract from the annual report of the railroad corporations in the State of Massachusetts for 1852, giving the length, cost, yearly earnings, expense of working, &c., of the roads in that State, may be found interesting.

Following it is an extract from the annual report of the State engineer and surveyor on the railroads of the State of New York, showing the length, cost, &c., of the roads in that State. I have made these extracts as brief as possible. It will be seen that the estimated cost of the route of the 32d parallel, after every consideration of the unusual circumstances that will produce an increased cost, is about the same per mile as the roads in these States:

Extract from an abstract of "Annual Reports of the Railroad Corporations in the State of Massachusetts," showing totals of the leading statistics of all the roads.

Capital	$56,236,600 00
Capital paid in	46,539,220 34
Cost	60,019,051 77½
Length	1,280.29 miles.
Length of double track	270.33 "
Length of branches	103.68 "
Speed of passenger trains adopted per hour	23.63 "
Speed of freight trains adopted per hour	12.98 "
Earnings	$7,713,208 35
Expense of working	4,541,468 31½
Net earnings	3,211,197 75
Dividends	2,483,545 94
Debt	16,009,095 77
Surplus	1,112,072 95

Extract from the "Annual Report of the State Engineer and Surveyor on the railroads of the State of New York—February, 1854."

The length of all the railroads in operation in the State is	2,432 miles.
The length of railroads laid is about	2,497 "
The length of double track in addition to the above is	664 "
The number of locomotives in use is	586
The number of passenger cars in use is	834
The number of baggage and freight cars in use is	6,895
The number of miles run by passenger trains is about	6,594,963
The number of miles run by freight trains is	4,227,807
Total number of miles run	10,822,770
The whole number of miles travelled by the passengers is about	531,572,298

The whole number of miles each ton of freight was moved, or the number of tons moved one mile, is 246,554,492
The capital stock of which is about.......... $112,038,131 45
The capital stock paid in is about.......... 61,238,829 22
The amount of funded and floating debt is.......... 59,669,478 38
The amount paid for construction and equipment is.......... 117,707,620 58

COMPARISON OF THE ROUTES.

The following table will enable a comparison to be made of the sum of ascents and descents, and the equivalent horizontal distances of the railroads connecting the Atlantic with the Mississippi, with those of the routes examined from the Pacific to the Mississippi. It will be observed, that in proportion to the lengths of the routes, the sums of the ascents and descents are less on the Pacific than on the Atlantic routes:

Roads.	Length in miles.	Elevation of summit above the sea.	Total rise and fall.	Number of miles of horizontal road equivalent in the cost of working the road to the ascents and descents.
Boston route	500	1,440	4,700	89
New York route, (Central)	440	650	2,100	40
New York route, (Erie)	460	1,720	6,500	123
Philadelphia route	340	2,400	5,600	106
Baltimore route	390	2,600 or 2,700	7,000	132
Charleston route	490	1,400	5,000	95
Savannah route	440	1,400	5,000	95

A table will be found at the conclusion of this chapter, giving some of the most important statistics of the several routes; following it, is a statement of the distances of the eastern termini of the routes to certain ports.

The sum of the ascents and descents given for the various routes does not take into consideration those minor undulations which sometimes largely increase the aggregate.

I think it probable that when detailed surveys are made, it will be found that this sum for the route near the 47th parallel will be more increased than those for the other routes, and that the sum for the route near the 32d parallel will be less increased than the others.

The equated lengths corresponding to these sums may give erroneous impressions. If the loads to be habitually carried over the roads are within the power of the engines over the greatest grades proposed, then the sums of ascents and descents really have little meaning or value. The wear and tear of rail and machinery and consumption of fuel would be somewhat greater on the road having the largest sum, but the difference would not be worth taking into account, unless there was an equality in all other respects between the routes.

If there are some grades so steep as to require the division of the loads habitually carried over other portions, the cost of the extra locomotives and of working them over those portions will show the extent of the disadvantage and yearly cost.

So far as any estimate has been made in this report of the amount of work to be done on the roads, these sums of ascents and descents have little practical value, since those portions of the routes have been indicated where it may be considered advisable to use steep natural slopes with extra engines, to expedite the completion of the road and save expensive road-bed preparation. With a full equipment and heavy freight business, the sum of ascents and descents becomes important.

The advantages and disadvantages of the several routes may be briefly recapitulated, as follows:

I. ROUTE NEAR THE FORTY-SEVENTH AND FORTY-NINTH PARALLELS.

The advantages of this route are—its low profile, which is important in relation to climate; its easy grades, and small amount of ascents and descents, both important if the road should be developed to its full working power; the great extension west of the prairie lands; in the supplies of timber over the western half of the route; the facilities which the Columbia river and its tributaries, and the Missouri, will afford to the construction of the road; in the short distance from the Mississippi to a seaport of the Pacific, (1,864 miles to Vancouver;) in the western terminus of the road on Puget Sound being nearer to the ports of Asia than the termini of the other routes; in the proximity of the eastern terminus to Lake Superior, from which a continuous navigation for seagoing vessels extends to the Atlantic ocean; and in the existence of coal on Puget Sound.

Its disadvantages are—the difficult and costly construction, including a long tunnel, through a mountain region of 550 miles, (comprising 90 miles on the Columbia river;) the delay in construction, and the liabilities of the road to great injury and destruction through a large part of this region from the high freshets on the Bitter Root, Flathead, Clark's fork, and Columbia rivers; in the severe and long winters on the prairies east of the Rocky mountains, and on the greater portion of the route suspending labor in the open air for such a large part of the year, and impeding the working of the road when built; in the distance of its western terminus from that port, (San Francisco,) which will give the only large travel, and business which may be counted upon with certainty; and, finally, its proximity throughout to the frontier of a powerful foreign sovereignty.

II. ROUTE NEAR THE FORTY-FIRST AND FORTY-SECOND PARALLELS.

Its advantages are—comparatively cheap construction, due to the favorable features of the Rocky mountain system in this latitude, and those of the Great Basin, both of which result in a low sum of ascents and descents, which would be a favorable element, should the full working power of the road be developed; in the mountains being passed without tunnels; the probability of its possessing extensive coal-fields in the middle of the route; and in the aid which its construction would receive from the population of Utah.

Its disadvantages are—the very difficult and costly construction along the Sacramento river for 136 miles; the construction through the cañon of the Timpanogos; the costly construction through the Black Hills to the South Pass, for nearly 300 miles, (the route by the Cheyenne Pass apparently giving an equally costly road;) in the great elevation of the summits in the Rocky mountain system; and in the great elevation of its plain, and the long and severe winters on it, and the prairies east of the Rocky mountains, suspending labor for several months of the year, and impeding the working of the road when completed, by their severity, and the snows on the prairies and in the mountain ravines and gorges.

III. ROUTE NEAR THE THIRTY-EIGHTH AND THIRTY-NINTH PARALLELS.

No peculiar advantage was developed in the exploration of this route, except the probability of the existence or extensive coal-fields in the valleys of the Grand and Green rivers.

The extraordinary difficulties to be overcome from the Coo-che-to-pa Pass to the Great Basin (500 miles) render the route impracticable. The elevations of the passes in the Rocky mountains are the greatest found, being 9,200 and 10,000 feet, the latter, the Coo-che-to-pa Pass, requiring a tunnel at an elevation of 9,500 feet.

IV. ROUTE NEAR THE THIRTY-FIFTH PARALLEL.

The advantages of this route consist in water and fuel being generally less scanty than on the others, excepting that of the 47th and 49th parellels; in a better supply of timber west of the Rio Grande; in the greater mildness of the winter than on the routes north of it; in the temperate character of the summer over nearly the whole route; in no tunnels being required on the Rocky mountain passes, and none on the route to San Francisco by the Tah-ee-chay-pah Pass; in the probability of the existence of coal-fields in the middle of the route; and in the assistance that the population of New Mexico and the Mexican provinces of Chihuahua and Sonora may give in constructing and supporting the road.

The disadvantages are—its greater length from the Mississippi to the Pacific than the route south of it; the apparently rough and broken character of the country through which much of it lies; its much greater cost, and the greater number of ascents and descents, the sum of which is the greatest of the four routes, and which would become seriously objectionable should the full working power of the road be developed.

V. ROUTE NEAR THE THIRTY-SECOND PARALLEL.

Its advantages are—the short distance from the eastern terminus to a Pacific port (1,618 miles;) the small cost of the road, it being to a Pacific port less than two thirds of the cost of the cheapest of the other routes, and to San Francisco $20,000,000 less than the least of the others, (the cheapness of construction being due to the location of the route upon more than 1,000 miles of table-lands and plains;) in the open and otherwise favorable features of the mountain passes; the lowness of their summits; in their natural slopes admitting of use without extensive and costly preparation; in the mild winters and temperate summers of all the route except that portion of the Gila and Colorado desert where, for 350 miles, labor in the open air must be suspended for three months of the year; in there being no reason to apprehend difficulties, impediments, delays, and dangers from snow and ice; in the coal-fields of the Brazos; and in the aid that the population of New Mexico and the provinces of Chihuahua and Sonora may give in constructing and supporting the road.

Its disadvantages are—the cost of construction of a portion between the Pecos and Rio Grande; the circuitous route to San Francisco from the plains of Los Angelos, which, unless further explorations determine a more direct route, requires a second crossing of the coast range, and a passage through the Sierra Nevada; in the sum of ascents and descents being the next largest after that of the 35th parallel, the extent of which objection depends upon the amount of business to be done on the road; and, finally, in the scanty supply of water and fuel on the route.

Table showing the lengths, sums of ascents and descents, equated lengths, cost, &c., of the several routes explored for a railroad from the Mississippi to the Pacific. (For the grades, see the profiles accompanying the report.)

	Distance in straight line.	Distance by proposed railroad route.	Sum of ascents and descents.	Length of level route of equal working expense.	Comparative cost of different routes.	Number of miles of route through arable land.	No. of miles of route through lands generally uncultivable, arable soil being found in small areas.	No. of square miles of sums of areas of largest bodies of arable land in uncultivable region.	No. of miles at an elevation above 0, and less than 1,000 feet.	No. of miles at an elevation greater than 1,000 and less than 2,000 feet.	2,000 and 3,000.	3,000 and 4,000.	4,000 and 5,000.	5,000 and 6,000.	6,000 and 7,000.	7,000 and 8,000.	8,000 and 9,000.	9,000 and 10,000.	Summit of the highest pass on the route.	
	Miles.	*Miles.*	*Feet.*	*Miles.*															*Feet.*	
Route near 47th and 49th parallels—																				
Route from St. Paul to Seattle.	1,410	2,025	19,100	2,387	a$140,871,000	535	1,490	b 1,000	631	580	720	130	97	28	...	...	..	..	6,044	Tunnel at elevat'n of 5,219 feet.
Route from St. Paul to Vancouver.	1,455	1,864	18,100	2,207	a 130,781,000	374	1,490	b 1,000	470	580	720	130	97	28	...	...	..	..	6,044	Tunnel at elevat'n of 5,219 feet.
Route near 41° and 42°, via South Pass from Council Bluffs to Benicia.	1,410	2,032	29,120	2,583	116,095,000	632	1,400	b 1,100	180	170	210	160	580	285	270	107	20	..	8,373	
c 38th and 39th—Westport to San Francisco by the Coo-che-to-pa and Tah-ee-chay-pah Passes.	1,740	2,080	49,986	3,125	....	620	1,460	b 1,100	340	276	165	348	466	170	60	155	80	20	10,032	Tunnel at elevat'n of 9,540 feet.
38th and 39th—Westport to San Francisco by the Coo-che-to-pa and Madelin Passes.	1,740	2,290	56,514	3,360	....	670	1,620	1,100	275	308	190	143	725	284	110	155	80	20	10,032	Tunnel at elevat'n of 9,540 feet.
35th—Fort Smith to San Pedro.	1,360	1,892	48,812	2,816	d 169,210,265	416	1,476	2,300	305	347	260	185	160	305	235	95	..	..	7,472	
35th—Fort Smith to San Francisco.	......	2,174	50,670	3,137	....	644	1,530	2,300	....	....	....	....	...	...	...	...	..	..	......	
32d—Fulton to San Pedro.....	1,400	1,618	32,784	2,239	68,970,000	408	1,210	2,300	485	300	100	170	503	60	...	...	..	..	5,717	
Fulton to San Francisco.	1,620	2,039	42,008	2,834	93,120,000	759	1,280	2,300	700	410	160	205	504	60	...	...	..	..	5,717	

a These are the estimates of the office, those of Gov. Stevens having been brought to the same standard of increased cost as the other routes, and his equipment reduced to that of the other routes. His estimates were $117,121,000 and $110,091,000.

b These sums do not include the areas of cultivable soil as far west as the Cascade and Sierra Nevada mountains.

c Supposing the route to be a straight line, with uniform descent from the Un-kuk-oo-ap mountains (near Sevier river) to the entrance of the Tah-ee-chay-pah Pass—the most favorable supposition.

d This estimate for the route near the 35th parallel is thought to be largely in excess.

The sum of the minor undulations (not included in the sum of ascents and descents here given) will probably be greater for the route of the 47th parallel than for the other routes; that for the route near the 32d parallel will probably be the least of all.

With the amount of work estimated for the roads in this report, the equated lengths corresponding to the sum of ascents and descents has but little practical value. With a full equipment and heavy freight business, the sum of ascents and descents becomes important.

Distances of the eastern termini of the several Pacific Railroad routes to the Mississippi river, Boston, New York, Charleston, and New Orleans, by railroad built, building, and projected, as measured on the "Railroad maps."

Route	Destination	Miles.
1. St. Paul	to Boston	1,316
	to New York	1,190
	to Charleston	1,193
	to New Orleans	1,198
2. Council Bluffs	to Rock Island (Miss. river)	267
	to Boston	1,374
	to New York	1,252
	to Charleston	1,195
	to New Orleans	1,075
3. Westport, mouth of Kansas, (near Fort Leavenworth)	to St. Louis, (Miss. river)	245
	to Boston	1,415
	to New York	1,220
	to Charleston	1,045
	to New Orleans	875
4. Fort Smith, on the Arkansas,	to Memphis, (Miss. river)	270
	to Boston	1,540
	to New York	1,345
	to Charleston	960
	to New Orleans	655
5. Fulton	to Gaines, (Miss. river)	150
	to Boston	1,530
	to New York	1,335
	to Charleston	950
	to New Orleans	402

CHAPTER VI.

NOTES BY LIEUTENANT G. K. WARREN, TOPOGRAPHICAL ENGINEERS, ON THE ROUTE FROM INDEPENDENCE TO SANTA FE, AND FROM INDIANOLA, VIA SAN ANTONIO, TO EL PASO.—(Compiled from the Reports of Lieut. Col. JOHNSTON, Top. Engrs., Lieut. SMITH, Top. Engrs., Capt. S. G. FRENCH, 3d Regt. Arty., and others.)

It will be seen from the results of the late explorations, that there are two practicable passes by which to reach, from the east, the New Mexican population of the Rio Grande valley, viz: by the passes near Santa Fé and by El Paso. As regards grade, a practicable route exists for connecting the former of these passes with Independence and St. Louis, (by the Cimarron route,) and probably a practical connexion of El Paso with San Antonio, or a part of the Gulf of Mexico.

The following notes relate to these two routes:

1st. *Route from Independence to Santa Fé.*—From Independence, Missouri, in latitude 39° 7′, longitude 94° 26′, to Santa Fé, in latitude 35° 41′, longitude 106° 01′, was barometrically surveyed by Dr. Wizlizenus in 1846, and the following notes are mainly from his report.

It is very direct, and lies mostly on a table-land gradually ascending towards the west, where little difficulty need be apprehended in obtaining easy grades. Its length is 765 miles.

From Independence to Council Grove, a distance of 143 miles, the route passes through a well-watered fertile prairie, which resembles the sea in its gentle undulations. There is sufficient wood along the water-courses to supply the railroad with ties and fuel. Westward the country undergoes a change, becoming gradually more sandy and barren, until we reach the Arkansas, a distance of about 200 miles. It still preserves its wave-like character, and can only be settled by a pastoral people.

The Arkansas is broad and shallow, with a sandy bottom. It has low bluffs or none at all. It is sometimes bordered with cotton-wood, but is generally quite bare. From this uninviting river to the lower springs of the Cimarron, a distance of 66 miles, the route lies over a barren, level desert, elevated 3,000 feet above the sea. It is scantily supplied with parched buffalo-grass; but is entirely without water, wood, or even buffalo-chips, the usual fuel in such inhospitable regions.

The lower springs of the Cimarron form a little green oasis with running water. From this point to Cold Spring, a distance of 80 miles, the desert character of the country continues. Water is sometimes found in the Cimarron river; but often it can only be obtained by digging in its dry and sandy bed. The want of it has often occasioned much loss and suffering in this barren wilderness.

From Cold Spring to the Canadian river, a distance of 110 miles, the route approaches and skirts a spur of the Raton mountains. Its character rapidly improves. The mountains are covered with cedar and pine forests, furnishing an ample supply for railroad purposes. The valley of the Canadian is fertile, and well adapted to settlements.

From this point to Galinas, a distance of 60 miles, the trail passes over an elevated plain nearly surrounded by mountains. The valleys of the streams are fertile. Water is abundant, and the mountains are thickly wooded with pine.

From Galinas, Dr. Wizlizenus says, "we shall now travel mostly in narrow valleys, and through mountain passes surrounded by high precipitous rocks." As he did not survey the route for a railroad, his information is not sufficiently definite to determine whether it is practicable for this purpose. Near this point it should, therefore, be considered as joining that of Lieutenant Whipple.

2. *From Indianola, via San Antonio, to El Paso.*—A route for a railroad has been surveyed and located between Indianola and San Antonio. It crosses the Guadalupe river at Victoria, about 30 miles from Indianola. Thence to San Antonio is about 100 miles.

A route was surveyed, barometrically, from San Antonio to Frontera by the Mexican boundary commission, and the profile was furnished to the Pacific railroad office, by Brevet Major Emory, of the topographical engineers, the distances being taken from the report of Colonel Johnston, topographical engineers. This profile gives the elevations along the route travelled, where the object was more to find good pasturage and water for the animals than to obtain easy grades. It, therefore, is only valuable as showing the general elevation of the country.

From San Antonio, the travelled road keeps along the foot of the hills, near the parallel of 29° 20′, as far west as the San Pedro or Devil's river, longitude 101°. It then ascends that stream 60 miles, and crosses over to the Pecos, and ascends this to the parallel of 31° north. It then proceeds west over the plains to El Paso, crossing the mountainous belt of country forming the continuation of the Guadalupe mountains on the north, the greatest elevation attained being 5,766 feet in the Wild Rose Pass of the Diabolo mountains.

Colonel Johnston undertook to explore a route north of this pass, and more directly west, but found it impracticable. Lieutenant Garrard, under orders from Captain Pope, explored this range about 30 miles south of the Guadalupe Pass without finding one more practicable; so there now remains but about 40 miles of these mountains unexplored.

There would probably be no difficulty of grade in continuing up the Pecos to the mouth of Delaware creek, and connecting with the route surveyed by Captain Pope in 1854, through the Guadalupe and Hueco mountains. This latter is usually known as the upper or northern, the former as the lower or southern El Paso routes. Distance from Indianola to Fort Fillmore, by the upper road, 820 miles; by the lower, 840 miles.

The lower route was first explored by W. H. C. Whiting, Corps of Engineers, and Lieutenant W. F. Smith, topographical engineers, in 1849; and subsequently surveyed by Colonel Johnston, who was followed by Captain S. G. French, of the quartermaster's department, in charge of a large train.

The upper route was first explored by Lieutenant Bryan in 1849, afterwards by Captain Marcy; was surveyed by Colonel Johnston in 1849, and again surveyed by Captain Pope in 1854, who added to our previous knowledge by giving us a profile. That route from the mouth of Delaware creek to El Paso forms part of the railroad route near the 32d parallel.

The following notes concerning the lower route are taken mainly from the report of Captain French, the distances being from Colonel Johnston's report:

From San Antonio to Rio San Felipe, 160 miles, most of the soil is excellent for agriculture or grazing. Wood is abundant on the banks of the streams. The road through this extent crosses numerous streams, some of which when swollen by rains are "large rivers." There is, however, sometimes a deficiency of water, particularly on the Rio Seco and Rio Frio. Bituminous coal is said to exist in abundance on the Nueces, 90 miles from San Antonio.

After leaving the San Felipe, a marked change takes place in the face of the country. Before reaching it, in the vicinity of 100° meridian, the surface becomes more rolling and hilly, and less covered with trees; and by the time we reach the San Pedro, on the 101st meridian, it is nearly barren. The valley of the San Pedro varies from a quarter to half a mile in width, and, owing to its vertical sides, it is difficult to approach. Much of the way it is very rough, and the road along it frequently takes the bed of the stream, and is in places submerged by the autumn freshets at least 20 feet. The travelled route usually avoids the lower part of the valley, keeping to the west of it.

After leaving the San Pedro, the first reliable water is 40 miles distant, at Howard's spring,

271 miles from San Antonio. The next at Live Oak creek, 304 miles from San Antonio. Afte crossing this creek the route follows it to the Pecos, and up this to the crossing. This portion of the Pecos is "narrow and deep, extremely crooked in its course, and rapid in its current. Its waters are turbid and bitter." * * * "Its banks are steep, and of clay. In a course of two hundred and forty (240) miles there are but few places where an animal can approach them for water with safety. Not a tree or bush marks its course."

The road crosses the Pecos 348 miles from San Antonio. It then proceeds west to the Escondido springs, 27 miles; thence to Comanche springs, 19 miles—(clouds of suffocating dust accompanied the passage of the train;) thence to Leon springs, 10 miles; thence to the Limpid, 37 miles. The country from the Pecos to this point, 93 miles, is exceedingly sterile, and, except a little cane and coarse grass about the springs and the mezquite, is barren; but it is favorable for grades. At the Limpid we enter the region of the Diabolo mountains, probably a continuation of the Guadalupe range. The country is beautiful, and the mountains in August were covered with green grass to their summits. Pine is found on them. The pass is called the Wild Rose Pass.

These mountains do not form a single continuous ridge, but are made up of single conical peaks, intersecting each other so as to form "an impassable barrier" had not some convulsion of nature seemed partly to have opened the pass and cañon through which the road runs. The cañon is deep and narrow, and in some places not more than 200 yards wide. The last encampment on the plain to the east is at the Painted Camp, 463 miles from San Antonio. We leave the mountains about 40 miles farther on and come upon an elevated plain with water in very limited quantities. Over this plain the road passes for 60 miles to Eagle springs. From Eagle springs the route leads by a cañon through the mountains on the left, and reaches the Rio Grande in a distance of 31 miles; thence to Fort Fillmore, 119 miles; making a total distance from San Antonio of 710 miles, and from Indianola 840 miles.

No reliable practical result could be obtained by the application of the equation of grade to the ascents and descents on this route according to the profile we have.

The elevations are: at Indianola, 0 feet; at San Antonio, about 700 feet; at leaving of Pecos, 1,900 feet; at summit of Wild Rose Pass, 5,766 feet; at Van Horner's well, 4,146 feet; on the mountains to the west, 4,714 feet; at first reaching the Rio Grande, 3,536 feet; at Fort Fillmore, 3,938 feet. Some of the grades are, for short distances, as high as 400 to 500 feet per mile, but could, no doubt, by proper location, be reduced to practicable ones. No wood could be relied on for railroad purposes from the San Felipe to the Diabolo mountains, a distance of 330 miles; probably none to the west of these mountains.

Water for working parties and for the use of the locomotives could probably be obtained as easy as on corresponding portions of the route of the 32d parallel.

MEMORANDA ON RAILWAYS,

PREPARED

OFFICE OF PACIFIC RAILROAD SURVEYS;

BY

CAPT. GEO. B. McCLELLAN,
CORPS OF ENGINEERS,

UNDER INSTRUCTIONS FROM

HON. JEFFERSON DAVIS, SECRETARY OF WAR.

MEMORANDA ON RAILWAYS.

WASHINGTON, D. C., *November* 21, 1854.

SIR: I have the honor to submit the accompanying memoranda upon various practical points connected with the construction, &c., of railways.

For the information therein contained I am chiefly indebted to Col. C. Crozet, Messrs. W. Raymond Lee, William P. Parrot, J. Edgar Thompson, and William Parker, civil engineers, who most kindly afforded me all the assistance I asked.

The article on tunnels is taken principally from a paper by Mr. W. L. Dearborn, civil engineer.

I am, sir, very respectfully, your obedient servant,

GEO. B. McCLELLAN,
Lieutenant Engineers and Brevet Captain.

Hon. JEFFERSON DAVIS,
Secretary of War.

GRADIENTS.

The following gradients are now, or have been, in use on American railways:

During the construction of the *Baltimore and Ohio* railroad a gradient of 528 was used on a temporary track, en boyau, merely to transport small loads of iron, &c. On the *Virginia Central* road the trains pass every day over a gradient of 275 feet—length two miles. On a part of this are curves of 300 feet radius (19° 6′) on a grade of 238 feet; 40 tons have been carried up this by a 30-ton engine on six drivers, with the utmost ease. Brakes of a peculiar construction are used, and found to answer well. On the "Virginia Central" the trains ascend at a velocity of about seven miles per hour, and descend at an average velocity of about four miles. In descending the steam is cut off and the wheels of the engine allowed to revolve, the brakes on the cars being "hard down." Reversed curves are frequent and sharp. On the *Baltimore and Ohio* road are grades of 116 feet for 17 miles. Auxiliary power is here employed, the trains being divided, and running up at the rate of 15 miles per hour. The trains descend these grades with a velocity of 25 miles under perfect control.

On the *Pennsylvania Central* road there are gradients of 95 feet for 9¾ miles; where curves occur the grade is reduced at the rate of 0.025 per 100 feet per degree of curvature. Passenger trains ascend this grade with a velocity of 24 miles per hour, and descend at 20 miles per hour. The ascent, when there are more than three cars, is effected by the aid of an additional engine. The working load of the heavy freight engines (weighing 65,000 pounds, and on eight drivers) on the 95-feet gradient is 125 tons net, or about 208 tons, including tender and cars. Over the 53-feet grades on this road (Pennsylvania Central) the general load of the engines (55,000 pounds, on six drivers) is 150 tons net, or about 250 tons, including tender and cars. On the *Massachusetts Western* road are grades of 83 feet for 1½ mile. Engines of 20 tons draw 100 tons over this grade. Passenger trains run up at about 18 miles per hour without auxiliary power. The average amount of wood consumed and cost of haulage, on the *whole* road, are no greater than upon other Massachusetts roads of lighter grades.

It is the opinion of many able railway engineers that, on a permanent track, grades of 200 feet, and even of 250 feet, may be advantageously overcome by locomotive power; it being clearly understood that such grades are to be resorted to only in cases of absolute necessity—economy in working the road rendering low gradients very desirable.

The accompanying formulæ and their applications show what work is to be expected from any given engine over given grades, and make the loss of economy in any particular case a question of easy solution.

It is evidently the fact that there is at present a strong tendency to use much higher grades than were formerly considered practicable or advisable. Even in England and on the "Continent," the American system of cheap roads, with high grades, to avoid the great expense of long tunnels, deep cuts, and high embankments, appears to be, to a certain extent, rapidly rising in repute.

The use of *inclined planes* with *stationary* power, (within the limits before mentioned,) may, as a general rule, be considered obsolete, except in cases similar to that of the Pennsylvania Central road, where the amount of traffic is becoming so great as to require more than a double or even triple track; in this case it has been proposed to pass the *surplus freight* over the mountains by means of stationary power, reserving the locomotive power for passengers and freight requiring rapid transportation.

Planes for stationary power should not exceed one mile in length. The number required to overcome any given ascent will depend more upon the elevation to be surmounted than the *length* of the ascent.

The opinion has been expressed by one of the most reliable railway engineers in the country, that where the gradient does not exceed 132 feet per mile, locomotive is cheaper than stationary power, without reference to the element of the first cost of grading for the two plans of operating the road; also, that the difficulty and danger in descending high grades is more important in determining their inclination than the resistance in their ascent.

In estimating the loss of economy of power in overcoming high gradients, the comparison should be made between the loads *habitually* drawn over the *more favorable* portions of the road, and the *maximum* load that *can be* drawn over the gradient in question.

FORMULÆ.

To obtain the maximum load due any engine of given weight, upon a given grade, and to obtain the maximum grade up which an engine of given weight can draw a given load:

$$\left.\begin{array}{l}(1)\ x = \dfrac{0.2A}{0.4242f + 8} \\[2ex] (2)\ f = \dfrac{0.2A - 8x}{0.4242\,x}\end{array}\right\}\ \text{The engine and rail being in good order.}$$

$$\left.\begin{array}{l}(3)\ x = \dfrac{0.143A}{0.4242f + 8} \\[2ex] (4)\ f = \dfrac{0.143A - 8x}{0.4242\,x}\end{array}\right\}\ \text{The rail being in bad order, slippery, greasy, \&c.}$$

In these formulæ, A represents the adhesive weight of the engine; that is to say, the portion of the weight of the engine actually supported by the drivers; it is expressed in pounds. In engines with four drivers about 0.6 of the whole weight of the engine rests upon the drivers, sometimes as high as 0.67; 0.64 may be taken as the average. With six drivers the whole weight of the engine will rest upon them, and, consequently, be the value of "A."

"f" is the grade in feet per mile.

"x" is the load drawn, including tender, and is expressed in tons.

Formulæ (2) and (4) are simply deductions by transposition from (1) and (3.)

In formulæ (1) and (3) the numerator expresses the *effective* adhesive weight; that is to say, it expresses the portion of the total adhesive weight which is found by experiment to be really effective in drawing a load in certain states of the rail. Now, since we know by experiment that on a level a force of eight pounds is necessary to draw one ton, if we divide the effective adhesive weight (expressed in pounds) by 8, the quotient will be the load due that effective adhesive weight, and formula (1) will read $x = \frac{0.2\,A}{8}$.

On a grade we know that, in addition to the force necessary to overcome the friction, it is also necessary to apply further power to counteract the effect of gravity.

Taking a load of one ton, and calling "f" the height of the plane, "l" the *length*, (for the value of which we may, in the slight inclinations given railway grades, substitute the value of the *base* of the plane, without appreciable error,) we have for the tendency of one ton to move down the plane $\frac{2240\ x\ f}{l}$, or substituting for l, 5280, the number of feet in a mile $\frac{2240\ x\ f}{5280} = 0.4242 f$, "$f$" being the height in feet of a plane whose base is one mile long.

This expression (0.4242 f) is, then, the measure of the force required to prevent one ton from sliding down the plane, and must be added to the force necessary to overcome the friction of a ton on a level in order to obtain the force required to keep one ton in motion up a grade.

Dividing, then, by this sum ($0.4242 f + 8$) the disposable power of the engine (0.2 A,) we have the number of tons that the engine can draw up any given grade.

Engines usually weigh from 20 to 24 tons; some as much as 30 tons: it is considered desirable to reduce the weight of engines as much as possible, in order to diminish the wear and tear of the rails.

Most engines now run with four drivers—the front of the engine resting upon a truck with eight small wheels; some engines, particularly those intended for heavy grades, are placed upon six wheels, all drivers, in order to increase the effective adhesive weight. The objection to multiplying the number of drivers consists in the increased number of joints, &c., with the consequent increase of friction and loss of power.

A common 8-wheel tender weighs, empty	14,000	lbs.
Water for 25 miles, (12,000 gallons at 8.35 lbs. per gallon)	10,437	"
Wood, (1.44 cord, at 3,180 lbs. per cord)	4,579	"
4 passenger cars, for 50 passengers each, at 12,000 lbs. each	48,000	"
2 baggage cars, at 16,000 lbs.	32,000	"
200 passengers, at 150 lbs. each	30,000	"
Baggage, at 100 lbs. each passenger	20,000	"
Add for contingencies	12,224	"
Total weight of train of 200 passengers	171,240	"

or 76 tons.

We will now take a 20-ton engine on four drivers and apply the formula.

The total adhesive weight will be about	28,600	lbs.
Its maximum load on a level, over a good track	715	tons.
Its maximum load on a level, over a track in bad condition, slippery, &c.	511	"
By formula (2) we have for the same engine the maximum grade up which it can draw the train of 200 passengers, as given in detail above	159¾	feet.
By formula (4) we have for same data a maximum grade of	109	"

By formula (1) we have the maximum load of same engine up a grade of 150 feet	79	tons.
By formula (3) for same data we have a maximum load of	56$\frac{3}{4}$	“
For a 20-ton engine on six drivers:		
The total adhesive weight will now be	44,800	lbs.
By formula (2) we have the maximum grade up which it can draw a load of 76 tons	261	feet.
By formula (4) a maximum grade of	181	“
By formula (1) with same data we have for a grade of 150 feet a maximum load of	124	tons.
By formula (3) with same data, a maximum load of	89	“
For a 22-ton engine on four drivers:		
The total adhesive weight is about	31,500	lbs.
By formula (1) maximum load on level	787$\frac{1}{2}$	tons.
By formula (3) maximum load on level	563	“
By formula (2) the maximum grade up which it can draw a load of 76 tons is	178	feet.
By formula (4) it is	122	“
By formnla (1) the maximum load that this engine can draw up a 150 feet grade is	87	tons.
By formula (3) it is	62$\frac{1}{2}$	“
For a 22-ton engine on six drivers:		
The total adhesive weight is	49,280	lbs.
By formula (1) the maximum load on a level is	1,232	tons.
By formula (2) the maximum grade up which it can draw a load of 76 tons is	289	feet.
By formula (4) the maximum grade for same load is	201	“
By formula (1) the maximum load this engine can daw up a grade of 150 feet is	137	tons.
By formula (3) the maximum load for 150 feet grade is	98	“
For a 24-ton engine on four drivers:		
The total adhesive weight is	34,406	lbs.
By formula (1) the maximum load on a level is	860	tons.
By formula (3) the maximum load on a level is	615	“
By formula (2) the maximum grade up which this engine can draw a load of 76 tons is	196	feet.
By formula (4) the maximum grade for 76 tons is	135	“
By formula (1) the maximum load this engine can draw up a grade of 150 feet is	95	tons.
By formula (3) the maximum load for same grade (150 feet) is	68$\frac{1}{3}$	“
For a 24-ton engine on six drivers:		
The total adhesive weight is	53,760	lbs.
By formula (2) the maximum grade up which this engine can draw a load of 76 tons is	317	feet.
By formula (4) the maximum grade for same load is	221	“
By formula (1) the maximum load this engine can draw up a grade of 150 feet is	149	tons.
By formula (3) the maximum load up same grade is	106$\frac{1}{2}$	“
By formula (1) the maximum load this engine can draw up a 200-feet grade is.	115$\frac{1}{2}$	“
By formula (3) the maximum load up same grade is	83	“
By formula (1) the maximum load up 275 feet grade is	86$\frac{3}{4}$	“
By formula (3) the maximum load up same grade is	62	“
For a 30-ton engine on four drivers:		
The total adhesive weight is	43,008	lbs.
By formula (1) the maximum load on a level is	1,075	tons.

By formula (3) the maximum load on a level is	770	tons.
By formula (2) the maximum grade for load of 76 tons is	250	feet.
By formula (4) the maximum grade for 76 tons is	173	"
By formula (1) the maximum load up a grade of 150 feet is	119½	tons.
By formula (3) the maximum load for same grade is	85	"
By formula (1) the maximum load on a 200-feet grade is	93½	"
By formula (3) the maximum load on a 200-feet grade is	67	"
For a 30-ton engine on six drivers:		
The total adhesive weight is	67,200	lbs.
By formula (1) the maximum load on a level is	1,680	tons.
By formula (2) the maximum grade up which this engine can draw a load of 76 tons is	401	feet.
By formula (4) the maximum grade for the same load is	281	"
By formula (1) the maximum load this engine can draw up a grade of 150 feet is.	186	tons.
By formula (3) the maximum load for same grade is	133½	"
By formula (1) the maximum load for grade of 200 feet is	146	"
By formula (3) the maximum load for the same grade is	104½	"

CURVES.

On the Virginia Central road there are curves of 300 feet radius on a grade of 328 feet per mile.

On a level, trains run on curves of 300 feet radius at a velocity of 20 miles per hour.

A radius of 150 feet, and even less, is practicable; but in such cases the velocity of the train must be greatly diminished.

There are various formulæ for the calculation of the resistance on curves, but the simple inspection of a wheel that has been some little time in use will show the inaccuracy of the results. The formulæ are based upon the supposition that the surface of the tire is conical; this shape is soon destroyed by what is called the channeling of the wheel.

The resistances in question can probably be determined only by the result of many experiments with a dynanometer.

On the Pennsylvania Central road the grade is reduced on curves at the rate of 0.025 per 100 feet per degree of curvature.

CONSTRUCTION.

To lay the rails.—The road-bed being prepared, cross-ties placed, and iron distributed, a party of six men will lay half a mile of track per day.

The cross-ties should be prepared with corrosive sublimate; the sulphurets do not answer a good purpose. 20,000 spruce cross-ties were prepared in this way, and laid in 1840; they are now perfectly sound, although the natural duration of the wood is but *five* years. Cross-ties average about twenty-five cents each.

Shallow excavations may be covered with workmen. In the case of *deep excavations*, where the earth cannot be removed laterally, sections of one-half mile, worked from both ends, are usually most advantageous; this distance, however, will depend chiefly upon the relation between the established gradients and the natural surface of the ground. The end of a cut composed of loose gravel or sand will accommodate a force capable of moving 15 to 20,000 yards in a month. In one case, 26,000 cubic yards of sand were moved in that time, the average haul being three-quarters of a mile.

Long, deep cuts of gravel, sand, or similar deposite, can be opened, (working two levels at each end,) with an average haul of one mile, at the rate of 15,000 to 25,000 cubic yards in 26 days.

Ordinary gravel can be dug, thrown into a car, and moved an average haul of 1,000 feet for

12 cents to 14 cents per cubic yard; for every additional 100 feet add a third of a cent. One man shovels into a car 15 yards to 18 yards per day.

STATEMENT OF WEIGHTS, COST, &C.

Locomotives weigh from 12 tons to 30 tons, generally from 20 tons to 24 tons. They cost from $5,000 to $8,500, freight-engines being rather more expensive than passenger-engines. This includes the cost of an ordinary eight-wheel tender.

A tender on sixteen wheels, carrying about 2,500 gallons of water, will weigh about 28,000 pounds empty.

A tender on eight wheels, of 1,250 to 1,500 gallons capacity, weighs 14,000 pounds empty.

A tank on eight wheels, holding 3,000 gallons water, will weigh less than an eight-wheel tender, and cost $650.

A tank on six wheels, of 2,500 gallons capacity, costs $550.

Baggage-cars generally weigh 16,000 pounds, and cost $1,200.

Passenger-cars for 50 passengers weigh 12,000 pounds, and cost $2,000.

Passenger-cars for 75 passengers weigh 14,000 pounds, and cost $2,500.

Freight-cars on eight wheels weigh 14,000 pounds, cost $650, and are of about eight tons to ten tons capacity.

Passengers are usually allowed from 50 pounds to 80 pounds of baggage each.

The weight of passengers may be estimated at 150 pounds each.

On the New England roads the average cost of the transportation of freight is 1½ cent per ton per mile.

The transportation of passengers costs about 1½ cent each per mile.

This is the average of the actual running cost, and does not cover depreciation of the road; to provide for this, and to secure a fair profit, it is generally stated that the freights and fares charged must be double the amounts given above.

In Massachusetts the average cost of *repairing locomotives* is (per annum) 6½ cents per mile run. For repairing tracks, exclusive of iron renewals, 11½ cents.

The average durability of iron in Massachusetts is not more than ten years. Old rails are re-rolled at a cost of $25 per ton; the ends may be rewelded for $5 per ton. In this connexion it may be remarked that the ends of the rails first give way, as a general rule; they are repaired by cutting off the injured part of the upper flange and welding on a piece of "Swedes" bar-iron. Small injuries in the middle part of the rail may be repaired, economically, in the same manner.

The average waste of steam while engines are at rest, stopping on the road, steaming up, &c., is one-third of the whole amount generated.

In Massachusetts, engines usually run with a pressure of 100 pounds in the boiler. The strength of the boiler is from 350 to 500 pounds.

Rails are now rolled from 18 feet to 23 feet in length; on the New England roads they average about 60 pounds to the yard; 90 pounds to the yard is recommended by many engineers as the proper weight for the Pacific railway.

A cast-iron wheel of the ordinary size will safely bear a weight of 1½ ton.

BRIDGES.

The railway wooden-truss bridges cost from $30 to $35 per running foot.

200 feet has been found to be about the maximum length that it can safely have; many engineers prefer reducing the spans to 50 feet.

Iron bridges have been successfully and economically used on some railways, and cost $40 per foot.

Many engineers prefer, whenever it is possible, using culverts and high embankments to the employment of bridges, as being the safer and more economical plan. This course has been adopted with embankments as high as 160 feet.

WATER AND FUEL.

The capacity and weight of tenders and tanks will be found on page 120.

To supply a passenger train, of 200 passengers, for 25 miles, under ordinary circumstances of track, &c., there will be required, of—

Water	1,250 gallons.
Wood (such as pine)	1.44 cord.
Or of coal (anthracite)	0.64 ton.
Or of coke	0.62 ton.

To supply same train 100 miles—

Water	5,000 gallons.
Wood	5.76 cords.
Or coal (anthracite)	2.56 tons.
Or coke	2.48 tons.

The quantity of anthracite as given above is on the supposition that the train makes no long stops; in that case, the amount would have to be increased.

The average of six trips on the *Boston and Maine* railway gives the following result:

A load of 170.5 tons (weight of cars and freight, exclusive of engine and tender, in tons of 2,000 pounds) was drawn 74 miles, at a velocity of 14.5 miles per hour, with an expenditure of 4,654.5 pounds of anthracite, and 3,348 gallons of water.

The average of eight trips gave as a result that 10.59 pounds of anthracite evaporate 7.48 gallons of water, or 0.78 ton to 1,250 gallons of water.

The trip with *Cumberland* coal indicated that 9.19 pounds of it will evaporate 7.48 gallons (1 cubic foot) water, or 0.64 ton to 1,250 gallons of water.

On the same road the average of ten trips results as follows:

A load of 210 tons (as above) was drawn 74 miles, at a velocity of 14.1 miles per hour, with an expenditure of 3.4 cords of wood, and 3,734 gallons of water.

These experiments were conducted in the winter season, and the track was more or less obstructed by snow and ice, giving a very unfavorable state of the rail.

1 cord of beech	evaporates	1,621	gallons water.
1 cord of spruce	"	1,200	"
1 cord of hemlock	"	1,028	"
1 cord of pitch-pine	"	994	"
1 cord of white-pine	"	906	"

Cotton-wood can be used, but is one of the least valuable species of timber as a steam-generator per pound; and its specific gravity is very low.

The result of a year's work on the Central road of Georgia shows that *one cord* of wood was used for every *sixty-six and four-tenths* miles on the road.

As pine wood is corded on the tender, one cubic foot will evaporate one cubic foot (7.48 gallons, or 62½ pounds) of water.

One cord southern pine weighs 3,180 pounds.

One cord common dry pine weighs 2,616 pounds.

For passenger trains the water stations are usually about 25 miles apart.

For freight trains 12 to 15 miles is found a convenient distance for replenishing the supply.

Over ordinary grades, say 30 feet to 40 feet, there would be no difficulty in carrying water and fuel for 100 miles, either by using additional tenders, or large ones made for the especial case, or tanks; the weight, &c., of these being given, it becomes a simple matter of calculating the extra weight to be drawn in any given case.

A partial remedy would be to condense the exhaust steam. This has been done in Scotland to a certain extent.

In ascending heavy grades water is required oftener than usual. Thus on the heavy grades of the Baltimore and Ohio road (116 feet) water is taken every eight miles; on the Western Massachusetts road the water stations are 10 to 12 miles apart on the heavy grades. It is to be remarked that on this road the average consumption of wood is not greater than on others of less heavy grades.

When the track is obstructed by snow it becomes necessary for the passenger trains to take in wood and water oftener than usual, using about double the ordinary amount.

STATISTICS OF VARIOUS RAILROADS.

Boston and Worcester road.

Length, 45 miles; maximum grade, 37½ feet; minimum radius, 541 feet. This distance is accomplished, by trains of four to six passenger cars, in 1½ hour; consuming 1¼ cord of wood, and evaporating 1,200 gallons of water; water is taken once on the road.

Freight trains with maximum loads take water every 12 to 15 miles.

An engine has run, with a train, from Boston to Worcester and back (90 miles) with one cord of wood.

Boston and Providence road.

Length, 43½ miles; maximum grade, 37½ feet.

Trains of four to six passenger cars run at a velocity of 25 miles an hour, maintaining the same up the maximum grade; they consume 3,500 pounds of wood, and evaporate 10,000 pounds of water; take water once on the road, but no wood.

Freight trains as on Worcester road.

In severe snow-storms passenger trains drawn by two or more engines take water every 12 to 15 miles.

Pennsylvania Central road.

Passenger trains wood and water at from 20 to 30 miles; freight trains at an average of 10 miles.

Boston and Maine road.

Trains of four to seven cars at velocities from 24 to 34 miles per hour; take water every 20 miles.

Boston and Lowell road.

Length, 26 miles.

Passenger trains pass over this distance in one hour; take neither wood nor water; evaporate 1,100 to 1,200 gallons, and consume three fourths of a cord of pine.

Freight trains carrying maximum loads due the engine take water once on the road, and travel with velocity of 12 miles per hour.

Burlington to Rutland.

Distance, 67 miles.

Passenger trains take wood and water once; freight trains take wood and water four times.

Rutland to Bellows Falls.

Distance, 53 miles; maximum grades, 60 feet.

Neither wood nor water is taken on the road in passenger trains. Velocity up maximum grade, 15 miles per hour.

With reference to the transportation of coal to be used as fuel, it may be stated that the freights by canal in New York and Pennsylvania vary from $1\frac{2}{10}$ to $1\frac{7}{10}$ cent per ton per mile; that the railroad freights on coal average about $1\frac{1}{2}$ cent per ton per mile; and, finally, that in Pennsylvania, under very favorable circumstances, coal can be delivered on the canal-boats, at the mine, broken, screened, and weighed, at 55 cents per ton. Taking the average weight of hard wood fit for generating steam at $1\frac{1}{2}$ ton per cord, the probable expenses of transporting it by railway would be $2\frac{1}{4}$ cents per cord per mile.

The experiments before alluded to on the Boston and Maine road show that 1 ton of anthracite =1.6 cord of wood (such as used there;) or one cord of wood = 0.625 ton of coal, taking evaporating power as the standard of comparison. The general result of these experiments was that coal is more economical, especially with heavy loads, than wood.

The presence of metallic salts in water is injurious to the boilers; if in large quantities, they they are prohibitory.

From the data given above, it would seem that the cost of transportation of wood for fuel would be about 2.4 times that of coal for the same purpose.

It will be remarked that freight trains habitually take water oftener than passenger trains; this arises from two principal causes: first, more steam is wasted in freight trains, on account of the great detentions, &c., as well as other causes; secondly, the various water-stations seldom give sufficient water to afford a *full* supply to several trains; a little is, therefore, taken from each, so that no one need be exhausted.

Relations between weight of water and fuel, and maximum load of engine.

For a 22-ton engine on 4 drivers, on a level:

Weight of water and wood for 25 miles = $\frac{1}{84}$ of maximum load of engine.
Weight of water and wood for 100 miles = $\frac{1}{22}$ of maximum load of engine.
Weight of water for 100 miles and wood for 200 miles = $\frac{1}{16}$ of maximum load of engine.
Weight of water and wood for 200 miles = $\frac{1}{10}$ of maximum load of engine.
Weight of water and coal for 25 miles = $\frac{1}{105}$ of maximum load of engine.
Weight of water and coal for 100 miles = $\frac{1}{26}$ of maximum load of engine.
Weight of water for 100 miles and coal for 200 miles = $\frac{1}{23}$ of maximum load of engine.
Weight of water and coal for 200 miles = $\frac{1}{13}$ of maximum load of engine.

The maximum load of this engine, on a grade of 40 feet per mile, is by formula (1) 252 tons; by formula (3) 180 tons.

The relative consumption of fuel and water on passenger and freight trains is in proportion to the resistance to be overcome, and may be determined when the velocity and weight of each train are known.

CHARACTERISTICS AND COST OF SIX RAILWAYS.

1. *Massachusetts Western road.*

Length of main road, $155\frac{1}{2}$ miles, of which 53 miles is double track; sidings, &c., $8\frac{1}{2}$ miles: equivalent to 217 *miles single track.* Maximum grade, 83 feet for $1\frac{1}{2}$ mile; total rise and fall, 2,085 feet; minimum radius of curvature, 882 feet; total degrees of curvature, 6,370°; weight of rail per yard, $56\frac{1}{2}$ pounds and 70 pounds; 33 way-stations, 59 engines, 48 passenger-cars, 17 baggage-cars, 1,666 freight-cars; miles run in one year, 947,382.

Graduation and masonry, per mile of main road........................	$22,352 50
Wooden bridges, (6,092½ feet,) per foot..................................	$38 08

Superstructure, per mile of single track.......... $7,243 78
Engineering, per mile of main road.......... $1,105 74
Total cost of road in complete running order, per mile of main road.......... $64,214 56
Total cost of road in running order, exclusive of land damages and stations, per mile of main road.......... $60,042 52

Velocity of express trains, 35 miles; accommodation trains, 28 miles; freight trains, 15 miles per hour.

2. *Boston and Lowell railway.*

Length of road, 26 miles, all double track; branches, sidings, &c., 16¾ miles: equivalent to 68¾ miles single track. Maximum grade, 10 feet for 6¼ miles; total rise and fall, 190 feet; minimum radius of curvature, 1,975 feet; total degrees of curvature, 665°; weight of rail per yard, 56, 60, 63 pounds; 9 way stations, 22 engines, 22 passenger-cars, 11 baggage-cars, 308 freight-cars; miles run in one year, 275,681.

Graduation and masonary, per mile of main road.......... $15,475 00
Wooden bridges, (2,397 feet,) per running foot.......... $18 81
Superstructure, per mile of single track.......... $4,967 60
Engineering, per mile of main road.......... $1,632 35
Total cost of road, equipment, &c., in complete running order, per mile of main road.......... $78,636 00
Total cost of road in running order, exclusive of land damages and stations, per mile of main road.......... $39,090 34

On the road the land damages and cost of depots, stations, &c., were enormous. Velocity of express trains, 35 miles; accommodation, 25 miles; freight, 12 miles per hour.

3. *Boston and Maine railway.*

Length of road, 74 miles, of which 46½ double track; branches, sidings, &c., 29½ miles: equivalent to 103½ miles single track. Maximum grade, 47½ feet for three-fourths of a mile; total rise and fall, 1,498 feet; minimum radius of curvature, 1,050 feet; total degrees of curvature, 1,988°; weight of rail per yard, 56 and 60 pounds; 18 way-stations; 28 engines; 35 passenger-cars, 13 baggage-cars, 585 freight-cars; number of miles run in one year, 516,328.

Graduation and masonry per mile of main road.......... $11,920 00
Wooden bridges, (9,619 feet,) per foot.......... $38 61
Superstructure, per mile of single track.......... $9,517 67
Total cost, in complete running order, per mile of main road.......... $55,558 71
Total cost in running order, exclusive of land damages, stations, &c., per mile of main road.......... $38,525 78

Velocity of express trains, 36 miles per hour.
Velocity of accommodation trains, 24 miles per hour.
Velocity of freight trains, 11 miles per hour.

4. *Boston and Providence railway.*

Length, 43½ miles, of which 15¾ double track; sidings, branches, &c., 19 miles: equivalent to 78¼ miles single track. Maximum grade, 37½ feet; total rise and fall, 505 feet; minimum radius of curvature, 1,910 feet; total degrees of curvature, 342°; weight of rail yer yard, 56 to 58 pounds; 26 way-stations; 20 engines; 31 passenger-cars; 9 baggage-cars; 125 freight-cars; number of miles run in one year, 305,734.

Graduation and masonry, per mile, main road.......... $17,625 50
Wooden bridges, per running foot.......... $32 00

Iron bridges, per running foot	$40 00
Superstructure, per mile, single track	$8,390 75
Engineering, per mile, main road	$2,294 00
Total cost in complete running order, per mile, main road	$81,273 00
Total cost in running order, deducting land damages, stations, &c., per mile, main road	$57,397 00

Velocity of express trains, 34½ miles per hour.
Velocity of accommodation trains, 25 miles per hour.
Velocity of freight trains, 14 miles per hour.

5. *Vermont Central road.*

Length, 124 miles.

Graduation, per mile	$14,517 00
Masonry and bridges	$6,599 00
Superstructure, per mile	$8,594 00
Engineering	$928 00
Total cost in complete running order, per mile	$55,685 00
Total cost per mile, excluding land, stations, &c	$49,852 00

6. *New York Northern road—Ogdensburg.*

Length, 118 miles.

Grading and masonry, per mile	$15,567 00
Superstructure	$9,545 00
Bridges	$1,203 00
Engineering	$1,099 00
Total cost per mile, in complete running order	$40,005 00
Total cost per mile, exclusive of land, stations, &c	$34,810 00

Average of the six preceding roads.

Graduation and masonry, per mile	$17,343 00
Wooden bridges, per running foot	$31 90
Iron bridges, per running foot	$40 00
Superstructure, including iron, per mile, single track	$8,042 50
Engineering, per mile, main road	$1,411 60
Total cost per mile, main road, in complete running order	$62,561 00
Total cost per mile, main road, in running order, exclusive of land damages, stations, &c.	$46,619 00

Average of fifteen New England roads.

Engineering, per mile of main road	$1,041 00
Total cost, per mile of main road, exclusive of land damages, stations, &c.	$36,305 00

The average of 36 Massachusetts roads gives as the velocity of passenger trains 23.8 miles per hour, and as the velocity of freight trains 13 miles per hour; and the average cost per mile of 1,415 miles of road in the same State, as $43,659 85 per mile of main roads.

DEPOTS, &C.

For a large depot of an important road an area of about 50 acres is necessary, to accommodate all the requisite shops, sheds, storehouses, &c.

For ordinary way stations, about 5 to 10 acres.

An engine-house for, say, 7 engines, costs, with turn-tables, about............ $3,500 00
A common way-station house, about.................................... $1,500 00

REPAIRS AND INSPECTION OF TRACK.

It is generally the case, on our roads, that one man carefully inspects about two miles of track every day. He makes all the small repairs that are necessary.

By the use of hand-cars, from five to ten miles of track could be daily inspected and repaired by one party.

TUNNELS.

"It is a rule which may be regarded as generally applicable, that to make a cutting more than sixty feet deep would be costlier than to 'bore,' unless the material is required for a neighboring embankment. Economy is the principal test in these matters; for in the present advanced stage of engineering, a tunnel may be made of almost any length, and through almost any substance, from granite rock to quicksand, and therefore the nature of the ground can hardly be said to oppose any other obstacle than that occasioned by the cost."

There is, however, an instance of an excavation 110 feet in depth in sand.

Shafts are usually sunk along the line of the tunnel at from 500 to 1,000 feet apart. On the Blaisy tunnel one shaft is 646 feet in depth; on the Nerthe tunnel one of 610 feet.

It is now a quite generally received opinion that shafts are not so necessary for the ventilation of the tunnel after its completion as was formerly supposed to be the case. Where it was proposed to use machinery for excavating, a tunnel of 7.5 miles miles has been projected without the use of shafts.

Shafts are usually from 7 to 11 feet in diameter.

The largest tunnel of which I can find a record is one in the district of Schemnitz, in Hungary. Its length is variously stated at from 10 to 11½ miles. It is used to drain an extensive series of mines, and also for the transportation of ore on railway cars.

The longest tunnel of large dimensions which I find recorded as having actually been completed is one in France. It is 3½ miles long, and a little more than 26 feet in diameter; 54 shafts were employed.

The section of railway tunnels varies considerably in different countries and on different roads. The dimensions of several will be found in the tables which follow.

Several machines for the excavation of tunnels have been invented. It does not appear that any of them have proved successful; so that in estimating the time necessary to construct any proposed tunnel, it will be safer to base the calculation upon the results of works actually completed.

As a general thing, headings, as they are called—small tunnels in fact—are first driven through, and afterwards enlarged, to form the large tunnel. This method of proceeding has great advantages in some localities, but is not always resorted to.

The grades can be so arranged in railway tunnels as to facilitate the drainage during the construction by establishing a summit in the middle of the tunnel, thus allowing the water to run out at each end without interfering with the work; there are instances of great embarrassment caused by the neglect of this simple precaution.

In *France* there are 56 tunnels on railways; eight canals, 36 of which have an aggregate length of 45.4 miles. The longest of small size is 7.45 miles, and that of large dimensions 3.5 miles. The Rouen and Havre road has eight tunnels; Paris and Lyons also eight.

The aqueduct from the Durance to Marseilles has three tunnels, whose aggregate length is 10.5 miles.

That through the Taillades had 7,320 gallons of water pumped out per minute during a part of the time it was under construction.

The *Nerthe* tunnel, near Marseilles, is 15,153 feet long; has twenty-four shafts, whose aggregate length is 7,589 feet—the deepest being 610 feet. It is in very hard limestone rock; is 29½ feet high by 26¼ feet wide. The shafts are lined with masonry; a portion of the body of the tunnel is lined with masonry, one, two, and three bricks thick; another portion is not lined at all. A semi-circular brick aqueduct, 4½ inches in diameter, runs the whole length of the tunnel under the floor. The time occupied in the construction is not stated.

The cost of the Nerthe tunnel was as follows:

For mining the body of the tunnel	$705,982 20
For mining the shafts	$109,081 08
Masonry for the shafts	$49,069 31
Lining for the body of the tunnel	$423,711 18
Cost of aqueduct	$10,607 10
Total cost of the tunnel	$1,298,450 87

The average cost of *excavating* the shafts, which are nine feet ten inches in clear diameter, was $43 per yard down; the average cost of the lining of the shafts was $19 40 per yard down. The deepest shaft cost, on the average, $73 per yard down, completed.

Cost of mining the body of the tunnel, $139 76½ per running yard.

On the *German* railways are ten tunnels.

The great "*gallerie d'ecoulement*" of the Clansthal mines, through the Hartz mountains, is 6.5 miles long. It was commenced in 1777 and completed in 1800, (twenty-three years,) and cost a little more than $350,000. Some authorities state this tunnel to be 7.5 miles long. Its dimensions are not given, but it is probably small.

In *Sardinia* there is a tunnel two miles long, through Mt. Giovi, on the Genoa and Turin railway. On this road, in 25 miles through the Appenines, are nine tunnels.

In *Austria* the Sommerung tunnel is one mile long.

England has 48 canal tunnels of an aggregate length of 40 miles; the largest being over three miles, on the Huddersfield canal. She has also 79 railway tunnels; 49 of which amount to 33 miles, the longest being three miles.

The London and Birmingham railway has eight tunnels; London and Dover, five; Newcastle and Dover, five.

The *Woodhead* tunnel, between Manchester and Sheffield, is a little more than three miles long. It has five shafts ten feet in diameter, which vary from 400 to 600 in depth. The character of the rock is granitic, being "mill-stone rock." The tunnel was about five years in construction, and its whole cost was $1,026,705.

Uppingham tunnel, 1,320 feet in length, cost $120 per lineal yard.

Saltwood tunnel, in very wet sand, cost $524 43 per lineal yard.

The United States has 67 tunnels on canals and railways, the longest of which is about one mile. Details are difficult to obtain. Many of them are short, however.

Baltimore and Ohio road has 16 tunnels; Parkersburg road, 17; Hempfield, seven.

The *old canal* tunnels cost, on an average, about $17 77 per running yard.

Those of *ordinary size for railways* cost from $88 per lineal yard, for those in soft sandstone not requiring a lining of masonry, to $444 and $710 per yard, in very loose ground, such as quicksand, &c., requiring a very tick lining.

Ordinary brick lining costs from $8 to $9 per cubic yard, including centering.

The *shafts* for the Blechingly tunnel, 10.5 feet in diameter, sunk in blue clay, and lined, cost $68 44 per yard down. The longest shaft is 97 feet.

Those of the Blaisy tunnel cost, lined, $139 11 per yard down. The soil was of clay, chalk, and loose earth. Deepest shaft 646 feet, and few less than 328 feet.

The cost of shafts varies in proportion to their depth, &c., &c.

The cost of those in the Black Rock tunnel, Pennsylvania, in hard slate, was $79 50 per yard down, or $18 72 per cubic yard. The shafts were seven feet in diameter, and 139 feet deep.

The cost per cubic yard of excavating tunnels has been in the—

Black Rock, hard greywacke slate, (U. S.)	$6.60
Lehigh, very hard granite, (U. S.)	$4.36
Schuylkill, slate, (U. S.)	$2.00
Union, slate, (U. S.)	$2.085
Blisworth, blue clay, lined, (Eng.)	$1.545
Box, freestone, marble, clay, &c., lined, (Eng.)	$3.464
Blaisy, exclusive of shafts, but including the lining, (France)	$3.176
Blue Ridge, cost per cubic yard	$4.000

The Blaisy tunnel cost, exclusive of shafts, $108 31 per lineal foot.

In comparing the cost of tunnels in different countries, the difference of the price of labor should be considered. This has not been done in any of the examples here given; the actual cost in pounds sterling, &c., being simply reduced to dollars.

The time required to drive the *heading* of the Black Rock tunnel was 1,243 days and 1,144 nights, or 2,387 spaces of 12 hours each, for 1,782.5 feet in length of tunnel.

For details of this tunnel, see the following tables.

In the Kilsby tunnel, a working shaft 129 feet deep, much troubled with water, was finished in seven or eight weeks.

In hard rock, where continual blasting is required, two expert miners can run a "branch" 40 inches by 32 inches to the length of 10.5 inches in 12 hours.

A tunnel cannot be pushed further than 500 feet without resorting to artificial means of ventilation.

Ventilation is found to be better in cold weather than in warm.

Headings are about 12 feet high; width at base, that of tunnel at that height.

In the table on the succeeding page,

P. L. means partly lined with masonry.
L. " lined with masonry.
N. L. " not lined with masonry.
Z. " not stated.
S. " has shafts.
S. S. " supposed to have shafts.
C. " average depth.
a. " average per running foot taken from total cost.
D. " was constructed to drain the lakes in the valley of Mexico, to prevent overflows.

Measures are in feet and decimals;
Time, in working days;
Cost, in dollars and decimals.

(X.)—For details of construction of Kilsby tunnel, see American Railroad Journal, vol. I, new series, (1838,) page 229 *et seq.*

Comparative Table of some of the largest Tunnels.

Name of tunnel.		Date.	Formation.	Shafts.	Maximum depth.	Section of tunnel.	Length, in feet.	Time required, in days.	Cost per lineal foot.	Total cost.	Locality.
					Feet.				*Dollars.*	*Dollars.*	
Nerthe	P. L.	Z ...	Hard limestone...	24...	610..	29.5 × 26.25	15,153	....	....	1,298,450	Near Marseilles, France.
Riqueval	P. L.	1803	Chalk	54...	210..	26.25 × 26.25	18,623	2,139	39.887	742,817	St. Quentin canal, France.
Pouilly	P. L.	1824	Chalk and clay...	32...	164..	20.34 × 20.34	10,928	2,504	113.965	1,245,412	Bourgogne canal, France.
Asschviller	Z	1839	Z	S. S.	Z ...	26.25 × 26.25	7,384	1,878	68.38	a. 504,897	Maine and Rhine canal, France.
Mauvage	Z	1840	Z	S...	Z ...	25.59 × 25.59	15,752	2,085	94.43	a.1,487,393	Maine and Rhine canal, France.
Rolleboise	Z	1841	Chalk	S. S.	Z ...	24.94 × 24.94	8,670	626	62.98	546,099	Rouen railway, France.
Roule	Z	1841	Z	S. S.	Z ...	24.94 × 24.94	5,645	522	62.98	355,513	Rouen railway, France.
Lioran	Z	1839	Z	S. S.	Z ...	21.33 × 21.33	4,548	2,087	56.98	259,178	National road, No. 126, France.
Kilsby, (X).	L	1834	Clay and sand	18...	164..	27 × 23.50	7,233	1,252	194.31	1,405,417	London and Birmingham railway, England.
Blechingly.	L	1840	Blue clay	12...	97...	24 × 25.05	3,972	626	102.86	423,271	London and Dover railway, England.
Thames and Medway.	P. L.	1822	Chalk	S....	194..	30 × 38.7	11,880	939	45.59	541,550	Thames and Medway canal, England.
Box.	P. L.	1837	Marble, freestone, marl, &c.	15...	400..	35 × 39	9,680	1,252	148.15	1,434,063	Great Western railway—shafts 25 feet diameter, one-third of tunnel in rock—England.
Hare Castle	L	1824	Rock and sand....	15...	187..	14 × 16	8,778	939	57.05	500,799	Trent and Mersey canal, England.
Nochistongo (D)..	L	1807	Clay and marl....	S....	164..	13.78 × 11.48	21,659	287	....	....	Lake Zumpango, Mexico; a Desagua.
Blisworth	L	1796	Rock and clay....	19...	59...	16.5 × 18	9,240	2,191	23.185	214,229	G. J. canal, England.
Sapperton	P. L.	1789	Rock	S. S.	246..	15 × 15	12,900	1,878	12.44	160,476	Thames and Severn canal, England.
Black Rock	NL..	1835	Greywacke slate..	6....	139..	19 × 17.23	1,932	....	77.18	149,120	Reading, Penn., railway, United States.
Blaisy	L	1846	Chalk, clay, &c...	22...	646..	26.25 × 26.25	13,455	1,043	136.06	1,830,730	Paris and Lyons railway, France.
Edge Hill	P. L.	1826	Clay and freestone	S....	Z ...	22 × 16	6,600	....	30.15	198,969	Liverpool and Manchester railway, England.
Littlebourg	L	1840	Z	14...	(c)177	27.5 × 24	8,607	590	129.61	1,115,544	Manchester and Leeds railway, England.
Woodhead	Z	Z ...	Millstone rock....	5....	600..	....	15,840	1,800	....	1,026,705	Manchester and Sheffield railway, England.

A tunnel has been projected at Mt. Cenis, on the line of the Lyons and Turin railway, of the length of 7.6 miles; the gradient in the tunnel to be 105 feet to the mile; the section of the tunnel to be 19 by 25 feet; *no shafts to be used.* By the aid of machinery it was expected to complete this work in five years, at an expense of $2,615,000.

The inventor of the machine and the engineer of the road is the Chevalier Mause. His plans and estimates were submitted to, and approved by, a board of eminent engineers and geologists, among whom was the celebrated Mr. Robert Stevenson.

The tunnel projected through the *Hoosack* mountain was to have been 4½ miles long, 23 feet by 22 feet; two shafts about 850 feet and 750 feet deep, 10 feet in diameter. The cost variously estimated at from $2,000,000 to $3,000,000. Time estimated by different engineers at from four to ten years. The machinery designed for boring did not succeed, and the project has not as yet been commenced seriously.

At the crossing of the Blue Ridge by the Virginia Central railroad there are four tunnels. The main tunnel is 4,280 feet in length; has been four years under construction, and is estimated to require two years more to complete it. No shafts are used. It is ventilated by machinery. A portion of it is lined. It is for a single track, and is in the clear 21 feet high by 15 feet in width. Where lined, the abutments of the lining are 4 feet thick; the arches 3 feet thick. The excavation in these places is 26 feet high by 23 feet wide.

A portion of one of the small tunnels is through a very difficult formation of loose rock and earth. In the main tunnel much trouble is experienced from the water.

The main tunnel is 700 feet below the crest of the mountain through which it passes. The workmen are arranged in three reliefs, and work night and day. No machinery is used for boring or excavating. It is the opinion of the engineer that no machinery can be applied when the tunnel requires lining, for want of space. He states that no excavating machine has yet been successful.

SNOW.

The roads in Massachusetts, with rare exceptions, find little difficulty in clearing the track from snow in the course of one day. They only fail to do so when the snow drifts badly, and packs hard.

To open the road, from two to five engines are attached to each train, with a snow-plough in front. The train pushes through until stopped, when it backs off and again advances.

Snow to the depth of five or six feet, as a maximum, can be cleared in this manner. With higher ploughs and additional power, it is possible that slightly greater depths of light snow may be worked through.

Snow a foot deep does not present a very great obstacle—that is to say, the train makes regular progress at reduced speed.

Embankments are far less obstructed than cuts.

Cuts of twenty feet deep, and upwards, are less obstructed than those of from five to ten feet.

Alongside of cuts like the latter, *snow fences* are used. These are board fences, about eight feet high, placed some twelve feet back from the edge of the excavation.

Drifting snow obstructs a train far more than a settled fall; for when the engine is brought to a state of rest, and finds it necessary to "back" in order to obtain a new impetus, the snow blows in under the wheels, and sometimes "blocks" the train so that it cannot move either way. In such cases a large manual force is necessary to clear all the wheels at once.

Men and shovels are always carried on the train when the fall of snow is great, in order partially to open heavy drifts and to provide for the contingency of the train being blocked.

Freight trains should be discontinued until the road is opened; the work being done by the passenger trains.

Light dry snow is by no means so serious an obstacle as wet heavy snow, except in regard to its liability to drift.

In opening the road over heavy gradients, commence working from the summit.

When the snow opposes a considerable resistance the engines use about double the usual quantity of fuel and water.

Snow-ploughs are generally of two sizes; the larger sizes are from nine to ten feet high, and about seven feet broad; the smaller are about four feet high by seven feet broad, and are sometimes of iron.

FREIGHTS.

Average freights during the last eight years from Calcutta to Boston $15 per ton.

Average for same time from Calcutta to London $17 per ton.

From Canton to the United States $10 to $18 per ton.

From Canton to England $26 per ton.

From Shanghai to the United States $10 to $20 per ton.

From Shanghai to England $26 to $30 per ton.

Freights from Boston to San Francisco average since 1849, $22 per ton; at present, $12 per ton.

Average freight from China and the East Indies to San Francisco $13 per ton.

Silks usually pay $5 per ton more than teas.

CATTLE, &C.

The total number of live stock carried over the Baltimore and Ohio railway during the year ending September 30, 1854, was 164,869, of which number 75,575 were transported a distance of 368 miles.

At the *same rate of freight* as on the Baltimore and Ohio road it would cost about $36 per head for horned cattle from Fort Smith to San Francisco, and about $42 per head from Memphis.

To transport horses and mules by railroad from Memphis to San Francisco, by way of Fort Smith, would cost about $47 per head.

REPORT

UPON

THE COST OF TRANSPORTING TROOPS AND SUPPLIES

TO

CALIFORNIA, OREGON, NEW MEXICO,

ETC., ETC.

BY

MAJOR GENERAL THOMAS S. JESUP,

QUARTERMASTER GENERAL, U. S. ARMY.

COST OF TRANSPORTING TROOPS, &c.

QUARTERMASTER GENERAL'S OFFICE,
Washington City, November 16, 1854.

SIR: In reply to your letter, dated the 8th instant, asking information in regard to transportation, I have the honor to report, in answer to the "1st.—The present cost of transporting troops to San Francisco and Fort Vancouver, via the Isthmus, how much for each officer and soldier; stating whether the price includes their food, and, if not, what additional amount is paid for food, or the transportation of their rations and arms,"—that the last troops sent to San Francisco, via the Isthmus, (in May, 1854,) their transportation was as follows: $225 for each commissioned officer; $150 for each enlisted soldier, laundress, &c.

The whole were subsisted by the contractor; 100 pounds of baggage allowed to each person on the steamers, and 25 pounds each across the Isthmus; *all over* the 25 pounds across the Isthmus to be paid for at 15 cents per pound. No troops have been sent from the Atlantic coast direct to Vancouver or Oregon, via the Isthmus. For those sent from San Francisco, California, to Vancouver or Oregon, in June, 1853, $75 was paid for each commissioned officer, and $40 for each enlisted soldier, &c., and $30 a ton for stores. In December, 1853, $15 a ton, and in February, 1854, $20 a ton, for stores.

From information received from New York since the receipt of your letter, I learn that the company now demands $300 for each officer, and $150 for each enlisted soldier, from New Orleans to San Francisco, including the transit of the Isthmus—extra baggage to be paid for at 15 cents per pound.

To the "2d.—What is the cost of the transportation of provisions, in bulk, to San Francisco and Fort Vancouver, via the Isthmus, and also via Cape Horn,"—I have to report that no provisions or other public stores, in bulk, have been sent to San Francisco or Fort Vancouver, via the Isthmus; but from information just received from New York, I learn that the present charges by that route are $14 a ton to Aspinwall, $300 a ton (15 cents per pound) across the Isthmus, and $80 a ton from Panama to San Francisco—say $394 a ton of 2,000 pounds. The agents of the line *think*, that when the railroad across the Isthmus shall be completed, the freight across will not exceed one-fourth of the above, $75 a ton—say $169 for the whole distance. Via Cape Horn to San Francisco, or Benicia, subsistence stores have been shipped during the present year from Baltimore at 90 cents per cubic foot, $4 50 per flour-barrel; and from New York at $3 70 per barrel for flour, and 60 cents per cubic foot for other packages.

To the "3d."—The same rates will apply to camp and garrison equipage and clothing; as all such freight, by sea-going vessels, is charged for by the cubic foot.

To the "4th," I have to report that ordnance and ordnance stores have been sent from New York, via Cape Horn, in June, 1854, at two cents per pound for ordnance, consisting of heavy guns, carriages, shot and shells; in August at $28 per ton for the same, and in October at two cents a pound for the heavy ordnance; and 60 cents per cubic foot for ammunition, and other boxes, &c. None have been sent via the Isthmus.

To the "5th" I report, that, during the present year, the contracts for the transportation of military stores of *all* kinds are as follows:

From Fort Leavenworth to El Paso, $14 per 100 lbs.

From Fort Leavenworth to Fort Fillmore, $13 75 per 100 lbs.

From Fort Leavenworth to Albuquerque, $10 83 per 100 lbs.

From Fort Leavenworth to Fort Union, $7 96 per 100 lbs.

No transportation has ever been paid for men, as they march, the only cost being for the transportation of their baggage, subsistence, &c., on the route. This may be estimated at about $15 per man to Albuquerque. The above are about the average rates for several years past, and it may be presumed will be those for the future.

As to what was the cost of transporting artillery and supplies from the city of New York to the northern frontier in the war of 1812–'14, this office furnishes no information, and I think it would be extremely difficult, if not impossible, to ascertain what were the average rates. There were no permanent or Macadamized roads in northern New York during that period, and the passage of heavy-loaded wagons, at the best of times, extremely difficult and slow. It may be fair to presume that each ton cost at the rate of $5 (the daily cost of a wagon and team) for each ten miles of distance from Albany to the different points on the frontier when the roads were in the best condition, and double this in the spring and fall of the year—say from fifty cents to one dollar a mile for each ton transported.

For General Harrison's army on the northwestern frontier, there were instances when the teams, loaded with forage, not only consumed all they were transporting to that army, but had to draw forage from the army depots to enable them to return. Much of the subsistence intended for the army was also consumed by the teamsters and escorts en route.

Since writing the above, I have information from New York that heavy freight can now be sent to San Francisco at about $15 a ton, and 30 cents per foot for measurement goods, and that a vessel could be chartered for Fort Vancouver at $20 a ton. These rates should not, however, be taken as ruling for the coming year, freight of all kinds being extremely low at this time.

I have the honor to be your obedient servant,

TH. S. JESUP,
Quartermaster General.

Hon. Jeffn. Davis,
Secretary of War.

www.ingramcontent.com/pod-product-compliance
Lightning Source LLC
LaVergne TN
LVHW010743120826
845150LV00009B/1921

* 9 7 8 1 4 2 5 5 1 0 2 4 4 *